aurora linnea had me on the first page, at 'men hate life'. Not all individual men, of course, but Man, the Man of Patriarchy. That's why men should read this spirited challenge to what patriarchy demands of us. *Man Against Being* is provocative, in the best sense, provoking us to ask why the dominant culture seems determined to escape from the limits of the larger living world on which we depend, the limits that make us human. linnea takes readers on a dizzying tour through thousands of years of patriarchal delusions, both sacred and secular. For me, *Man Against Being* is a call to men to make peace — with ourselves, with each other, with women, and with our fears.

 —Robert Jensen, Emeritus Professor, School of Journalism and
  Media, University of Texas at Austin, author of *The End of*
  Patriarchy: Radical Feminism for Men and *It's Debatable:*
  Talking Authentically about Tricky Topics

This remarkable book is a passionate, intelligent, and erudite exposition of the continuous age-old attempt at derogation of the female body (and thus of women's bodily wisdom) and a warning of the future deadly consequences for humans, animals, and the earth if we don't collectively resist Man's aspiration for a transhumanist, non-corporeal future.

 —Heather Brunskell-Evans, author of *Transgender Body*
  Politics

aurora linnea forces Man to bare it all in her expansive, impressively researched and vivid account of patriarchy's true foundation: fear of body, and so, of life. With breathtaking prose, one is guided through a grim journey from which one cannot help emerge shaken but strangely reinvigorated as well. This must-read book reminds us of the power of Man's mythology but also — more importantly — its antidote: even more powerful *reality*.

 —Syl Ko, co-author of *Aphro-ism: Essays on Pop Culture,*
  Feminism and Black Veganism from Two Sisters

aurora linnea weaves a searingly beautiful polemic that painstakingly demystifies the patriarchal delusion of mind/body duality as a sick death cult and argues for a return to embodied intimacy as a path of healing that is 'alienation's antivenin'. We are our bodies. What is more beautiful, powerful, and mystical than our intimate participation with all planetary life? The poetry of linnea's prose reminds one of Susan Griffin, and her unflinching ability to expose patriarchal lies is positively Dworkin-esque. This book is as enlivening as it is enlightening.

    —Amy E. Sousa, MA Depth Psychology, author of substack
    www.theknownheretic.com

aurora linnea has issued an urgent call to the women of the world: it is long past time to face the obvious: the men of patriarchy hate life. On page after pounding page, she lets them explain exactly why and how much. Meanwhile, our ravaged planet shows that they mean it. It will take courage to read this book but it will also lend you courage, for Man Against Being is, in the end, a fierce and tender reminder that our animal bodies — like the earth herself — are holy and calling us home.

    —Lierre Keith, author of *The Vegetarian Myth: Food, Justice, and Sustainability*

In beautiful and thought-provoking prose, aurora linnea invites us to examine the destructive power of mind-body dualism and warns against the perils of a 'post biological future'. Her thesis, that it is 'Man's culture of rigorous estrangement' coupled with a consuming death-fear that rationalizes horrors against the body and natural world, warns us against the lionization of the technological above the physical. In the tradition of Susan Griffin, linnea calls for a feminist return to reality vis-a-vis an embrace of the living in defiance of a culture of disembodiment.

    —Genevieve Gluck, journalist, co-founder of Reduxx

Photo credit: Tanner Wilcox

aurora linnea is a radical ecofeminist writer committed to poetic dissidence and uncompromising disloyalty to male dominion. She has authored poetry chapbooks, horror stories, and zines, and contributes regularly to the media disruptions of Women's Liberation Radio News. In the past, she has served women as a shelter worker and rape crisis advocate. Aurora is no longer in collusion with the predator.

MAN AGAINST BEING

BODY HORROR AND THE DEATH OF LIFE

aurora linnea

We respectfully acknowledge the wisdom of Aboriginal and Torres Strait Islander peoples and their custodianship of the lands and waterways. The Countries on which Spinifex offices are situated are Djuru, Bunurong and Wurundjeri, Wadawurrung, Gundungarra and Noongar.

First published by Spinifex Press.

Spinifex Press Pty Ltd
PO Box 200, Little River, VIC 3211, Australia
PO Box 105, Mission Beach, QLD 4852, Australia

women@spinifexpress.com.au
www.spinifexpress.com.au

Edited by Pauline Hopkins, Renate Klein and Susan Hawthorne
Indexed by Belinda Nemec
Cover design by Deb Snibson
Typeset by Helen Christie, Blue Wren Books
Typeset in Macklin Text
Printed and bound in Australia by Pegasus Media & Logistics

A catalogue record for this book is available from the National Library of Australia

ISBN: 9781922964120 (paperback)
ISBN: 9781922964137 (ebook)

10 9 8 7 6 5 4 3 2 1

for my wolf-sisters
and the swamps and saintly cows
for lymph, dirt, the Atlantic Ocean
the thrum in your blood
the lives that could be ours
and for someone who told me
"you can't legislate reality"
and how i didn't understand at first
but then i knew: the truth of it

*The feminist revolution is
accept the body and destroy society.*

—*It Ain't Me Babe*, 1970

CONTENTS

ACKNOWLEDGMENTS

I will be forever grateful to Renate Klein and Susan Hawthorne for creating a home for this book, and for their endless support through the process of releasing it into the wild. I thank them, too, along with Pauline Hopkins, for the many careful, painful re-reads and refinements of the text, which benefited immeasurably from their combined rigor, care, and expertise.

I thank the women whose writing spared me a life spent sleepwalking or desolate. I will not try to name them, for the list would go on and on, but they are cited amply in these pages. Thank goodness for writers, writers with guts and hearts and spines, and for books written with real purpose.

I thank the women of Women's Liberation Radio News, for affording me the space to write as I wish to, and for all they do to uplift women's voices. Thank you Thistle, April, Jenna, and the rest, past and present.

I thank my parents, for raising me to be a feral creature and for showing me true nonconformity. Thanks to you both, I wasted less time than most trying to fit in.

I thank everyone who has graced me with their friendship over the years I've spent working towards this book, even as I became an insufferable recluse carrying on about any number of unappetizing topics. Thank you especially to Crystal Dyer, Sherryl Kleinman, Deanna DeMatteo, Tanner Wilcox, and lots of excellent dogs.

Finally, I thank Roswell Spook-Magnet (2009–2024), who saw me through the agonies of every project I've published in my adult life, as research assistant, book warmer, dinner bell, fluff distributor, and sweetest boy. What a joy to have known you, bunny.

INTRODUCTION

I n the urgency of my heartbreak as a ravaged world succumbs to plunder and the killing won't slow but only accelerates with the unstoppable surge of years, I write because I want to scream it: men hate life. By 'life', I mean the substance of creation, the creatures that men themselves are, their existence as bodies and the matter from which their bodies are made. 'Life' is being alive on the earth, being an animal, being a body. Life means *being*. I realize how it could come off as extreme, flippant even, to say that men are making it impossible to live by destroying the living world for the simple stupid reason that they despise life. We have been taught to distrust this sort of simplicity. Surely the truth must be more complicated. And surely it is — yet if one cuts through manufactured complexity's glut to the pith of things, one finds that what is truest is always rather shockingly and painfully simple. It is an oversight to shrink from what is clear to see. So we observe that men have spent thousands of years articulating their hatred for life and acting on it. Men have made themselves clear — why not take them at their word?

A man writing in the twelfth century addresses himself to life as he knows it:

Worldly life, future death,
Permanent ruin,

Worldly life, evil thing
Never worthy of love

...

Life, stupid thing
Accepted only by fools,
I reject you with all my heart.
For you are full of filth.[1]

---

1   Anonymous monk, quoted in Delumeau (1990, p. 15).

3

This concise execration epitomizes the attitude that took root as medieval Christianity's governing dogma, circulated in literary form through the genre of *contemptus mundi*. As doctrine *contemptus mundi* — 'contempt of the world' in English — denounces life as a wellspring of ceaseless torment. Likewise, the living world is a debased wasteland lorded over by Satan himself, the foil to god-the-father's ethereal extraterrestrial heavenly kingdom in the sky. Just below the earth's crust, hell lies boiling. Originating at the end of the Classical Era to bolster the resolve of ascetics self-exiled to the Egyptian desert, by the twelfth century *contemptus mundi* had spread from hermitage to monastery and from there entrenched itself as Christianity's standard position vis-à-vis being alive on the earth (Delumeau 1990). Writers taking up this theme breathlessly cataloged the profusion of horrors that made life such a scourge: dirt, bad smells, flies, fleas, cold, heat, hunger, thirst, worms, wild animals, fire, lightning, fierce winds, poisonous plants, hard labor, poverty, deprivation, surfeit, fear, desire, sex, childbirth, disease, injury, aging, death, decay.

Pope Innocent III's *De miseria humane conditionis* (*On the Misery of the Human Condition*), authored prior to his papacy in around 1195, was one of the most widely read theological texts of its era. A classic of *contemptus mundi* literature, the treatise includes among its 90 chapters commentary on such concerns as the "Vile Matter from which Man is Made," the "Brevity of Joy," the "Innumerable Kinds of Illness," the "Varied Forms of Torment," and "The Putrefaction of the Dead Body." It concludes with an account of "The Unspeakable Anguish of the Damned" (dei Segni 1195/1969). From his conception to the decomposition of his corpse, life afflicts the person unfortunate enough to exist; each instant he spends living he senses himself banished from his god, a helpless prisoner of the flesh, degraded and defiled. Even life's supposed 'pleasures' so swiftly evanesce that, in their vanity, they serve only as cruel aggravators of human misery. We suffer, we perish, we become wormfood: that's life. What sane response is there but to shun it?

Thus it was a wise man who said, "This is the highest wisdom: through contempt of the world, to strive for the kingdom of heaven."[2]

In the centuries that have passed between the Middle Ages and now, men have given lavish, violent display to their rejection of the life they called stupid, evil, and unworthy of love. They have razed field and forest, felling trees by the thousands, grinding them into sawdust, clearing the land for cities and suburbs and feedlots, leaving the earth scarred, the creatures who once lived in and amongst the trees displaced, the air thinner for the loss of the trees' enlivening breath. An estimated ten million hectares of forest are destroyed each year (Food and Agriculture Organization of the United Nations, 2020). More than three-quarters of the earth's arable land has been commandeered for 'livestock production', converted either into cages to warehouse captive exploited animals or monocultures of the pesticide-drenched genetically modified crops grown to fatten the bodies bound for slaughter (Ritchie 2017). The total global biomass of the sacrificial beings we term 'livestock' — cows, pigs, sheep, goats — is today fifteen times greater than that of wild mammals (Ritchie et al. 2022). And the wild creatures who have survived are ruthlessly hunted down as pests or prizes for patriarchy's mantel. Men track pregnant wolves to kill them in their dens, so their pups will never be born. Men shoot down wild horses from helicopters. Men set traps jagged with steel teeth to snare the limbs of 'nuisance animals' — foxes, coyotes, raccoons, bears, bobcats, dingoes — to hold them pinioned while they break their own bones twisting to free themselves until the men return to make the kill, a mercy now for the broken body.

And where men have erected cities to house themselves in isolation from the world they abhor, the earth enervates interred under miles of tons of concrete, today the single most abundantly used substance after water. And the denizens of these cities spend their days gazing into glaring blue-lit boxes of metal and tangled wire, their bodies sustained on cheap sugar and preservatives and the flesh of frightened animals, anxious minds buckling bent to submission by

---

2   Thomas à Kempis, quoted in Lawson (2021, p. 39).

regimens of compulsive desensitizing overstimulation. In the cities, there are state-sponsored megabrothels where men go to pay to violate the bodies of dispossessed women, while in other buildings, men pay to ejaculate into lifeless silicone mannequins; and online, men amass enormous collections of photographs of raped children which they trade with other men and masturbate to. And when the cities are bombed, their denizens — the men and the dispossessed women and the raped children alike — will be reduced to black smears, blast-shadow silhouettes scorched onto sidewalks, stairways, garden walls. The bombs that men have built and stockpiled to date could snuff out virtually all life on earth several times over.

The approximate death toll of the Nazi regime's Holocaust, 1941-1945: 6,000,000. Approximate death toll of the Cambodian Genocide, 1975-1979: 2,000,000 (Heuveline 2015). Approximate death toll of the Darfur Genocide in Sudan, as of 2015: 400,000 (Straus 2015). These are merely estimates. At the time of this writing, the Israeli government has killed nearly 40,000 Palestinians with its months-long bombardment of Gaza, a figure that leaves out those buried in the ruins of shattered homes and schools and hospitals, their bodies as yet unrecovered and uncounted (Al Jazeera 2024).

And the oceans are dying. The guts of fish, turtles, and seabirds bloat clotted with plastic dregs. And countless gallons of unknown, unknowable chemicals leach into the soil and into the groundwater, so humans and other animals are born deformed and diseased and rapidly decline. Forests turn arid into tinder and catch fire, polar ice melts, the permafrost thaws, topsoil erodes. We breathe the ashes, our lungs blacken. A mountain's peak is blown to rubble, so men can mine for coal to keep electric lights burning through the night in vacant office parks, while the earth stews sickening in the toxic miasma our cities, highways, factories, and farms cough up. Grasslands desiccate into deserts. Then nothing grows, then nothing eats, then nothing survives, nothing lives. Today, at least one million species are estimated to be under threat of extinction; the current extinction rate is tens to hundreds of times higher than it has been on average during the last ten million years (Brondizio et al. 2019).

And as the living world thrashes in its death throes, men intoxicate themselves placated with self-soothing fantasies of excarnation, ascension, myriad raptures both religious and technological. They are convinced that they can live without their lives. That they will be better off without them. And the killing continues apace.

"If patriarchal males loved life, the planet would be different," Mary Daly wrote in *Gyn/Ecology* (1978/1990, p. 352). She diagnosed men's terminal pathology as necrophilia, defined here not as a lust for corpses, but instead as a consuming, compulsive, enthralled fascination with the unalive. This form of necrophilia, endemic in patriarchal societies, has been the engine for men's long procession towards mass deadening. In other words, Daly theorized: men do not love life, they love death; because they love death, they want to be dead, hence they are killing the world.

There can be no question that men's inexhaustible brutality against life on earth will prove suicidal, but I do not agree with Daly's analysis that men desire to die. If men truly longed for death, why would they have spent the last several thousand years frantically hatching schemes to immortalize themselves? True though it is that many of men's strategies for securing eternity have entailed dying in the strictly physical sense, they have cast this dying as a welcome, indeed a blessed release, the prerequisite for passage into the more perfect, enduring existence that men deserve, which they fully expect to enjoy elsewhere, far from the contemptible earth.

Fearing death, insulted and affronted by it, men have hardened themselves against life, for in mortal material reality there is no living without dying. Yet to scorn life and to wage war against it sets men at no safer distance from mortality; they have not preserved themselves but, by damaging the creation their lives depend upon, only expedited their own demise. By disavowing themselves as animals, the beings they are by nature, they have harshened their own suffering, for now their lives are spent in paranoiac denial. Paradoxical as it seems, it is men's hatred of death, not any necrophilous craving for it, that is the source of their madness, the malignant terror that poisons the heart and mind of the civilization in which we now find ourselves entrenched.

I am not being polemical, I am simply stating a fact: patriarchy is the end of the world.

In her novel *Ice* (1967), the British writer Anna Kavan describes an earth glaciated by men's assault on living:

> The ultimate achievement of mankind would be not just self-destruction, but the destruction of all life, the transformation of the living world into a dead planet ... By rejecting life, Man had destroyed the immemorial order, destroyed the world; now everything is about to crash down in ruins (pp. 188-189).

For Kavan, it is Man who destroys the world; she believes the destruction of all life will be mankind's crowning achievement. I share her assessment of the situation, and in the pages to follow, I take up the same terminology. 'Man', as a generic term for the human species, is male-supremacist language. Feminists have been right to object to it, for how it abandons females outside of humanity or otherwise absorbs women into a male-defined category as anonymous ancillary appendages to the men who matter. History has been charted as if Man did this and that and everything else of any significance; religion has concerned itself with Man's soul, psychology and philosophy with his mind; while science has been the chronicle of Man's ever-advancing knowledge. Man is the genius, the innovator, the engineer, the artist, the poet, the hero.

Obviously, women belong to the human species no less than men do, for whatever that particular 'honor' is worth. Likewise, it is obvious that women's contributions to human cultures have been invaluable. Limning humanity's tale as if its every accomplishment were men's doing is as inaccurate as it is unjust. Yet it is nevertheless the case that, since the advent of recorded history — or at least that which is dignified as 'History', meaning: the history of the predominantly white patriarchal imperium known as 'Western Civilization' — men have been in power. Males have been at the wheel of human societies, the masters and authors of our social reality, designing and presiding over the political and cultural systems, the religions and ideologies that have defined civilization for the past five or six millennia. All civilization's exalted institutions have functioned as fraternities, instrumental in the production and reproduction of male dominion. Its myths, cultural traditions, entertainments, and recreations have served the same purpose. Because this civilization and its cultures developed under male dominion, and because men continue to dominate as the global ruling class, 'Man' is an accurate shorthand for the subset of humanity culpable for the cataclysm no longer imminent now but already underway.

Man is men. Imagine a composite figure, like those unsettling 16th-century paintings of faces made up of fruit and vegetables, but formed instead from a lurching heap of mostly (but not uniformly) white males — however many centuries' worth of kings, colonizers, real estate developers, loggers, financiers, oil company executives, philosophers, pornographers — and you'll get the gist. 'Man' the generic was not intended to include women, despite men's lame insistence otherwise, and it does not. But then why would we aspire to be included in such a rancid brotherhood? Rather, women can be proud of our history of exclusion, and choose actively to exclude ourselves, in principled refusal of complicity. For the *contemptus mundi* rejection of life that has rendered patriarchal civilization irremediably morbid is men's madness. The violence and sadism that define this civilization are male violence, male sadism; its endless wars have been men's wars, whether against rival male factions, or against women, non-human animals, or the earth itself. Accordingly, I write of the manmade world, of manmade society and manmade culture; and I charge mankind with the outrages that patriarchal civilization has perpetrated against life. I deem the wasteland as it spreads sallow into distance the Kingdom of Man, undeniably doomed.

None of this is to say that men, by dint of their maleness, are in some helpless way constitutionally cursed to be biocidal maniacs. Maleness itself is neutral: the body damns no one. I believe this to be true. But it is also true that it is men who have made civilization the atrocity complex it is today, a vampiric industrialized monstrosity vomiting for its yield a seemingly endless deluge of oppression, strife, needless suffering, and world-devouring violence. Only now it is plain to see that the end is bearing down on us at last, and this dying earth is what men have to show for themselves after 5,000 years of dominion.

So I have written: Man is the Destroyer, the Enemy of Life.

Yet I am not Man. Nor are you. Even men need not be, for they can make the decision to renounce and resist their Manhood. Redemption is possible. It is a choice. If we are to deliver ourselves from manmade annihilation, we are called to purge the maddening horror Man spilled into us, his legacy, our inheritance. To learn to be other than the blight he became. We are called, too, to dethrone Man, to tear down the failed structures that have scaffolded his reign, the collapsing cities and extractive machineries, yes, but also those subtler edifices he raised inside our skulls. And once Man is overthrown and we're no longer acting as his loyal acolytes, couldn't we resuscitate our vital grace as the creatures we are, living not in hostile denialist opposition to the material reality of the world but peacefully within it, willing participants in the vast ceaseless churning of its flux? What could we become, and how would we be transformed, and how might this planet be different, if we loved life? Every wet-hearted cell that thrums within the soft flesh of the animal I am cries out to see the answers born. To feel their weight, hold them in my hands. For our bodies to know them.

This book, then, is about what it will take to unearth those answers. I have been told that what I have written is grim. If it is, it's because male dominion is a grim ordeal, for women and for the world, and I am committed to telling the truth about its atrocities. Not to wallow in the abyss of the status quo, despairing, but to confront it as honestly as I can, without shrinking back in fear or sorrow. Because to fail to confront reality honestly is to forfeit finding any real answers at all. Andrea Dworkin (1974) wrote that to be a writer "means telling the truth. It means being incorruptible. It means not being afraid, and never lying" (p. 25). What I ask you to understand is that my purpose on the pages ahead is not to dwell on horrors, but to do my part to get us out of the hole. I do love life. I have no other reason to write.

BODY
HORROR

> *The shape is there, and most of us come to realize what it is sooner or later: it is the shape of a body under a sheet. All our fears add up to one great fear, all our fears are part of that great fear — an arm, a leg, a finger, an ear. We're afraid of the body under the sheet. It's our body.*
>
> **STEPHEN KING**, *Night Shift* (1978, p. xvi)

A BLOB, A SLIME, A JELLY THING

The Blob (1988) is a horror film about an alien substance. Pink and gelatinous, illuminated by a weird inner glow: a yolk of ooze seething and roiling inside the black stone that carried it crash-landing to the earth. The black stone is a meteorite, jettisoned from outer space. In the forest at the edge of a quaint cozy quiet little all-American town, the local vagrant watches a streak of flare slice the night sky over his shack before arcing to strike down in a nearby clearing. The light draws him, he follows it. Seconds later, we see the man crouched over the crater where the black stone now rests smoldering, embedded in the earth, cracked open. Something pinkish pulsating in its depths. The man's dog growls and scrambles back from the pit, retreating, but the man is curious. With a long stick he pokes at the crack in the stone, probing the fissure. When a dripping clot splits off from the yolk and grips his stick and hangs there, like a living thing, the man goggles uncomprehendingly. And when it squirms upward along the length of the stick to latch onto the man's wrist, where it throbs, thickens, wrapping itself around his forearm like a viscid sleeve he cannot pry loose, the man screams uselessly into darkness. Pulse by pulse the vile pink stuff spreads.

A young couple out for a date-night drive almost run the man over as he staggers dazedly onto the road. Nice kids — the high school quarterback, the star cheerleader — they take him to the hospital. But the Blob's first victim is already worse than dead. There is something hideous inside him. On a cot in the hospital he convulses, his body bulging and buckling as whatever has gotten into him heaves its bulk up his throat: he chokes on this incursion. The man is no longer himself, and what remains cannot rightly be called a man. The doctor lifts the sheet to show what's left of him: a mangled torso, rapidly dissolving; shredded gristle in a plash of bloody froth and bile.

The rest of the film follows the Blob along its rampage through the town, as its slick substance undulates and distends, swells, slithers, devouring everything in its path. "Whatever it is, it's getting bigger," a perceptive onlooker observes. True: all the Blob does is eat and grow, eat more and overgrow, eating and growing on and on uncontrollably. The Blob fleshes itself out, its candied pinkness inflaming to meatier crimson as it floods the streets.

Whatever the Blob is, it's obscenely organic. Anatomically speaking, it most resembles the mesentery: that membranous ruffle of connective tissue that holds our bowels contained within our abdomens. But then in other scenes it is more placental, a sack of jellied blood spat from the black-hole womb of the universe. Like a cancer, the Blob metastasizes into a writhing fabric of cysts, polyps, abscesses. It is tumorous, its constant growth malignant. The Blob is a diseased organ gone rogue, sentient but severed from any reasonable rational mind that might temper its frenzy. Instead, it obeys only the compulsive insatiable carnal drive that animates it: appetite. The Blob is voracious.

Although the Blob eats anything/everything indiscriminately, the film's most gruesome scenes spotlight the meals it makes of men. Our handsome teenage quarterback's head caves in under a goo-sheened lamina as the Blob drags him out of the orderly whiteness of a hospital office into the black night beyond. Tentacles of Blob-stuff burst through a dead girl's chest to seize a boy's head and smother him. In the town diner, the Blob sucks a muscle-bound macho dishwasher facefirst down the kitchen drain. Thus, we can make certain inferences about the Blob's eating habits: it goes for the head. The head houses the mind that Man says defines him, his face the prized symbol of the unique individual essence he names the Self. His identity, his personhood. For Man, the apex anatomical structures of head and face represent the singular humanity that sets him apart from the rabble, while the body below is derogated and discounted as an anonymous, impersonal mass of flesh. Hence, in losing their heads, faces melted from their skulls by acid mucilage, men lose themselves completely to the Blob. Engulfed by an inescapable fleshy onslaught, they disintegrate irreparably.

To be consumed is to be incorporated, the Self captured then annulled, metabolized into the pulpous immensity of soft moist pink matter that is the monster. Forced into violent collision with revolting materiality — his own body merging, melding with the body of the Blob — Man is no longer in control of himself. His most desperate and delicate ambition collapses: he is powerless to separate himself from the horrific substance that surrounds him.

The philosopher Jean-Paul Sartre, in *Being and Nothingness* (1943/ 1992), relates a horror story about a substance he calls slime:

> I open my hands, I want to let go of the slimy and it sticks to me, it draws me, it sucks at me ... It is a soft, yielding action, a moist and feminine sucking ... and I sense it like a dizziness; it draws me to it as the bottom of a precipice might draw me (p. 776).

Slime is insistent as it closes in to envelope Man in its clinging embrace. Drawn into the sliminess, Man is no longer his own master; he has been usurped: undone and overthrown. "To touch the slimy is to risk dissolving into it" (p. 777). Encounters with slime terrorize Sartre inasmuch as they threaten to absorb him into "the whole of being." Slime, for Sartre, is materiality's revenge; it is substance reasserting its dominion over Man, who has made it his mission to sequester himself from the flesh and flux of life. Yet try as he might he cannot free himself.

> The sucking of the slimy which I feel on my hands outlines a continuity of the slimy substance in myself. These long, soft strings of substance which fall from me to the slimy body ... symbolize a rolling off of myself in the slime (p. 777).

He is powerless, the longed-for separation impossible. The slime is in him; when the slime drips from his skin onto the slimy earth, some little droplet of the man leaks out with it. Recognizing his body as continuous with the slimes of the world, Sartre fears that, like "the wasp that sinks into the jam," he will drown in the mire.

Harlan Ellison's oft-anthologized sci-fi story 'I Have No Mouth, and I Must Scream' (1971) details a punishment he deems more horrifying than execution, inflicted on the world's final living human by a sadistic supercomputer with centuries to spend perfecting its tortures:

> I am a great soft jelly thing. Smoothly rounded, with no mouth, with pulsing white holes filled by fog where my eyes used to be. Rubbery appendages that were once my arms; bulks rounding down into legless humps of soft slippery matter. I leave a moist trail when I move. Blotches of diseased, evil gray come and go on my surface, as though light is being beamed from within.
>
> Outwardly: dumbly, I shamble about, a thing that could never have been known as human, a thing whose shape is so alien a travesty that humanity becomes more obscene for the vague resemblance (Ellison 1971, p. 32).

The last man on earth is condemned to exist in this degraded state until eternity gutters out. To endure the misery of such a soft, blobby and lumpish, slime-drenched, shapeless and faceless inhuman and yet hatefully familiar body is the harshest sentence the author can imagine for a man.

A TOMB, A PRISON, A MEATSACK

Plato, writing in the fourth century BC, invoked the Orphic doctrine of *soma sema* (body = tomb) when he compared the body to a grave in which the soul lies buried. Taking up a second, slightly less morbid metaphor, he likens the body to a prison in which the soul, caged, does penance. "[T]his which we carry about with us and call the body, and are imprisoned like an oyster in its shell," Plato wrote, apparently forgetting that oysters tend to fare rather poorly once shucked (Plato 370 BCE/1928, p. 485). Elsewhere, the philosopher maligns the body as an "impediment" and "imperfection" that handicaps the soul, forever "interrupting, disturbing, distracting and preventing us from getting a glimpse of the truth" (Plato 360 BCE/1961, p. 49). The body puts "pure knowledge" out of reach, for as long as Man's soul remains "a helpless prisoner, chained hand and foot in the body," it is doomed to "view reality not directly but only through its prison bars" (Plato 360 BCE/1961, p. 66). The thinking man should therefore have as little to do with his body as possible:

> It seems that so long as we are alive, we shall continue closest to knowledge if we avoid as much as we can all contact and association with the body ... and instead of allowing ourselves to become infected with its nature purify ourselves from it until God himself gives us deliverance (p. 49).

The deliverance knowledge-seeking men must eagerly await is death, the ultimate release by which their souls will once and for all be "liberated ... from the desires and evils" of the corporeal sepulcher (Plato 388 BCE/1961, p. 441).

The Exorcist, 1973. Across the bruised belly of the daughter the childish scrawl rises like a scar, the girl's skin embossed as if the words were being carved by some clawed writer penned up in her guts. The wound spells: "Help me." Tonight, the daughter is a detainee inside her own body, though in fact that body ceased to be hers when the demon slipped in. Because the flesh is such tawdry stuff, it is corruptible, easily broken into, infiltrated and overtaken. How readily a body succumbs to evil — a girl's body especially, since female, hence faultier, hence frailer, more inclined to sin and submission both. From whatever secret cell interred deep in the bowels of her infested body within which the possessor holds her captive, the girl pleads to be set free. Her soul wants out.

In *Timaeus* (360 BCE), Plato outlines his personal take on Man's creation story. In the beginning, he writes, the Craftsman fashioned the Soul of the Universe, and it was perfect. From the remnants of the celestial substance he used to make the Soul of the Universe, the Craftsman next creates the souls of Man, "equal in number to the stars" (p. 42). The task of making Man's body, however, along with the nonhuman animals and plants, the Craftsman passes on to lesser gods. These lesser gods are fit for the job because in their inferiority they have the power to create imperfect things, while the Craftsman is only capable of perfection. Already it has been determined that the body will be second-rate. So, the lesser gods take the celestial immortal soul and encase it inside of a sphere sculpted in the image of the world. This noble sphere where the soul makes its home is Man's head. But alas the soul is not entirely safe sealed off in its tower room; inevitably, the base influence of the body's lower parts sullies it. According to Plato, corporeality is a test imposed by the Craftsman: once instilled into an imperfect body, each immortal soul must master the tempest of impure sensations, passions, emotions, and appetites emanating from the flesh. "And if they shall master these, they will live justly, but if they are mastered, unjustly" (p. 42). The soul that dominates "by force of reason" the "burdensome mass" of his body "shall return again to his abode in his native star," where he will enjoy "a life that is blessed and congenial" in his "first and best" immaterial state. (Meanwhile, the soul that lapses, overpowered by flesh, will find itself reborn into "woman's nature" — i.e., a female body – or some other bestial form bespeaking its wickedness.)

Slang popular among contributors to Reddit and gamer forums refers to the human body as a 'meatsack', 'meatbag', and 'meat suit', as if one's flesh were a layer of dead matter wrapped around the soul like some vulgar and embarrassing garment. Meatsack: "a filthy, fleshy sack of meat, gland-juice, bone, stupidity, and other fluids."[3] Meatbag: "a human or another living creature with flesh in their composition."[4] Meat suit: "the human body, especially one's flesh, suggesting the burdens of corporeality for an otherwise ethereal being."[5] We learn that these terms originated in television shows about robots and demons. "Meatbag," as an insult hurled by machines

---

3   Urban Dictionary. <https://www.urbandictionary.com/define.php?term=meatsack> (accessed 26 February 2024).

4   Wiktionary.org. <https://en.wiktionary.org/wiki/meatbag#:~:text=meat%20 %2B%E2%80%8E%20bag.,the%20Star%20Wars%20fictional%20universe> (accessed 26 February 2024).

5   Urban Dictionary. <https://www.urbandictionary.com/define.php?term=meat%20 suit> (accessed 26 February 2024).

— fleshless, inorganic, built of metal – ridicules the pathetic crudeness of humanity's biological, corporeal nature. When demons possess people they are said to wear their victims' bodies like "meat suits."[6] One Reddit user tells us, "My body is not me. It's just a meat sack that I live in."[7] Another stares into the pale blue light of the screen and implores, "Why am I trapped in this disgusting meat suit?"[8]

In her analysis of the virulently body-negative rhetoric that permeates the great philosopher's oeuvre, Elizabeth Spelman diagnoses Plato with a syndrome she has christened 'somatophobia': a paranoid terror of the mortal material biological body, characteristically expressed as abhorrence for all things physical (Spelman 1982). It is a condition by no means unique to Plato. Instead, Spelman argues, it is endemic, saturating the western philosophical canon with anxious antipathy for human bodiliness. For Spelman, somatophobia stems from the division of the immaterial soul from the material body. And out of this schism, a dualistic theory of ontological reality emerges: body and soul are separate and discrete from one another, composed of entirely different materials, however inextricably bound together they may seem in life. The soul is associated with the immortal, the other-worldly and divine, while the body belongs to earthly organic nature. Soul and body are set at opposite poles, with the soul nearer to god, i.e., goodness, and the body closer to dirt. Which is to say: badness. The soul is valued over and above the body, as unquestionably superior to it as immortality is superior to mortality, immateriality to materiality, heaven to earth. As Spelman observes, "all the good and hopeful and desirable possibilities for human life … are aligned with the soul, while [the] rather seedy and undesirable liabilities of human life are aligned with the body" (Spelman 1982, p. 119) Predictably, Man makes his camp with the soul. The body gives him the creeps.

---

6   Supernatural Wiki. <http://www.supernaturalwiki.com/Meatsuit> (accessed 26 February 2024).
7   Reddit. <https://www.reddit.com/r/fatlogic/comments/7kdxux/my_body_is_not_me_ its_just_a_meat_sack_that_i/> (accessed 26 February 2024).
8   Reddit. <https://www.reddit.com/r/Psychonaut/comments/4mlz4t/meat_suit/> (accessed 26 February 2024).

Inasmuch as soul and body are entangled during Man's life on the earth, their union endangers soul. The downward drag of the dark, dense, leaden earthbound body depresses the long-suffering soul, debauches it; flesh hangs from the soul like a filthy cerement. Ceaselessly, the body assails and assaults its prisoner-victim, preventing the soul from enjoying the least moment of peace. Wendy Brown, who like Spelman has probed the somatophobic undercurrents of patriarchal philosophy, writes that Man experiences his body as "a demanding demon — foreign, irascible, and infantile" (Brown 1988, p. 195). Now the body is not merely a passive tomb/prison/oyster shell confining and constraining Man. No, now it has become an active aggressor: the soul's monstrous adversary, an alien enemy for Man to vanquish or else allow himself to be degraded and destroyed.

SOMATOPHOBIC FOUNDATIONS

Manmade culture's proud tradition of somatophobic thinking launched roughly 2,500 years ago with the emergence of Orphism. Orphic theology staged a never-ending battle between the divine soul and the ignoble body, reputedly formed from the ashes of evil giants (Russell 1987, p. 137). The theory held that matter in general, and the human body in particular, was malevolently conceived as a cage for Man's soul. Man's mission, it followed, was to disburden himself of evil matter in order to unite his soul with the immaterial heavens. Socrates (469-399 BCE) was partial to the Orphic view, instilling it in his student Plato (c. 429-347 BC), who then passed it on at the Academy in Athens to his own most illustrious pupil, Aristotle (384-322 BCE). Neoplatonists like Plotinus (204/5-270 BCE) drew upon Plato's *soma sema* attitude to hone their own contempt for matter and the body as "total deficiency, total privation, total non-being, and hence a total lack of good" (Russell 1987, p. 162). Being totally deficient in goodness, the material body was to be despised as totally bad.

The early Jewish philosopher Philo of Alexandria (20 BCE-40 CE) wrote that the body was evil because it resisted the work of God; Man's sins resulted from the soul's contamination by the body, rendering him susceptible to "the demands of matter" (Russell 1987,

p. 167). And it is to Saint Paul the Apostle (5-62 CE) that we owe our thanks for pioneering the Christian habit of overwrought ambivalence towards corporeality by on one hand bidding the faithful to revere their bodies as "temple[s] of the Holy Spirit,"[9] while elsewhere writing that within the flesh there reigns "a perverse law that rebels against the spirit," and pleading to be delivered from his own "body of death."[10]

The Stoics, for their part, berated the body as "but clay and corruption" — to quote the philosophizing emperor Marcus Aurelius (121-180 CE) — and looked forward to death as "a release from impressions of sense, from twitchings of appetite, from excursions of thought, and service to the flesh" (170 CE/1964, p. 97). Meanwhile, the assorted Gnostic sects that gained popularity during the first century CE were teaching their members that the human body was not the product of any divine creator, but had been crudely molded out of "dark substance" by the Archons, bestial demons who ruled over the material realm (Williams 1989, p. 135). By this demon-wrought body the soul, likened to a pure and immortal pearl, was befouled as if "dipped into the excrement and slime of matter" (Keen 1995, p. 126). Gnostic doctrine advised Man to disclaim his body — "Woe to you who put your hope in the flesh and the prison that will perish," warns a passage from *The Book of Thomas the Contender*[11] — and maligned reincarnation as Man's punishment for failing to attain 'gnosis', or spiritual knowledge.

Manichaeism, founded in second-century Babylonia, elaborated upon Gnosticism's basic precepts in the making of its own unique somatophobic mythos. Manichean legend waxed nostalgic about a blissful golden age when opposed substances — spirit and matter, good and evil, light and dark — were perfectly isolated from one another. So it was in the good old days before demons gave birth to Adam and Eve and thereby instigated the soul's downward spiral to the material realm (Doniger 1999). On the premise that earthly beings were made up of particles of pure light trapped inside corruptive bodies,

---

9   Corinthians 6:19-20
10   Romans 7:23-24
11   Quoted in Williams (1989, p. 136).

Manichaean monks were forbidden from any actions that could promote the reproduction of animals or plants, since to encourage new life would cruelly delay the inner light's liberation from matter (Tardieu 2008). As long as living things persisted in living, the light was in exile; only when life on earth died out would it finally be set free.

St. Augustine of Hippo (345–430 CE), the so-called Great Church Father and theologian whose influence is said to have "affected all subsequent Christian thought, attitudes, and practice," dabbled in Manichaeism in his youth, and though he later publicly renounced the sect, his account of the mortal material body as original sin incarnate tempers somewhat any claims of his reconciliation with corporeality (Bottomley 1979, p. 97). According to Augustine, the human body was by god's original design immortal, incorruptible, and fully obedient to Man's will; it was only after the fall that bodies began dying, growing ill, suffering erections during sexual arousal — the latter indignity being Augustine's favored illustration of the flesh's baleful unruliness (Bottomley 1979). Because he accepted the idealized (and wholly hypothetical) prelapsarian body as a suitable vessel, Augustine's complaint was not with bodies per se, but the earthly body in particular:

> To obtain blessedness, we need not quit every kind of body, but only the corruptible, cumbersome, painful, dying bodies — not such bodies as the goodness of God contrived for the first man, but only such bodies as man's sin entailed (425/1913, p. 540).

Given that no bodies besides earthly ones actually exist, Augustine's clarification does little to redeem the mortal material biological body, which retains its low status as sin's penalty. Yet Augustine's view does come to seem almost sunny when compared to the wrathful antipathy given vent by later Christians. Take, for example, the monk John Climacus (579–649 CE), who cried out, "Let us kill this flesh ... let us kill it just as it has killed us with the mortal blow of sin!"[12] This attitude inspired several centuries of stringent asceticism amongst

---

12   Quoted in Piero Camporesi (1988, p. 45).

pious Christians, during which "the hideous maceration of the body was regarded as the highest proof of excellence" (Lecky 1869, p. 114) and "devout penitents burned ... with a desire to annihilate and deform their physical selves" (Camporesi 1988, p. 43). Popular self-torture practices intended to subjugate the sin-sodden body included flagellation, starvation, grueling open-air vigils atop pillars, truly bleak personal hygiene, sleep deprivation, and periodic bouts of rolling naked through thorny brambles.[13]

St. Peter Damian (1007-1072/73 CE) set the tone for a new somatophobic millennium when he proclaimed the body to be corruption itself: "It could be said that human flesh, which now seems to be alive, does not in fact bring forth decay in itself after death, but only then declares itself openly to be the rottenness which it has always been."[14] This revulsion failed to wane with the Reformation, but instead found a fervent and eloquent spokesman in Martin Luther (1483-1546 CE), whose preferred epithet for the body was *Madensack*, translating to "maggot-sack" (Cortright 2011, p. 216). Luther was of the view that the body's constitutional nastiness revealed itself in its many and diverse secretions, excretions, and afflictions, an offensive spectacle culminating in the vermicular explosion that bursts forth from the flesh after death. Upon dying, Luther asserted, the sinful stuff from which Man's body was composed comes spilling out into the world as a spew of "vilest worms, adders, toads, and snakes" (1973, p. 185). A century later, the Jesuit Jeremias Drexel (1581-1638 CE), court preacher to the Duke of Bavaria, was no less disgusted: "To be sure the body is very like a tomb and gives off noxious vapours in all directions ... [like a] tavern for worms, an inn for serpents, an hostelry for toads, a bilge full of dirt."[15]

13　St. Benedict of Nursia recalls throwing himself into "sharp thorns and stinging nettles" and rolling until he was covered with bloody scratches in order to squelch temptation aroused by memories of women. See Jane Tibbetts Schulenberg (1998, p. 315).

14　Quoted in Camporesi (1988, p. 78).

15　Quoted in Camporesi (1991, p. 36).

THE STUFF OF NIGHTMARES

*He would be inevitable, like a pure idea ... and he finds himself
shut up in a body of limited powers ... This quivering jelly which
is elaborated in the womb ... evokes too clearly the soft viscosity
of carrion for him not to turn shuddering away ... Because he is
horrified by needlessness and death, man feels horror at having
been engendered; he would fain deny his animal ties; through
the fact of his birth murderous nature has a hold upon him.*

SIMONE DE BEAUVOIR, *The Second Sex* (1949/2011, p. 165)

*The body must bear no trace of its debt to nature: it must be
clean and proper in order to be fully symbolic.*

JULIA KRISTEVA, *Powers of Horror* (1980, p. 102)

The body Man desires is a smooth surface, with nothing inside it to
stink or decay, no gurgling bowels nor blistering stinging nerves, no
blood, no guts. Man wants his body clean, a proper temple for the
soul. He wants his body separate from the world that surrounds it and
completely independent from it; Man needs nothing from the world.
His body should be under his own rational control, immune to the
forces of nature. The body Man desires is the living symbol of his
sovereignty.

But the body he has is horrid: blighted by the stigma of its debts,
it does not conform to Man's image of himself, but instead disgraces
his ego by defying his will. This horrid body — the horror body — does
not grant Man the comfort of forgetting his contingency: that he is
a corporeal creature, dependent on the earth's generosity for every
aspect of his existence. Murderous nature's mark screams lurid upon
the horror body's sweat-damp skin; its smell of afterbirth cannot be
rinsed nor perfumed away. Like a savage animal the horror body eats
Man alive.

Because the horror body does not conceal its monstrousness,
Man takes it as his model for all the scary-movie mythic monsters he
invents. It is the body that marks and makes the monster, recognizable
as an enemy by some physical or physiological anomaly that alerts
us to respond, as philosopher Noël Carroll writes, "not only with fear

24

but with loathing, a combination of terror and disgust" (1990, p. 23). To glimpse the monster's body is to know the evil of its nature, and the sight sparks terror, yes, the urge to flee — yet in an odd way the monster is also a comfort. For when Man looks upon the monster, he is reassured by the manifest differences between its physicality and his own. He has one head whereas the monster has three; his skin is smooth not scaly nor seeping fetid discharge; his limbs attach at their proper places, in their proper number. Relatively speaking, Man's own body is clean and proper and unmarked. This is a relief, and there is another: now, at least, Man fears something he can run from. From the menace of monsters, if not his own body, Man can preserve some hope of escape.

Body horror is externalized in the figure of the monster, situated outside of society and opposed to it as an object lesson in "all that must be repudiated by the human spirit" (Gilmore 2012, p. 12). As the antithesis of the taintlessly civilized symbolic body Man covets, the monster is cast out to the furthest margins, where it prowls permanently through twilit primeval forests, the fathoms of blackest ocean, abyssal subterranes or the mist-shrouded back alleys and sewers of the bleakest parts of town. Should it come too close, Man swears he will hunt the monster to the ends of the earth and slaughter it. There is no other way: it is only through distance that Man can save his soul. In horror movies and horror myths, when the monster encroaches upon the city, undaunted by the borderlines Man traces to mark his territory, the terrifying potential the monstrous body incarnates is nothing less than total dissolution, manmade civilization's collapse. It is Godzilla, trampling Tokyo to rubble; the vampire that bleeds the castle dry; the zombie horde that leaves no survivors but just faceless bloodied lumps of meat strewn across parking lots. The monster's return from exile is an existential threat precisely because Man founds his civilization on the conceit that he can separate himself from the matter he calls monstrous. But the monster has no respect for Man's authority. Ferociously, the monster resists Man's desperate attempts to banish it; time and time again it comes writhing back from baleful wildernesses to collect Man's debts. For how it reveals the flimsiness of Man's bulwarks, the return of the monster threatens to topple all that Man has built, to unmake all his hard-won progress.

The horror body is the monster that breaches every boundary Man exhausts himself laboring to draw in the sand, violating Man's sanctuaries and checking his transcendental ambitions, dragging mankind backsliding down and out from the 24-hour industrial electric dazzle of the sterile, meticulously under-control hypermodern megacity heart of empire, down and down deeper still into the turbid green-dark swamp of those primordial nightworld wastelands where nature reigns, where men are denied refuge from the reality that terrorizes them: Man is not the ruler of this world, he will never be King.

IT IS DEFORMED

The body horrifies because it is mutable and ever mutating; in the perpetual flux of cells dividing and self-digesting the flesh shapeshifts promiscuously, heedless of Man's will. The body is subject to external forces, be they natural or occult, as well as those forces that emanate from the obscure inner realms of the body itself. A man's body is altered by elements outside his control; he can do nothing to stop it. A volatile thing, the body cannot be trusted: in a moment of turbulence it warps and he is disfigured, he no longer recognizes himself, he is not what he once was. Alterations in bodily form and function — however abrupt or gradual, whether resulting from accident or illness or simply the slow coursing of years through his tissues — leave Man feeling hijacked and betrayed. Horrible is the mark that appears on his surface, unwilled — for it is mutiny. A blister, a pimple, a cold sore, a carbuncle, an ingrown hair: these defects he dreads as signs of sedition.

The mutinous body is a monstrous creature. On some moonlit night, the man is mauled by an enormous ferocious animal and bitten, the beast's curse injected into his blood like a virus. Now each month when the moon is full, black hair bristles down the man's spine, he falls on all fours, his teeth lengthening into fangs. In the morning he will wake to find clots of fresh gore under his nails. "He was said to exhibit much uneasiness and discomfort when the wolf-hair began to break out and his bodily shape to change" (Baring-Gould 1865, p. 59).

In David Cronenberg's 1988 update of the 1950s sci-fi B movie *The Fly*, we see Jeff Goldblum's fingers slough their nails, his teeth drop from his gums, his jaw unhinge, his skin redden with an ugly rash that begins to weep pus and then molts, revealing raw wet flesh, as he is reconfigured by a painfully protracted metamorphosis into an unrecognizable 'man/fly'. Cronenberg's film is considered the paradigmatic example of the cinematic subgenre of 'Body Horror', also dubbed 'Biological Horror' by film theorist Ronald Allen Lopez Cruz. Cruz defines Body/Biological Horror as "characterized by the manipulation and warping of the normal state of bodily form and function" (2012, p. 161). What distinguishes this brand of horror's transformations from those played out in other subgenres — the slasher film, for example, in which endless successions of (typically female) bodies undergo brutal alteration as they are run like grist through the mill of some maniac's violence — is that the underlying anxiety is not the fear of attack from without, but of the body's own instability. What horrifies is the potential, inherent in Man's own nature as a corporeal being, that his substance will turn against him, that the flesh will rebel and he will find himself overpowered from the inside out.

In Junji Ito's horror manga trilogy *Uzumaki* (2000), a town and its residents are violently unraveled by a supernatural force that spins air and matter alike into deadly spirals. A scar on a teenage girl's forehead curves into a crescent moon that spirals deeper day by day until it opens a black hole into her skull. Her classmates' hair grows long, spiraling to the sky, coiling around telephone poles to string the girls up, as the overgrowth drains the life from their bodies like parasitic vines. Whorled shells swelling heavy on boys' backs signal these unfortunates' imminent transformation into giant snails. When men eat the snail-boys, their own bodies contract the spiral, tongues looping and twisting from their mouths. The spiral-sick resemble eels, serpents, worms; they have ceased to be human. They have lost all control of themselves. They drool slimes, they wriggle on the earth.

Man's powerlessness to mold his substance to his will is evidenced by the unwelcome metamorphoses the unstable mass of his body abandons him to, each transmutation a nightmarish reminder of his mastery's limits. Again and again he is thwarted in his struggle to govern his own body; his will is overruled. And so it is by fact of his bodiliness that nature keeps Man in its thrall. As long as he is prisoner to this out-of-order organic body, through the chokehold it has on his flesh, murderous nature will maintain the upper hand. Injury, disease, age, a glitch of the genes, random mutations vandalize him: he is not sovereign. Deformed, Man is dethroned.

PERMEABLE IT IS PARASITIZED

"The conception of the individual as *homo clausus*, a little world in himself who ultimately exists quite independently of the great world outside, determines the image of man in general," writes the sociologist Norbert Elias (1978, p. 249). *Homo clausus*: the Closed Man, safely divorced from the world and ensconced inside the impenetrable shell of his surface, his skin the wall dividing his inner self from the chaos outside. In the *homo clausus* model, the body is conceived as a material edifice inhabited by Man's immaterial ethereal essence. He tells himself it is possible for the soul to be saved shut tight inside such a fortress. Yet the skin is not so steely a defense as he desires it to be; it is no impervious barricade, it neither seals nor shields Man from the world. As partition, the skin is porous. Through its orifices and apertures, fissures and ruptures, Man drips out from his body; and through this same compromising constellation of holes, the world creeps seeping in. It is corporeality's appalling incontinence that elicits the disgust expressed by the fifth-century Buddhist scholar Buddhaghosa when he describes the human body as

> ... constantly dripping and trickling like a grease pot, inhabited by a community of worms ... perpetually oozing from the nine orifices like a chronic open carbuncle, from both of whose eyes eye-filth trickles, from whose ears ear-filth, from whose nostrils snot, from whose mouth food and bile and phlegm and blood,

from whose lower outlets excrement and urine, and from whose
ninety-nine thousand pores the broth of stale sweat seeps ...[16]

Untold strains of exudate dribble from the body everywhere,
unstoppably. It is this same suppurative wide-open body that Mikhail
Bakhtin (1965) classified as "grotesque," marked by its continuity with,
rather than its separation from, the physical world. The grotesque
body "swallows the world and is itself swallowed by the world,"
sucking and guzzling matter through its holes into its bowels only to
expel matter out again by way of yet more holes as sweat, seepage,
ordure (p. 317). Aghast at how being an eating and excreting creature
caught in perpetual interchange with the material world shatters
his *homo clausus* fantasies, Man has labored diligently to deny the
'grotesqueness' that threatens to undo him.

Julia Kristeva, in *Powers of Horror: An Essay on Abjection* (1982),
labels as "abject" those substances Man repulses in order to sustain
the illusion that he is not grotesquely open but instead hermetically
sealed, his fortress walls leak-proof and impenetrable. The word
'abject' derives from the Latin *abicere*, meaning to cast off or rebuff,
and as an adjective it has come to designate that which has sunk to the
lowest states of degradation, deprivation, and indignity. For Kristeva,
however, the abject is any form of matter that compels Man to recall
the permeability of his body, and which he aggressively rejects as a
result. Scabs, excreta, spit, vomit, mucus, blood — all are abject, Man
wants nothing to do with them. "Any secretion or discharge, anything
that leaks out of the feminine or masculine body defiles" (p. 102).
As an action, abjection is the strategic, systematic exclusion of these
unacceptable leakages in an attempt to reassert and reinforce one's
borders. The material Man rejects as abject is what he refuses to be;
it is what he disavows and disowns. He will not swallow it, nor will
he let it swallow him. "The abject has only one quality of the object —
that of being opposed to I," Kristeva writes (p. 1). "Such wastes drop
so that I might live" (p. 3).

With the corruptive scums of corporeality expelled beyond
the barricades, Man can rest assured that his inner self stays clean

---

16   Quoted in Hamilton (1995, p. 59).

and pure, secure within its carapace. Thus the process of abjection enables him to believe he has isolated himself from the material world, otherwise known as filth. It is an excision and expulsion by means of which he strives to forget what he has — what he *is* — inside. Yet what Man repels as vile is ultimately inescapable: the whole horrible earth is lousy with the stuff. Encounters with the abject are inevitable and each new encounter is a chilling ordeal, in which Man is forced to confront his terror that the fortification separating Self from world can and will be violated. William Ian Miller (2009) defines horror as a kind of fear-infused disgust, specifically: "... that disgust for which no distancing or evasive strategies exist that are not in themselves utterly contaminating" (p. 26). Horror sets in when Man, pressed close to some disgusting substance, senses that he cannot save himself, cannot extricate himself from this insidious enemy that, even after he casts it out, finds its way slithering back inside to subsume the Self. Thus subsumed, the Self dissolves into the horribleness of all matter. There can be no separation. There is no safe haven.

The constant vigilance required to police his borders makes Man paranoid. He spies a twitch in the slime puddle, feels a moist stroke coaxing open the shuttered pore. The sickly caress of the abject, which would lure him out of himself only to drown him in the mire. Disgusted, horrified, Man cannot forgive his body for leaving him so exposed to the vileness of the world.

The permeable body is also penetrable, and what can be penetrated is prone to invasion. The soul's sanctum can become infested. Physical invasion is parasitization, Man's corporeal residence breached and re-purposed as a cask for vermin. Through the Middle Ages, Man tormented himself with lurid visions of bodies brimful with worms, lice, caterpillars, serpents, eely invertebrates, all manner of "vile and minute animals" devouring the living flesh and feasting on Man's innards, a plague of miniscule anthropophagic monsters swarming and spawning unceasingly, their teeming a harbinger of apocalypse for the host (Camporesi 1988, p. 94). Of all the pests that plagued Man, worms were the worst. The human body was believed to be an inhabitation "highly conducive" to the proliferation of flesh-eating worms, on account of the "unrefined humors" that suffused it (p. 81). Women, being "fuller of bad juices and phlegmatic humor," tended by their nature to be wormier (p. 82). The vermicular enemy was legion: ashen worms with vipers' heads, worms generated exclusively in the partially decayed extremities of lepers, worms like "little snakes that came forth from [men's] skins and gnawed at their arms and legs" (p. 98). Because Man's body is open to the earth and, more horribly still, made from the same foul matter, Man is fated to be wormfood not merely after he dies, but for the awful entirety of his earthly existence.

Alien, 1979. Its skeletal extremities curl around the astronaut's head as he lies unconscious and inert on the table. Clamped to his skull the thing covers his face like a mask, its tail tightening in coils that wind around his neck. Into the immobilized man's mouth the alien deposits its larva, a parasitoid embryo that will incubate within the dark recesses of its human host's body, maturing unseen inside the man until one night during dinner he starts to cough, sputters, shuddering. Falls, convulsing. With a spray of blood, the red stain a shock against the bright white sterility of the spacecraft, his sternum cracks, and the alien births itself thrusting up through the astronaut's ruptured body. It comes out sharp-toothed and screeching, coated in slime like amniotic fluid, before it speeds away. An abandoned host, useless now, spent, the man twitches and bleeds and dies on the table. There's simply no saving him.

Parasitization's metaphysical parallel is possession by demons and unclean spirits. Evil entities take advantage of the body's porosity — slipping underneath girls' fingernails, like the fox-spirits of Japanese lore (*kitsune*), or sliding between lips parted in anticipation of a kiss, or stealing in through nostrils and anuses inadequately guarded — to invade, overthrow the resident soul's rule over his members, and seize the corporeal vehicle for their own diabolical purposes. In Elizabethan England, demonic entry via the mouth was considered standard, though the airy, shapeshifting bodies of demons were thought capable of entering and exiting at will by whichsoever orifices suited them. Acts of consumption carried a special risk of spiritual contamination, since demons could be swallowed in a sip of milk, or eaten along with the leaves of unblessed lettuce (Katajala-Peltomaa 2020). The demon would then make its home in the belly of the possessed, "dwelling amidst the filth in the entrails."[17] Once again it was women, with their frailer bodies fuller of bad juices, and their anatomy putatively 'designed' for penetration, who were considered most susceptible to possession.

In 1563, a young woman possessed by a "white thing" (Satan, we presume) that appeared in her path while she was out herding her father's cows into a nearby field fell ill and languished bedridden for months. Her possession was apparent in how her belly swelled "up and down, sometimes beneath her chest, sometimes up to the throat, in such vehemence that a man would have thought she would burst" (Sands 2004, p. 17). Regarding the seventeen nuns besieged by demons in 1694 at an Ursuline convent in the French town of Loudun, it was reported that "their faces became so frightful one could not bear to look at them; their eyes remained open without winking; their tongues issued suddenly from their mouths, horribly swollen, black, hard, and covered with pimples" (Des Niau 1634/2020, p. 98). The Jesuit priest Malachi Martin, in his bestselling memoir *Hostage to the Devil: The Possession and Exorcism of Five Living Americans* (1976), remarks that "[v]iolent transformations seem sometimes to make the lives of the possessed a kind of hell on earth. Their normal processes of secretion and elimination are saturated with inexplicable wracking and exaggeration" (p. 10). He writes that a putrid stench accompanies the possessed, like the dankest commingling of sulfur, sewage, and rot.

Exorcism is the remedy prescribed to drive out demonic invaders and restore the raided body to the soul to which it rightfully belongs. The demoniac is restrained, the presiding priest reads the Bible aloud over the thrashing body, prayers are spoken in the name of the Lord Almighty. Yet even if Man has faith in these rites of salvation, his horror is at best only temporarily assuaged. How will he ever feel safe, the tenant of an abode so violable, its every pore a doorway swinging

---

17   Caeser of Heisterbach, 13th century, quoted in Katajala-Peltomaa (2020, p. 30).

open, impossible to lock? He is forced to concede that his body is no fortress. Instead it is a dilapidated hovel into which untold horrors are bound to worm their way, and from which Man himself, despite his claims to ownership as the proprietor of the derelict structure, can be so readily evicted.

IT IS PERISHABLE

Its habit of dying is by far the body's gravest, most unforgivable offense. Nature is murder and the body, in conspiracy with it, ensures Man's demise as it follows organic creation's morbid coursing towards the River Styx. Man's matter makes him mortal:

> The body comes from the earth, the seed comes from the body, blood comes from the seed, the body from blood. Just as man's body is formed in the womb, so will it rot in the bosom of the earth. The body engenders corruption, corruption engenders worms, worms create ashes, and ashes make earth. Thus the mother of the human body is the earth, and to the earth it shall return.[18]

Another medieval Christian was more concise: "After man comes the worm. After the worm, stench and horror."[19]

Though death is for Man "an impossible and contrary monster,"[20] the ghastly fact of the matter is that his body will die and when it does he will perish right along with it. Of course he tells himself his soul is eternal and immortal, that it will persist after the body's extinction. But since he cannot be sure that what he tells himself is true until he dies, it is necessary for him to suffer death, the source of his terror, if he wants to see his hypothesis confirmed. The comforts offered by the immortal soul theory are therefore somewhat limited.

In panicked recognition of his mortality, Man obsesses over what he perceives as death's emblems, detected everywhere within his body and scattered across its surface. In life he is death-laden, his flesh

---

18 Attributed to St. Anselm, as quoted in Delumeau (1990, p. 43).
19 From the *Speculum Peccatoris* attributed to St. Augustine, as quoted in ibid., p. 42.
20 Jean Molinet, 15th century, quoted in ibid., p. 40.

already rancid. He sickens, sensing his last meal moldering in his belly. His skin falls away in flakes of dander, he finds his hair clumped in the shower drain. A welt yellows with purulence and widens. His body "naught but foam made flesh and covered with a flimsy garment,"[21] life diminishes for him into an immersion in sustained decomposition. "Worldly life, future death, permanent ruin,"[22] Man laments, wracked with self-pity. Steadily rotting his way through life, Man is condemned by corporeality to a state chronically swamped by rank corruption, the spoilt meat of his person ever-dying, breeding death and feeding its familiar, the Conqueror Worm. (It was Edgar Allan Poe who wrote: "And seraphs sob at vermin fangs/In human gore imbued": 1858, p. 31).

Between the 14th and the 16th centuries, a procession of decayed corpses and goggling skulls paraded through European popular culture, the morbid iconography of an age tinged a darker shade of grim by regular repeated outbreaks of plague and war. This was the era of the *danse macabre* and the Triumph of Death, when church walls were adorned with murals depicting mortality in the person of a bat-winged hag, trampling nuns beneath the hooves of her spectral steed; and princes petitioned to have their tombs carved with their likenesses in the latter phases of decay, with skin peeling tattered from their skulls and toads nibbling at their eyeballs (Delumeau 1990). A popular guide to "the art of death" from this period advised its pious readership that, each time they gazed at their physical forms, they'd do well to pause a moment and contemplate how soon the flesh would putrefy and turn to ash.

Writing in the 14th century, the French poet Guillaume de Deguileville imagines his soul's reaction to the unpleasant discovery of its former body, post-evacuation:

Among several bodies there lying
I saw my own
Those bones that I once knew so well ...
Are you, said I, that evil body

---

21 *Meditatio de humana conditione*, attributed to St. Bernard, as quoted in ibid., p. 45.
22 Unnamed 12th century monk, quoted in ibid., p. 15.

That very vile body, so filthy and malodorous
Meat for worms and putrification,
That horrible and ugly creature?[23]

The lesson woven into this macabre whirl of skulls, gristle, and worms was an entreaty not to wallow in the vain and fleeting sensual pleasures of the physical world, best understood as a quagmire of putrescence. Rather, the righteous should disavow the world and the body, which lives only to die in the most disgusting fashion, and focus instead on the soul's salvific return to bodiless purity in the finer cleaner air of heaven.

The queasy obsession with death and decay ought not be mistaken for some eccentricity of European Christendom, since the same morbid tendencies can be found to surface elsewhere in the Kingdom of Man. Early Buddhist texts describe the monastic custom of sitting alongside decomposing corpses as a meditation on the miserable impermanence of the material world. The pedagogical function of these contemplations was to help the monks along in their process of detachment from worldly things and carnal desires, amplifying their yearning for the enlightenment that would release them from the mortal cycle of birth-life-death through graphic demonstration of that cycle's true grotesquerie. Theravada Buddhism, founded in Sri Lanka during the third century BCE, advocates a form of death awareness meditation known as *Maranasati*, wherein the practitioner imagines a human cadaver transformed by the nine stages of decomposition. Commencing with the "swollen, blue, and festering" days prior to the dead body's initial disposal at the charnel ground, the meditator tracks his object through its gradual decay and consumption by scavenging dogs, vultures, and worms, until, in the final stage, all that remains is "rotted bones, crumbling to dust" (Thera 2005, pp. 133-134). The instructions specify the intended effect of the meditation upon the meditator: "Independent he dwells, clinging to nothing in the world" (p. 134).

---

23   Quoted in Delumeau (1990, p. 67).

In one particularly memorable Buddhist tale of carrion contemplation, the Buddha orders that the "fly-blown corpse" of a formerly beautiful and much-desired courtesan be dumped in the charnel field as an object lesson for a young monk. The monk had been in love with the woman when she was alive, but this love bound him to the mortal material world, impeding his progress towards transcendence, and he would have to be released from it if he wished to know enlightenment. What could extinguish the snag of love more efficiently than to gaze upon the flesh that had once attracted such ardor as it disintegrated back into the dirt from whence it came? For the Buddha and his disciples, once-lovely female flesh now rotting on the ground exemplified the chicanery of the material world, matter's intrinsic foulness, and, crucially, the treacherous nature of men's own sensual desires. "Look at this diseased body," the Buddha instructs his followers, "Look at this decorated image, an elevated mass of wounds. This diseased thing is highly fancied [although] it's neither permanent nor stable."[24] In another anecdote, a monk overcomes his carnal urges by visualizing "the process of decay of the impure body of a beautiful woman" until he is able to calmly conclude that "attachment to the body is akin to relishing the droppings of maggots in a toilet" (Kanda 2005, p. 25). Sufficiently reassured by this thought, he recommits to total renunciation of material reality.

A contemporary analog to the pious macabre pageants of plague-era Europeans and the funereal ruminations of Buddhist monks is the zombie film. Like its precedents, the zombie film treats the viewer to a grisly extravaganza of human bodies laid waste, ravaged, and reduced to hunks of rancid carnage, as the screen spills over with corpses rendered at every stage of decomposition, from bloated to viscous to desiccated. Strips of grey-greenish skin dangle like seaweed from mildewed skulls; darkly enslimed entrails unravel from ruptured bellies and tumble to the dirt. Severed heads and limbs pile up pell-mell in spreading lakes of congealed blood.

---

24 Quoted in Elizabeth Wilson (1995, p. 84).

The zombie is the horror body defined by mortal matter's perishability forced to its most repulsive extremes. In the figure of the zombie, we see the body torn to pieces, mutilated and degenerated and disassembled until it is deteriorated to a state of dissolution surpassing even death — and yet the body remains unthinkably, miserably, wretchedly alive. The zombie is alive in its body — it shuffles around, pursues and consumes its prey — but braindead, stripped of the selfhood that resided in the flesh subsequent to zombification. That the zombie remains in the barest sense sentient makes its degraded state all the worse, since the zombified person's former richness of thought and feeling has attenuated to a single, shameful objective: appeasing the body's appetites. Stupidly lugging around its burden of blood and guts, the zombie is a body hunting down other bodies its hungers mean to convert to meat. Appetite, as we saw in the case of the Blob, is a serious bugbear for Man, the steady twinge within that never lets him forget his dependencies or limitations. A 16th century monk decried appetite as "the lowest part of our soul ... that which debases us, which pulls us down to earth and estranges us from heaven,"[25] and Man's sentiment has scarcely shifted over the course of the last 500 years. In its implacable hunger as a body eating bodies such that there is nothing at all in its voided world but bodiliness, the zombie is contemptible.

Zombie movies source their deepest terror from the suggestion that, though the despised body dies, even death might fail to put an end to corporeality's depredations. Even as it disintegrates, the body, in becoming a zombie, continues to victimize Man. Prevailing zombie lore holds that the undead maintain their own mindless bodies by feeding on the brains of the living. When a zombie feasts on its victim, the victim's own brain is destroyed. The brain: the mind, the soul, the self. Destruction of the brain implies the death of the soul. Man as he knows himself is annihilated — but still the body persists. Presuming he has enough carrion left on his bones to undergo zombification after being killed and eaten, the victim then 'turns' and joins the ranks of the living dead, in which condition he will endure indefinitely the

---

25   Louis of Granada, quoted in Delumeau (1990, p. 25).

deathless torments of an abjectly corporeal existence, ruled by the exigencies of the flesh. We look on, revolted, as its body staggers and oozes, putrid and anonymous in the welter of the horde, a beast glutting itself on bleeding flesh until the eater itself falls to pieces. (And still its teeth chatter, its milky eyes rolling in their undying search for the next meal.) The zombie's mindless, soulless carnality is more disgusting, and more dreadful, than death.

Similarly better-off-dead are Buddhism's hungry ghosts, the spectral form into which people in life "unable to stop desiring and consuming, unable to release from this world of suffering" are fated to be reincarnated (Wetmore Jr. 2021, p. 131). Its body "a corporeal chamber of horrors" (Rotman 2021, p. 50), the hungry ghost is forever ravenous yet physiologically forbidden from satisfying its appetites: through a mouth "like the eye of a fine needle,"[26] the hungry ghost can ingest only the tiniest portions at a time. Therefore it must eat continuously. Some hungry ghosts dine on corpses, while others are resigned to scrounge for trash, cremains, or excrement. One story tells of a large company of hungry ghosts who dwelled in the city moat, their only food "pus-filled blood and shit, which they eat, then vomit and defecate, then eat again" (Rotman 2021, p. 46). Buddhist scholar Andy Rotman writes that hungry ghosts "fully embody suffering": they are suffering incarnate, their own carnal loathsomeness the bane that torments them (p. 51). With the hungry ghost as with the zombie, it is the very fact of the body, its substance and its needs, that constitutes damnation. The body is horror's origin and crux.

Set against the gory, lurching and appetitive hellscapes of zombification and hungry ghosthood — the curse of eternal bodiliness — death is refigured as a blessed release, an end to the myriad persecutions of mortal materiality. And thus Man circles directly back to Plato's lesson: extinction is the soul's liberation from the fleshy tomb of the body. Which means that there shall never be harmony between these two warring elements. Body and soul are irreconcilable. For Man, there is no peace on earth.

---

26 "Bhaktam," quoted in Rotman (2021, p. 64).

MAN'S REVOLT (THE FIRST WAR)

Horrified by the gruesome ordeal of being a body — a mortal biological being, vulnerable to injury, disease, decay, death — Man rejects corporeal reality, and this phobic refusal to accept what he is makes his life impossible. Because he depends for his very existence on the flesh he loathes, living is a nightmare. Every sensation, every pang of hunger, every rich-blooded throb that cycles through his racing heart is laced with terror. It is too monstrous to be true: that he is damned to live and suffer and die and rot a meatsack, his innards stinking pulps and sludges, food for worms. He doesn't believe it, he denies it, he casts himself adrift from the material reality of his body and seeks consolation in delusion.

Man says he is a soul, immaterial and pure, his source some resplendent paradise waiting for him above and beyond the lowly earth. The Body — an abstraction now that it is safely separate and 'outside' — is only a temporary sort of thing. Soon, Man shall be free of it. His god will liberate him, or he'll free himself. At which point, bodiless now, Man will rise to his true potential; at last he shall know heaven.

Rejected corporeality is replaced by male fantasy: Man swears he is not 'mere matter'.

Yet the body remains; it does not release him, does not slacken its grip in deference to Man's desires. Flesh does not capitulate to Man's daydreams of blissful disincarnation. In moments of hunger, thirst, arousal, and injury, his earthly materiality reasserts its realness; with every breath he is conscious of how its continual, repulsive presence sours his existence. And he is afraid. When the body resists his control and reminds him he is not his own master, never mind master over all the world. When he strains for transcendence, only to slump heavily down to earth again, subsumed in the substance from which he is inseparable. When the boy loses his head swallowed up in the pink swell of the Blob, when the slime clings to Sartre's fingers and he shudders.

Seeking a cure to this chronic terror, Man has tried to extricate what of his person he accepts as Self from the horror he calls the

Body. He has striven to install a safe distance between the two. Yet he has wasted his energy: there is no separating something from itself, from that which it is. Man fails and fails again to realize the division he desires. Instead, he is defiled by a dread intimacy, his body unshakable as ever.

The narrator of H. P. Lovecraft's story 'The Outsider' (1926/2005) finds himself in a strange castle in a strange land, face to face with a revolting creature. An "inconceivable, indescribable, and unmention-able monstrosity" (p. 12), the man calls it, an "unholy abomination" (p. 13):

> I cannot even hint at what it was like, for it was a compound of all that is unclean, uncanny, unwelcome, abnormal, and detestable. It was the ghoulish shade of decay, antiquity, and desolation; the putrid, dripping eidolon of unwholesome revelation; the awful baring of that which the merciful earth should always hide. ... to my horror I saw in its eaten-away and bone-revealing outlines a leering, abhorrent travesty on the human shape; and in its mouldy, disintegrating apparel an unspeakable quality that chilled me even more.

Careening in panicked flight from the "terrible object," the man loses his balance and stumbles forward, pitched closer to the monstrosity he is so frantic to escape. And, falling, he is "suddenly and agonisingly aware of the *nearness* of the carrion thing" before him. He puts out his hand to ward it off, and in the "cataclysmic second of cosmic nightmarishness" when his fingers touch the "outstretched paw of the monster," a "fleeting avalanche of soul-annihilating memory" slants down blackly to crush him. For a single shattering instant he can comprehend what he is seeing, can recognize the abomination that leers at him in that castle room.

For the first and last time before his mind recoils into amnesiac derangement, the man is forced to confront reality. What his fingers grazed when he held out his hands to drive away the monster, that accursed vision staggering towards him, was neither moldered rags nor the outstretched paw of some beast. What the man touched was nothing more than "a cold and unyielding surface of polished glass" (p. 14). His soul annihilated, the man reels in horror from the mirror.

He feels himself transformed into "a great soft jelly thing," moist and faceless, festering cocooned within a cortex of slickly slithering plasma. His soul, desperate for release, founders in the slime. Escape is impossible, he has no way out. His tortured soul dizzies as the maggot-sack beckons.

Terrorized by the brute fact of his body, Man pits himself against material reality, initiating what Ernest Becker in *The Denial of Death* (1973) calls Man's "revolt against existence itself" (p. 84). Reality defies and defiles Man, denies him the power to exist indefinitely in his own immortal image, clean and pure and spiritualized. Unstigmatized, unindebted. Thus he abhors reality as adversary and oppressor. He tells himself that it is his destiny to overthrow this enemy, to finally bring reality's reign of terror to an end. Yet Man's crusade is a hopeless farce: with each new day the warrior awakens still a body, and each new day he recommits to his fantasy that he is other than what he is. He dares not admit defeat because to resign himself to reality would be to surrender to certain death. Instead, he is prepared to die defending the delusions he has devised to shield him against dying. This is the essence of Man's madness, which is the madness that plagues the manmade world.

Body horror churns septic at the core of Man's delusional mentality, from which fear leaches steadily out congealing into the anxious alienation and anguished rancor that pollute to pathological the sum total of Man's relations with the living world and its creatures, his fellow Man and himself not least of all. The revolt he launches against material reality striving to defend himself from his own being is the original war, the primary antagonism that turns Man against the world. Because he rejects his own being, Man's life on earth is ugliness and torment; he is tainted by living, he is enslaved, but ...

Man says he will be liberated. He will win his sovereignty.
Man says he will have his revenge and by his wrath be redeemed.
Man says he will crown himself king, so the sundered world
bows down before him.

Yet he wakes another day, still flesh and blood. Before him, a foetid apparition rots in the cold glass. Material reality upholds its dominion over and against the Kingdom of Man. He wakes, another day closer to death.

SEVERED HEADS FOREVER:
DISEMBODIMENT AND IMMORTAL MANHOOD

The basis of horror — and difficulty in life in general — is that we cannot comprehend how we die. Why should a healthy mind die, just because the body is not healthy? ... There seems to be something wrong with that.

DAVID CRONENBERG, *Cronenberg on Cronenberg* (1992, p. 79)

I was born to a greater destiny than to be a mere chattel of my body ...

SENECA THE YOUNGER, *Epistulae Morales* (64 CE/1917, p. 457)

THE CARTESIAN DECAPITATION

The Father of Modern Philosophy was a sickly child. Pallid and listless, afflicted with a cough he likely inherited from his mother, who was dead of tuberculosis by the end of his first year, René Descartes spent much of his youth bedridden. His doctors did not expect the boy to survive to manhood. And though survive he did, he did not come through unscathed, the imprint of his morbid childhood a lasting blot, subtle yet unmistakable in the grooves of his adult mind. Writing to friends and colleagues, Descartes confessed his hopes of living a century at least, while biographers have noted his penchant for health fads reputed to stall the reaper. Descartes was a vegetarian, not out of any sympathy for animals — classing nonhuman animals as insensible automata, he had no moral qualms with their slaughter — but because he regarded vegetables "much more proper to prolong human life, than the flesh of animals."[27] Biographer Richard Watson characterized Descartes as "something of a health nut," a passionate avoider of anything he perceived as a potential hazard to his longevity, be it alcohol or bad air (2007, p. 38). The Father of Modern Philosophy was a man determined not to die.

---

27   Father Adrien Baillet, quoted in Stuart (2007, p. 135).

Descartes was 40 years old when he published his *Discourse on the Method* (1631), in which he announced his vow to "employ [his] whole life" to freeing Man from disease "and perhaps also even the debility of old age" (p. 103). Clearly sensing the urgency of his task, it took the philosopher only a few short years to settle on a solution: the yearned-for reprieve clinched through proof positive that immortal mindhood is Man's true nature.

Descartes stated his purpose in no uncertain terms with the title of his book: *Meditations on the First Philosophy: in which are demonstrated the existence of God and the immortality of the soul* (1641). The promised demonstration begins with Descartes' confident dismissal of reality. Although in real life, in the real world, it may appear undeniable that men die, reality is not a trustworthy source for the facts. Not being trustworthy, it can be discounted. Descartes writes that the world around him may very well not exist, for couldn't it be false, like dreams are false? His own body, too, could be as a dream, the sensitive flesh as much a deception as the pangs that spark through an amputee's phantom limb. And since there are persons who believe themselves to be pumpkins, and still others who suppose their heads are made from porcelain, isn't it conceivable that humans in general are no less deluded when they presume that their bodies actually exist?

The senses are unreliable: prone to error at best; at worst, shameless deceivers. Any data one receives through these channels is open to doubt. All Descartes is willing to say exists for certain is his own mind, since his ability to doubt the world relies upon the existence of some entity capable of doubting. That which doubts is, for Descartes, the Thing that Thinks: "a mind, or soul, or intellect, or reason" (1641/1979, p. 19). With nothing to confirm that there's really anything else to him — the physical body already having been debunked — Descartes concludes that he must be in essence this Thing that Thinks. He cannot doubt he is a doubting mind: undoubtedly, then, he does exist! And because he (his mind) undoubtedly exists, his existence must therefore be independent from all that is subject to doubt, such as the material body/world. What is indubitable cannot hinge upon the dubious:

Now I will shut my eyes, I will stop up my ears, I will divert all
my senses, I will even blot out from my thoughts all images of
corporeal things ... (p. 23).

Having demonstrated that Man without a doubt exists as a mind,
Descartes moves on to demonstrate the existence of god. He explains
that god exists beyond doubting because the mind can imagine god
in his full perfection, yet there is nothing in the whole flawed illusory
mirage that constitutes material reality sufficient to inspire imaginings
of perfect things. Hence, it is impossible that Man could have dreamt
up god. What arises immaculate within the mind, unsullied by input
from the faulty senses, is far more real than anything perceptible in
the world. Thus it is concluded that god is real because Man's mind is
able to conceive of him even in the total dearth of tangible evidence
suggesting his existence.

Next it occurs to Descartes that he is not a body. Because this
inkling hatches fully formed as an evidence-free mental impression,
it qualifies for undeniable fact status and Descartes trusts it
unreservedly. The spontaneous impressions ripening rapid-fire now
in the mind that he is, Descartes has another thought. Acknowledging
that he was perhaps a touch extreme in his incredulity to start with, it
occurs to him that the body might in fact exist. But if so, then it would
have to be in every way separate from the mind. In 1641, Descartes
wrote, "the concept of the body includes nothing at all which belongs
to the mind, and the concept of mind includes nothing at all which
belongs to the body" (Kenny 1988, p. 145). This is the division of
mind from body known today as Cartesian Dualism, though in truth
Descartes was more a devotee of the schism than its progenitor. Once
established, the dualistic mind/body split enables the philosopher to
conclude with total confidence that his mind is "entirely and absolutely
distinct from [his] body, and can exist without it" (1641/1911, pp. 1-28).
To land at last on the balmy shores of this conclusion must have been
a tremendous relief, for though the body "can easily cease to be ...
the mind by its nature is immortal" (1641/1979, p. 9). Because Man
is not the wretched corporeal creature spurious reality makes him
out to be, but in actual fact a higher mind — or soul, since Descartes
admits he makes scant distinction between the two — death is a non-

issue. Severing his head from the dying body to place it aloft and afloat in heaven's starry vault, Descartes reassures himself that his immortality, like the existence of god or the fact of a triangle's three sides, is beyond doubt: "I am; I exist; this is certain. But for how long? For as long as I think" (p. 19).

In the synopsis of the *Meditations*, Descartes declares his intention to show "that the annihilation of the mind does not follow from the corrupt state of the body" and therefore to "[give] mortal men hope in an afterlife" (p. 9). He affords his fellow Man this hope by means of an intricate regimen of mental gymnastics aimed at wresting from the morass of mortal matter an affirmation of Man's deathlessness ready to withstand any challenge, impervious to argument. Since reality has already been scrapped as a hotbed of delusion, and the body as a dream, and the world as a phantasmagoria of hallucinatory apparitions cast flickering across cavern walls, none of the above can be invoked to controvert the theory that Descartes has proposed. All evidence gleaned from the world outside of Man's mind is inadmissible, so unless it occurs to Man apropos of nothing that he's going to die, he can be sure he's guaranteed to live forever. Man is he who thinks himself into existence. And if he thinks it, it must be so. Man thinks he is immortal, therefore he never dies.

It was a cold winter in Sweden in February of 1650 when Descartes, aged 54, contracted pneumonia. He would be dead within the month.

DEATH & DENIAL

Man is afraid to die. Such is the astonishing thesis of Ernest Becker's *The Denial of Death* (1973), for which the author was awarded the Pulitzer Prize (posthumously, we can't help but note). Becker writes that, "of all the things that move man, one of the principal ones is his terror of death" (p. 11). Man's terror is unabating, its presence unspoken, submerged, but like some ancient leviathan the fear quietly circles the abyssal zones of his unconscious, its shadow the dusky tint coloring his perceptions, clouding his thoughts, steering his behavior as he scrambles feverishly to evade the inevitable.

Becker does not question Man's chronic terror nor his panicky labors to console himself. Instead, the author accepts paralyzing dread as a rational, sensible, appropriate response to mortality. Of course Man has every reason to be terrified. How else could any intelligent being react to earthly life, grimly limned by Becker as "the nightmare spectacle taking place on a planet that has been soaked for hundreds of years in the blood of all its creatures" (p. 283)? For indeed it is precisely Man's exceptional intelligence that allows him to perceive death as a horror and which compels him to invent methods for dodging it. Man's anxiety and avoidance, his staunch refusal to reconcile himself with the fearsome reality of mortality — pathological though these traits may seem, they are, by Becker's estimation, the mark of a singular genius. An ennobling endowment, Man's terrorized mind is the attribute that elevates him above every other animal, those creatures of limited intellect who creepeth humbly across the earth, mindlessly submitting to death without fear, without a fight.

If Man's genius for terror is what elevates him above all other creatures, his body is the demeaning encumbrance that hurls him earthbound into sordid kinship with the world's mass of creeping crawlers. Regarding the "degrading animal body," which he identifies as "the human burden sans pareil" (p. 31), Becker writes:

> The body ... is one's animal fate that has to be struggled against in some ways (p. 44).

> The body is definitely the hurdle for man, the decaying drag of the species on the inner freedom and purity of his self (p. 226).

> [Man's] body is a material fleshly casing that is alien to him in many ways — the strangest and most repugnant way being that it aches and bleeds and will decay and die (p. 26).

Becker considers it a given that Man should detest corporeality and devote his life to perpetual conflict with the being/body he is. Man's loathing is warranted, because the body is inherently restrictive/repugnant/ugly/lethal. Not only will the body one day be the death of him, it threatens to debase Man every single day of his life, reducing him to as much of a brute beast as any other animal. "The body cannot be allowed to have ascendancy," declares Becker, since if the body were to overtake him, then Man would cease to be Man (p. 32). "The ego, to develop at all ... must stop the body" (p. 262). By Becker's analysis, it is anxious repudiation of the body that makes Man 'human', by which he means separate from and superior to all other animals and the living earth itself.

Man is exceptional because he alone has the wits to stand in opposition to the "inadmissible reality" of mortality. Rather than accept his fate, he cultivates "healthy repressions," "explicit immortality-ideologies," and "myths of heroic transcendence" to facilitate ongoing denial (p. 285). Together, these repressions, ideologies, and myths form the basis for what Becker dignifies as "human culture." According to Becker, Man's terrified rejection of bodiliness is fundamental to his 'humanity' (i.e., his superiority over other animals), while his terrified rejection of material reality is fundamental to the development of his 'human' (i.e., manmade) culture. Denial drives Man to replace reality with a world of his own making, composed of more reliable, controllable materials than organic matter. This counter-natural otherworld is the patriarchal civilization in which we currently find ourselves: Man's artificial fiefdom, its systems, structures and institutions engineered by the founding fathers to extricate Man from "the cycles of life and death that characterize all other organisms" lift him onto the "special immortal plane" he claims as his birthright (p. 231). If he shuns murderous nature, if he draws himself up and out from the biological rabble, why shouldn't he be free to live forever? Unlike the other animals, too dimwitted to fantasize their way out of their deathly bodies, Man is subject to neither "the real nature of the world" nor his own "real situation on this planet" (p. 63). He renounces reality and rests assured that what he denies cannot destroy him.

The realm of immaterial symbols/dreams/myths/rituals we know as 'culture' serves to distinguish Man in his own mind as more than "a blind glob of idling protoplasm" born only to die (p. 3). Super-imposing culture over nature, Man labors to "[prevail] over the natural order," to suppress and supplant it, tame and transform it into a death-free zone (p. 238). In this way, manmade culture operates as a kind of alternate dimension, cut off from nature and built exclusively from

Man's own fantasies, fictions, and artifices. Ensconced within this protective bubble, his placid plastic hideaway in which mortality is not reality, Man can indulge in imagining he has mastered the earth, altered the order of things and thereby averted his fate: surely he will not die.

For Becker, everything Man has made of himself, his sprawling empire of cities and citadels spiring up to scrape the gates of god's good heaven, all his works of genius, his glorious achievements, his discoveries and inventions, can be understood as the relics of a millennia-long campaign against mortal material reality. For Becker, it is terror that makes the Man, and terror that rules the manmade world: Man's is a kingdom of fear.

IMMORTALITY CULTURE

It is commonplace — "uncontroversial and unoriginal," Buddhist scholar Steven Collins writes — to observe that the complex metaphysical systems known as religions, around which manmade cultures have long revolved, take as their source and sustenance Man's "aspirations to avoid death and impose control and order on life" (Collins 2000, p. 187). Of the many social functions religion serves — the consecration of male supremacy, for example, and the sanctioning of male dominion — its most basic is to palliate people's terror of death and dying. This it achieves by promising believers protection from mortality. For Colin McGinn, the balm with which religion soothes the death-fearing mind is the conceit that it is "merely a passing illusion that we are disgusting biological creatures," fated to die and decay (2011, p. 220). All Man's major religions are founded on dualism, with the body imagined as vessel for the immaterial and immortal soul that is Man's essence, his true Self. The Torah conceives of the soul as god's breath, inhaled from the expiring body at the moment of its death back into the great cosmic lungs of the divine (Hayon 2009). In Shintoism, all things contain a spiritual essence, called the *kami*, and it is said that when a man dies, his *kami* can, under proper conditions, be glimpsed leaving the body as a fireball blazing towards eternity (Gollner 2014).

If Man is not his biological body but instead a supernatural soul briefly interned within it, then Man does not die when the body-vessel dies but, as his soul, will persevere beyond death. The Hindu god Vishnu, called the preserver and guardian of men, affirms this logic:

> Unborn, undying ancient, perpetual and eternal, [the Spirit of Man] hath endured and will endure forever. The body may die; be slain; be destroyed completely -but he that hath occupied it remaineth unharmed ... Weapons pierce and cut not the Real Man, nor doth the fire burn him; the water affecteth him not, nor the wind drieth him nor bloweth him away. For he is impregnable and impervious to these things of the world of change — he is eternal, permanent, unchangeable and unalterable, Real (*Bhagavad Gita* 1907, pp. 27-28).

The celestial idols and heroes with whom Man populates the cosmos — like Vishnu, like Zeus, like the Christian godhead — provide further evidence of religion's death-defying function. Man's gods are not tethered to the putrefactive earth, they do not die and become its dirt. Gods neither degenerate nor decompose; they are not "mass[es] of flesh vulgarly subject to life and death," to quote Simone de Beauvoir (1949/2011, p. 186). Wholly self-determining, gods have no need for the world, so they cannot be betrayed by it. Murderous nature never gets the best of them. Man creates his gods as he would have created himself, given the opportunity: perfectly dissevered from the perishable world, uncontaminated by foul nature's morbid influence, immutable, autonomous, all-powerful and all-knowing, deathless.

Denied the privilege of self-creation, Man creates gods through which he can recreate himself. If Man is a product of the earth, then dust he is and to dust he shall return. But if god created Man in his own divine image, then Man partakes of god's otherworldly nature. Man says that, fashioned in the image of god, he is the closest of all living creatures to godliness, which is deathlessness. Man says he is very nearly immortal and his god-the-father loves him and soon, soon, he will be saved.

To the faithful, obedient masses, religions relieve mortality-induced anxiety by paving straightforward roads out of death. Dutifully conform to the good books' commandments, follow the instructions of the holy men, say your prayers and pay your dues, and you too can earn your ticket out of expiry! Rather than face down death as a black chasm in which the self dissolves worm-gnawed into nothingness, the pious can expect their virtuous submission to god's will to earn them paradisiacal afterlives of milk and honey, winsome pearly-eyed virgins, choirs of pink-and-blonde cherubic harpists blithely fluttering over some gilded cream cheese cloudscape, and so on. Man crowds the skies and the recesses beneath the earth's surface with eternal accommodations. On high we find Heaven, Elysium, Svarga (Hinduism's Abode of Light), Valhalla, Nirvana. And below: Hell, Tartarus, Niflheim. For the Mayans the underworld was Xibalba, the "Place of Fright," its capital city home to six baleful houses through which the deceased must pass: Dark House, Rattling or Cold House, Jaguar House, Bat House, Razor House, and Hot House (Ardjis 2017, p. 214). The Aztecs cremated dogs to accompany their masters on the journey to the Land of the Dead, while the Ancient Egyptians furnished the tombs of their pharaohs with the housewares, provisions, and servants they'd require for a well-appointed hereafter. Even the damned in their various and sundry underworlds are spared the indignity of finitude, instead suffering tortures without end.

An alternative loophole is reincarnation, the transmigration of souls. The immortal soul is not yoked to any one corporeal receptacle but passes instead from one body to another over the course of its never-ending existence. When one body perishes, the soul is reborn into another, and on and on it cycles, until eventually the soul evolves to its highest state, expiates all past sins, and earns its freedom from the mortal world. Reincarnation is customarily associated with Asian religions like Buddhism and Hinduism, but it has been a consistent feature of western belief systems as well, with Orphism, Gnosticism, Pythagoras and Plato all teaching variations on the theme. More recently, past life regression has modernized the theory of reincarnation to suit the secular-yet-spiritual sensibilities of New Age mysticism. Though subscribers to these ideologies run the risk of being reborn as beggars, flies, or females in penance for the impure deeds of their former selves, at least they needn't fear dying as a dead end. Life after life, Man lives on.

Christianity's golden ticket is resurrection. After sacrificing his body to absolve Man's sins, Jesus Christ arose from the darkness of the cave in which his corpse was stored and journeyed skyward to reign over all creation alongside his father. Christ's return from the dead was his most spectacular miracle: conclusive proof of his immortality and divine parentage, of his incorruptible nature, the purity that marked him a savior worth adoring. It was well-known, too, that Jesus' power could salvage even humble mortals from death's predations: Lazarus had been four days a corpse — asked to open his tomb, Lazarus' sister demurred that her brother would stink — by the time Jesus called him staggering out of the sepulcher into daylight, still draped in his sere-clothes.[28] "I am the resurrection and the life," the son of god announced to awe-struck onlookers, "He that believeth in me, though he were dead, yet shall he live: And whosoever liveth and believeth in me shall never die."[29]

In Christian doctrine resurrection is not an exclusive pardon reserved for the select, nor a party trick to prove divine favor. Instead, it is the destiny awaiting everyone. When the Day of Judgment arrives, all dead bodies shall be reunited with their souls to stand before god and be dispatched to their eternal abode. Sinners will be hurled back into hell's sulphurous lakes, while the pious are blessed with redeemed bodies, beautiful and harmonious as the human form was before the Fall, their members cleansed of carnal evil and placed firmly under rational control — St. Augustine is overjoyed to inform us that, once resurrected, Man shall be safe from the ignominy of unwilled erections — never to be weakened by age or debility, never to sicken nor perish, but instead to dwell nestled forever at the feet of the godhead in an earthly paradise "where every tear is wiped from their eyes and death shall be no more."[30]

---

28 John 11: 38–45
29 John 11: 26–27
30 Revelations 21: 24

To the east, another of Man's great saviors writes:

> Verily this world has fallen upon trouble — one is born, and grows
> old, and dies, and falls from one state and springs up in another.
> And from the suffering, moreover, no one knows any way of
> escape, even from death and decay. O, when shall a way of escape
> from this suffering be made known — from decay and death?[31]

Similarly dour denunciations litter the Buddhist canon, suggesting
that however much its path may deviate from the one charted by the
Abrahamic creeds, Buddhism has been no less directed in flight from
mortal material reality. "There is no sorrow like existence," laments
the Buddha in the *Dhammapada* (trans. Wagiswara and Saunders
1912, p. 51). Disciples retreat from the reality of death by renouncing
sorrowful life on a decaying earth so scrupulously that their sojourn
finds its ideal end in self-obliteration: the Buddhist paradise is not
a perfected extension of existence, but rather existence's absolute
negation. It is not an afterlife that followers of the Buddha seek, but
a nonlife. "[E]xistence is the greatest sorrow. Sure knowledge of this
is Nirvana, highest bliss" (p. 51). When it achieves Nirvana, the soul's
sentence on earth is finished; no longer shall it suffer the horrors and
humiliations of birth, life, death, rebirth. Nirvana — which translates
to "blowing out," like a candle snuffed — is freedom from the body, its
life and its death.

The Sanskrit scholar and Indologist Wendy Doniger observes
a parallel yearning for nonexistence in Hindu texts. She quotes a
passage from the *Markendeya Purana*, in which an embryo expresses
remorse for its imminent birth:

> ... [the embryo] begins to remember its many previous existences
> in the wheel of rebirth, and that depresses it, and it tosses from
> side to side, thinking, 'I won't ever do *that* again, as soon as I
> get out of this womb, I will do everything I can, so that I won't
> become an embryo again'. ... it comes out crying, because it is
> pained by the misery in its heart.[32]

---

31   The *Digha Nikaya*, XIV, as quoted in Piven (2003, p. 503).
32   Quoted in Doniger (2000, p. 174).

In *The Masks of God: Oriental Mythology* (1959/1976), Joseph Campbell pinpoints the historical moment when Man turned his back on living. Around 600 BCE, weary of the existence he perceived as a "fiery vortex of delusion, desire, violence, and death, a burning waste," Man veered into an impassioned embrace of death as that existence's ending (p. 211). Campbell calls this paradoxical about-face the 'Great Reversal': spurning life as the cause of all hardships, Man welcomed death as friend and saving angel, whose arrival would rescue him from the miseries of being.

An Egyptian papyrus dated 1900-1700 BCE documents a suicidal man's wistful reflections on his imminent deliverance:

Death is before me today:
Like the recovery of a sick man,
Like going forth into a garden after sickness.

...

Death is before me today:
Like the home that a man longs to see
After years spent a captive.[33]

In Greece, before Plato escorted western philosophy "out of the prison-house of the body into a new realm of incorporeal truth" (Jantzen 2004, p. 130), Sophocles cried out for death as a boon second only to never having been born, while Euripides puts his words on the tongue of a sacrificial female who prays to be spared the unpleasantness of an afterlife:

For if we
Whose short life ends in death must there too suffer pain,
I do not know where we can turn; since death has been
Thought of as our great remedy for all life's ills.[34]

Alphonse de Lamartine, a 19th-century French poet and statesman, welcomed death as a godsend, the "Liberator divine": "Thou dost not destroy, thou deliver'st."[35] This sentiment was shared by the more

---

33 Quoted in Campbell (1959/1976, p. 138).
34 Quoted in Jantzen (2004, p. 138).
35 Quoted in Aries (1981, p. 411).

famously morbid French poet Charles Baudelaire, who pronounced death the "goal of life," and "our only hope."[36] In his poem 'La Mort Joyeux', Baudelaire gleefully anticipates the feast his carcass will make for saprotrophs:

> O worms! Black friends, who cannot hear or see,
> A free and joyous corpse behold in me!
> You philosophic souls, corruption-bred,
> Plough through my ruins! eat your merry way!
> (1857/1922, p. 26).

In 1994, members of Heaven's Gate, an American cult fated to disband three years later when its inner circle committed suicide in preparation for their souls to board the spacecraft they expected to ferry them to their extraterrestrial forever-home, warned that

> THE SHEDDING OF OUR BORROWED HUMAN BODIES MAY BE REQUIRED IN ORDER TO TAKE UP OUR NEW BODIES BELONGING TO THE NEXT WORLD.
>
> IF YOU WANT TO LEAVE WITH US YOU MUST BE WILLING TO LOSE EVERYTHING OF THIS WORLD TO HAVE LIFE IN THE NEXT. CLING TO THIS WORLD AND YOU'LL SURELY DIE.[37]

In the 1990s, however, Heaven's Gate's severely literal-minded Great Reversal theology placed the cult at the extreme fringes of U.S. culture. Though the destructive 'death instinct', diagnosed by Sigmund Freud as *thanatos*, flowed on unebbing as manmade culture's Stygian undercurrent, by the late 20th century the urge to rapturous self-obliteration had lost much of its mainstream appeal. Man had formulated a new antidote to his mortal terror.

From the Age of Enlightenment to the present day, science has surpassed religion as Man's primary fantasy/weapon in his arsenal for the war he wages against mortal material reality, the faith he once placed in his god(s) re-invested in technology and medicine. Man trusts that, through rigorous unsparing study of the material

---

36 Quoted in ibid., p. 474.
37 Quoted in Zeller (2014, p. 123).

world — 'Mother Nature', as men of science have liked to call the earth they strap down to the dissection table — he can force it/her to divulge its/her secrets until there is nothing that remains unknown to him. Knowledge is power, as Francis Bacon, that great Father of the Scientific Method, once said. So Man will never again be made nature's fool. Quite the opposite: it (she!) will be Man's slave, shackled in his service.

By eliminating the middleman, science outperforms religion as a buffer between Man and his mortality. Man need no longer rely on the generosity of the god(s) he invented, then came to resent when gifts were less than forthcoming. Now, through his own brilliance, he can extricate himself single-handedly from death's clutches. Science thus affords Man greater autonomy than religion ever could: wielding its miracles, Man unseats god and ascends to the throne as his own lord and master; it is he alone who rules.

Having traded in religion for the shinier miracles of science, Man's first move is to banish his enemy death from his sight. He develops methods for disappearing death, disguising its realities via the production of increasingly lifelike corpses. The dying, meanwhile, Man stows away in hospitals and hospices and 'homes', the scandal of their terminal decline quarantined to closed wards. Physicians, trained as trench fighters in the war on death, abominate mortality as a sign of failure, "never to be an accepted outcome of medical intervention" (Moller 1996, p. 26). Since modern medicine's charter is to beat back death as long as possible, heroic efforts are made to stall the flatline — even if the cost is more acute or prolonged pain for the patient in whose name the battle is ostensibly fought. When death is equated with defeat, the protraction of suffering becomes best practice.

Although Man for all his dogged efforts has so far failed to bring the global human death rate down from 100%, he has greater cause for confidence than he ever managed to wring from religion. Scientific advances in medicine, technology, and sanitation have more than doubled the average life expectancy since 1900 (Roser et al. 2013). Today when an organ malfunctions it can be replaced, either by a second-hand part excised from a donor, a readymade organ

3D-printed or grown in a lab, or an organ-simulating machine. We have machines to keep our hearts beating, and machines to filter our blood, and machines that breathe for us, inflating our lungs with precision-timed sighs before siphoning out the spent air. Man is optimistic that soon he will know the joy of microscopic robots ('nanobots') swarming through his bloodstream, surveilling his tissues, vigilantly scanning cells for signs of damage and making any necessary repairs. With science on his side, Man is closer to eternity than ever. Immortality is Man's destiny: if he thinks it, it is so.

Organizations like the Church of Perpetual Life, Human Longevity, Inc., the Immortality Institute, and the Fuck Death Foundation are dedicated to overthrowing the gloomy "deathist paradigm," their sights boldly turned "beyond the past of dying to a future of unlimited living" (Moshakis 2019). Rejuvenate Bio, a biotechnology firm founded by Harvard professor George Church, employs gene therapy to code 'anti-aging' instructions into DNA. Church reports that his experiments on mice and dogs have been promising (in Gabbat 2019). Another company, Unity Biotechnology, focuses its research on so-called 'senescent cells', cells which no longer function nor proliferate yet refuse to die, stagnating instead in a zombified state and seeping a "noxious goo" of proinflammatory cytokines and proteases. Neighboring cells that come into contact with this goo tend to follow the malefactors into senescence, leading to tissue dysfunction — and so the dying process begins. According to Unity Biotechnology staff scientists, the selective elimination of senescent cells via 'senolytic' drug treatment increases median murine lifespans by 35% (Friend 2017).

In 2016, a California start-up calling itself Ambrosia — ambrosia, food of the gods, from the Greek *ambrotos*: immortal — merged luxury wellness with dystopian vampire nightmares by peddling plasma extracted from the blood of young donors as an anti-aging elixir for the modest price of $8,000 per liter (Brodwin 2019). The company folded in 2019 after the U.S. Food and Drug Administration issued a statement warning against 'young blood' treatments, but it has since re-opened in answer to popular demand. Ambrosia's website claims that their 'patients' experience "subjective improvements in athletics, memory, skin quality, sleep, and other areas" (Robitzski 2019).

Ambrosia's approach is based on research investigating a procedure known as parabiosis: the stitching or stapling together of live rodents in order to fuse the two animals' circulatory systems. Channeling a young mouse's blood into the body of an older mouse to whom it has been annexed has shown some promise of promoting tissue regeneration, neuronal growth, and improved cognitive and physical performance for the senior rodent (Kaiser 2014). Yet parabiosis is not without its hazards: the authors of a 1956 study warned future investigators considering the technique that, "[i]f two rats are not adjusted to each other, one will chew the head of the other until it is destroyed."[38]

By 2027, the global market for anti-aging products is projected to reach $47.8 billion (Global Industry Analysts, Inc. 2022).

Aubrey de Grey, founder of the Strategies for Engineered Negligible Senescence Research Foundation, denounces aging as "the greatest embodiment of our failure as a species to escape the yoke of nature."[39] His organization invests in "rejuvenation biotechnologies" engineered to pitch that crushing yoke by "reconstructing the structured order of the living machinery of our tissues" (SENS Research Foundation 2022). In 2020, de Grey was awarded the Bacon Prize for Thought Leadership in Super Longevity from the Coalition for Radical Life Extension, the director of which refers to himself as a "visionary anti-death activist" (Coalition for Radical Life Extension 2022). Since 2016, the Coalition has been crowding hotel convention halls around the United States with the aspiring immortals who fly in from across the globe to attend its annual RAADfest. "RAAD," of course, is an acronym for Revolution Against Aging and Death. Such a revolution is necessary, conference-goers assert, because mortality violates our basic human rights. It is a person's sovereign right to say when and if he or she stops living, hence death is tyranny and a coup the only self-respecting response (Raphael 2018).

---

38 Quoted in Friend (2017).
39 Quoted in Solomon et al. (2015, p. 95).

Dave Asprey, 'biohacker', founder of the body-optimizing Bulletproof Diet and author of *Super Human: The Bulletproof Plan to Age Backward and Maybe Even Live Forever* (2019): "I decided that I was just not going to die."[40]

Dr Joon Yun, healthcare hedge fund manager and sponsor of the Palo Alto Longevity Prize: "Thermodynamically, there should be no reason that we can't defer entropy indefinitely. We can end aging forever."[41]

Arram Sabeti, Silicon Valley entrepreneur and tech startup investor: "The proposition that we can live forever is obvious."[42]

Martine Rothblatt, transgenderist/transhumanist thought leader and billionaire biotech entrepreneur, whose company United Therapeutics Corp. is busily pioneering the manufacture of transplantable organs custom-made from consumers' own DNA: "Clearly, it is possible, through technology, to make death optional."[43]

Men like the futurist Ray Kurzweil, author of *The Singularity is Near: When Humans Transcend Biology* (2005) and *The Singularity Is Nearer: When We Merge with AI* (2024), have placed their faith in an upgrade from biological to technological existence as the final solution to the death crisis. Kurzweil believes that by 2045, we will be able to upload the contents of our brains wholesale into computers, transferring the Cartesian immortal mind/soul from its perilously perishable corporeal husk into a more durable receptacle, namely: a manmade machine. Inspired by Kurzweil, a wealthy Russian entrepreneur has developed the 2045 Initiative, which someday soon will offer consumers the opportunity to purchase personalized avatars destined to supersede their bodies once the mass body-to-machine transfer gets underway. The 2045 Initiative plans to provide consumers with a range of post-organic lifestyle options, from a "full-body prosthesis topped off by [the buyer's] transplanted head" to a "top-of-the-line, wholly artificial body containing [the buyer's] uploaded essence" (Friend 2017).

---

40 Quoted in Horn (2018).
41 Quoted in Friend (2017).
42 Quoted in ibid.
43 Quoted in ibid.

All of this is a ways off, since even perennial optimists like Kurzweil don't expect Man's blissful merger with the supercomputer to occur for another twenty years. Fortunately for those men anxious that their subpar organic bodies will sputter out before the day when Man's scientific genius finally frees him from the death-curse that is being biological, there's cryonics. At Alcor Life Extension Foundation's facility in the Arizona desert, dead bodies are immersed in ice baths, injected with anesthetics, antacids, anticoagulants, and antibiotics — "a postmortem cocktail designed to keep the cellular apparatus preserved in the best possible condition" (Walter 2020, p. 29) — then wrapped in sleeping bags and placed inside aluminum pods. These pods are then lowered into vats of liquid nitrogen for 'vitrification', the industry jargon for freezing. Once vitrified, bodies are ready for transfer into vacuum-insulated metal capsules for long-term storage.

The aim of this procedure is to "[pause] the dying process," so that, in the future, chilled 'patients' (see: corpses) can be thawed, revived, and reintegrated into society (Alcor 2020a). No cryogenically frozen 'patient' has been revived to date; the human heart cannot survive even five hours of freezing — but Alcor is unfazed. The cryonicists have faith that "foreseeable technology" will soon make possible full recovery of the dead. Moreover, they buoyantly note, "[i]f indeed cryonics patients are recoverable in the future, then clearly they were never really dead in the first place" (Alcor 2020b). If what can be 'recovered' was never really dead, then nothing ever really dies! Exposed as an illusion by cold hard future-science, death effectively ceases to exist.

In anticipation of their temporary hiatus from living, Alcor 'patients' must choose between chilling their bodies whole, or, for a lower price point, freezing just their heads. Christine Quigley outlines the 'neuropreservation' process in her book, *The Corpse: A History* (1996):

> The head is severed at shoulder level and placed in a silicone oil bath, a can of liquid nitrogen, and finally transferred to permanent cold storage (with several other heads). The headless body is then cremated (p. 234).

Underlying the severed head method is Man's conviction that, by the time foreseeable future-science has obviated human mortality, furnishing the neuropreserved with new-and-improved replacement bodies will be a no-brainer. While the head harbors the mind understood as Man's True Self, the body is impersonal, expendable; as a rudimentary technology, it will be relatively easy to replace. Full-body transplants are one possibility; robotic body prostheses onto which reanimated heads can be grafted are another. Perhaps synthetic bodies could be conveniently 3D-printed on demand, like replacement organs. Better still, the contents of the thawed heads might be uploaded into the Kurzweilian cloud. Whatever state-of-the-art receptacle Man intends to upgrade himself into, he's confident that in the future he is creating, he'll have no need for his present meatsack. He expects to get along just fine — so long as he can keep his head.

One would-be cryonics customer tantalized by the attractions of neuropreservation was Jeffrey Epstein, the American financier and pimp to the ruling global male elite. Following Epstein's arrest for sex trafficking, acquaintances told *The New York Times* that the billionaire had mentioned plans to have his head and penis frozen after his death, in hopes they might one day be resuscitated (Stewart et al. 2019). To be clear, neither Alcor nor its competitor, Michigan's Cryonics Institute, currently offer penile preservation services. And since Epstein died in prison without the luxury of having any of his parts put on ice, we should be spared from that particular phallus ever coming back to haunt us.

As of 2020, Alcor served as the interim resting place for 181 crusaders against death, 134 of whom were men (Alcor 2021).

TERROR MANAGEMENT THEORY

American social psychologists Jeff Greenberg, Tom Pyszczynski, and Sheldon Solomon developed Terror Management Theory (TMT) in the 1980s to test the thesis of Becker's *Denial of Death*. They wanted to prove it: that fear of mortality is man's primal motivator, culture's *raison d'etre*, and the key to understanding human behavior.

Simplifying Becker's analysis in order to probe it empirically, the psychologists proposed that humans cope with the terror stoked by our knowledge that we will one day die — true to their forefather, they took it for granted that death is by default terror-inducing — by cultivating a two-pronged psychic defense mechanism. First, one must subscribe to a cultural worldview, or shared belief system, by which Man's mortal condition is swapped out for the consolations of an 'eternal reality' imbued with structure, order, meaning, and stability. The second component of the 'anxiety buffer' is self-esteem, which the individual achieves by striving to live up to the standards of his culture. He who meets or exceeds these standards secures himself a place of honor as a valuable member of and contributor to his 'eternal reality' of choice. A potent palliative, self-esteem enables humans to believe that we are "enduring, significant beings rather than material creatures destined to be obliterated" (Solomon et al. 2015, p. 9).

Having formulated Mankind's defensive strategy against death terror, the psychologists hypothesized that, induced to think of death — or brought into a state of "mortality salience," to use the TMT term of art — experimental subjects would react by "clinging to and defending their cultural worldview" (Goldenberg et al. 2001, p. 428). For culture to function as a sturdy bulwark against death, one's faith in it must be unfaltering. It follows that individuals with death at the fore of their minds will seek to reinforce the worldviews upon which their salvation depends, to thicken the fortress walls. Likewise, when a challenge to someone's worldview plants the seed of doubt, the bad old death terror comes slithering blackly back again to cloud the subject's mind with morbid brooding.

Since the publication of Greenberg, Pyszczynski, and Solomon's initial paper, researchers around the world have conducted hundreds of studies to test their theory.[44] This body of research has shown

---

44 Most TMT research has been conducted in the United States and Europe, such that its findings reflect those worldviews dominant within U.S. and European ('western') cultures. Yet there are noteworthy exceptions: TMT research in Israel showed that death primes increased Israeli study participants' support for nuclear strikes as well as their desire to serve in the military (Horschig 2022; Tubman-Ben-Ari and Findler 2006); studies in South Korea found that participants induced to mortality salience were more in favor of violent reprisals in response to North Korean aggression

that, when reminded of human mortality — by what's termed a 'death prime': the word 'CADAVER' flashed across a screen, for example — individuals steel their anti-death defenses by means of staunch, even aggressive, adherence to the ideologies that comprise their worldviews of choice.[45] Nationalism, sexism, racism, political partisanship, religious sectarianism, dogmatism and extremism of every stripe: all appear to be amplified when death's shadow steals across our consciousness. Struggling to shake off the pall, we recommit to culture over reality.

Reminded of death, individuals respond more negatively to persons outside their own cultural clans, to those their worldview maligns, and to anyone who criticizes their belief systems. Conversely, death awareness moves people to respond more positively to their cultural peers, members of the 'in-group' to which they themselves belong. People are also more inclined to conform to cultural standards and impose, then enforce, those same standards on others, and to experience discomfort when compelled, in the context of an experiment, to violate some cultural norm or taboo ('mishandling' an American flag, for example).

Reminded of death, people struggle to attain "simple, consistent, orderly conceptions of the social and physical world" — to institute structure on reality, to establish order and control (Swanson and Landau 2019, p. 150).

(Hirschberger et al., 2016); and in a study conducted in Côte d'Ivoire during the country's civil war, people residing in 'pro-government' areas were more likely to affirm the government's actions when prompted to think about death (Chatard et al. 2011). TMT's thesis is not that there is one universal, monolithic response to death anxiety. Rather, it holds that individuals attempt to manage their anxiety through conformity to the norms and value systems of the cultures to which they belong, whatever those norms and values may be. Where the culture is patriarchal, masculinist, hierarchical, and violent, terror management approaches will be shaped by these cultural tendencies. In cultures characterized by different norms and values, it can be assumed that terror management would differ accordingly. The handful of TMT studies conducted in Asian countries, where collectivism is emphasized over western-style individualism, provide some evidence to support this hypothesis (Kashima et al. 2004; Watanabe and Karasawa 2012; Otsubo and Yamaguchi 2013).

45 For a broad review of Terror Management Theory research and its findings, see Pyszczynski, Greenberg and Solomon 2015.

Reminded of death, people attempt to distance themselves from animals and the biological world. They express disgust for nonhuman animals, support killing them (in medical research and similarly 'valid' contexts), and tell themselves that animals and humans are radically different kinds of creatures. While death primes induce denials of animality, reminders that humans are in fact animals — mammals, primates — prod mortality closer to the surface of study participants' conscious minds. The prospect of time spent in "wild nature" likewise dredges up morbid thoughts, while, thinking of death, people are markedly less enthusiastic about the "intrinsic value" of the mortal material natural world (Fritsche and Hoppe 2019, p. 165).

Reminded of death, people feel alienated from and disturbed by bodies, their own as well as those of others — especially if those others happen to be female. Study participants were disgusted by bodily secretions and recoiled from physical experiences, whether the experience was unpleasant — such as dipping one's arm in ice water — or something generally agreed to be pleasurable, like a foot massage (Goldenberg et al. 2006). Under the sway of mortality awareness, heterosexual men's self-reported attraction to a 'sexually alluring' woman has been shown to wane (Goldenberg et al. 2019, p. 234). People of both sexes, reminded of death, exhibit a decided distaste for menstruating and pregnant women. In one study, participants assigned to write about their own demise, and then later introduced to a woman they were told had recently been breastfeeding, placed their chairs at a greater distance from the woman compared to individuals in the control group, to whom breastfeeding was not mentioned (Cox et al. 2007).

Women reminded of death along with a reminder of their femaleness — by another woman asking for a tampon, for example — are moved to imagine themselves in objectifying terms, retreating into self-imposed lifelessness to neutralize the threat posed by their own culturally execrated biological bodies (Goldenberg et al. 2019).

Reminded of death, study participants have been found to support authoritarian policies, favor jingoistic leaders, justify violence as righteous, and call for revenge against perceived enemies (Pyszczynski 2013; Chatard et al. 2011). Studies show that death primes also increase individuals' support for military intervention, including the use of nuclear weapons (Pyszczynski et al. 2006; Horschig 2022). And the endorsement of political violence excited by reminders of one's mortality remains resolute even when the violence is explicitly described as strategically useless. What the death-terrorized mind demands is retribution (Reiss and Jonas 2019).

In one 2016 study, men (but not women, notably) reminded of death reported experiencing a heightened urge to achieve power and dominance in the days that followed. During the week subsequent to death prime exposure, the men told researchers that they engaged in more domination-oriented behaviors. They became more aggressive in their interactions with others, trying to intimidate them, to assert control; they sought to compel others by force (Belmi and Pfeffer 2016). Another study showed that "subtle reminders of personal death" increased participants' enthusiasm for violent resistance in the face of an impending life-altering upheaval (Hirschberger and Ein-Dor 2006). Significantly, this zest for violence spiked most dramatically among those individuals who most adamantly denied the realities of their situation.

Man, committed to the culture he has authored, a fanatical believer in its doctrine of mankind's deathlessness, operates in a state of permanent denial. Yet he is continuously besieged by reminders of what he denies. His body, which refutes the conceit of Man's severance from matter. All other living creatures, whose births, sufferings, deaths rouse Man's suppressed memories of his own. The earth whose substance his existence depends upon. Confronted in each instant by these challenges to his cherished fantasies, Man's confidence in his own immortality is a fragile thing. It flags, falters, and he is afraid. His recourse is rigid adherence to the rules of manmade culture, a hardening of the mind to overrule the soft body; he demands structure, control; craving power he strains to dominate; he declares supremacy over every/body he condemns as carnal and demotes to lowliness. And because denial is Man's primary defense against terror, because he has cultivated no better methods for coping with his life or his death, he is predisposed to violent rages when he perceives a threat on the horizon. Prey that he is to an inconsolable fear, Man sees mortal threats worming at the core of everything. Terror turns to an addiction to dominion turns to world-destroying violence in the service of delusion.

Such is Man's state of mind. Manhood, it seems, is a mental disease.

REBORN: THE MAN OF STEEL

Masculinity, as a mode of being, originates from the dualistic Severed Head ideal preached by Descartes and made flesh in the neuropreservation tanks at Alcor. Man takes as his own and calls masculine all talents he claims derive from the mind: intelligence, rationality, logic, willpower, objectivity. Masculine wisdom is absolute and changeless and best attained through mathematics — the manliest of all disciplines, according to Plato. Also masculine are those traits posed in polar opposition to bodiliness. Since the body is palpable and concrete, Man retreats into abstractions. Where flesh goes soft, Man hardens. While the body needs and hungers, Man is self-sufficient, self-contained, self-determining. The body is dependent, so Man must be autonomous. The skin may be a flimsy garment riddled with holes, but Man is armored. And though the body can be wounded — pierced flesh bleeds, pain wells up screaming from the cut — to be masculine is to be impenetrable. Stoically enduring any injury he betrays no sensitivity, as if, above and apart from it all in the locked-box command center of his skull, nothing can touch him. Klaus Theweleit, in his study of the embittered German paramilitary fighters who would become the first and most fervent Nazis, characterizes Man as "a monstrosity that expends every ounce of its energy making itself invulnerable" (1987, p. 202).

So furiously does Man strive to enforce his law of mind over matter, so arduous is the program of self-discipline by which he means to subdue the beastly body, that his experience of being is saturated with an antipathy inevitably absorbed into the fabric of masculinity. Perennially on guard against corporeal subversions, Man sees omens of insurrection everywhere. Anxious that these rebellions, like those of his body, will spell his undoing, Man resolves to squelch every challenge to his power. The rancor he feels for his own defiant defective body filters into his daily life as a slow-burn outrage that keeps him forever primed for combat. Because Man must always be in command of the situation or else risk perishing, the paramount attribute of masculinity emerges as control, both "the capacity to exert control and resist being controlled," as sociologist Michael Schwalbe writes (2014, p. 59). And this will to power, this paranoid vigilance for the least signs of insurgency, this antagonism that swerves so swiftly and feverishly into aggression — these too are integral to what it means to be Man, the MasterMind.

Wendy Brown writes in *Manhood and Politics* (1988):

> Once man alienates his head from his body, once he conceives of the body as something to be mastered ... he is set upon a course in which he strives to conquer, master, dominate or control all that threatens his precious freedom from the body (p. 80).

But the fearsome reality is that everything that Man experiences and encounters threatens that freedom, because he encounters and experiences everything through his body. Never and in nothing is he actually free from it. Hence Man's life on earth is permanent war, and the more willing he is to fight to the death to defend his fantasized deathlessness, the more real is his Manhood. The broader the trench he carves out between his mind and body, the more he isolates himself suspended in the ivory citadel of his skull, the more raging his estrangement, the harsher he lashes out in his struggle for absolute mastery, the more he proves himself a Man.

Of course, we know that no matter how rigorously he conforms to masculinity's code, the male's body persists. However suppressed, neglected, beaten down and driven to the margins, there is the body, and there it is again, never leaving his mind in peace, becoming what Susan Griffin in *Pornography and Silence: Culture's Revenge Against Nature* (1981) describes as "a continual and silent presence which is above all ominous" (p. 147). And so, Griffin continues, "a frenzy grows, and a desperate realization, which the mind must want to quiet, that this vulnerable self will always return and cannot be destroyed" (p. 127).

He catches sight of the fleshly mass down below his head, a sting splinters from its sloppy depths to strike a nerve he cannot quiet, its shrills shrieking and in answer, Man stiffens. He is aggrieved: how repulsively tender is his burden! Death is there, lurking in the pulp; terror drives him nearer to a total loss of control. Thus he sickens, full of shame. Because the mortal material body he is humiliates him, what Man desires, what Man says he deserves, is a new body, one worthy of his mind and his Manhood. A body that is indestructible, dependable, amenable to discipline; a body to serve and to glorify the MasterMind. Devising ever harder forms for himself, he nurses an infatuation with metals. He will be Superman, the Man of Steel: faster than a speeding bullet, more powerful than a locomotive, able to leap tall buildings at a single bound.

The unforgivably sensitive, porous skin he exchanges for a chromium carapace, nerves for wires, circuits; he wants motor oil in his veins, and through this metamorphosis Man senses he becomes more authentically himself. It is a process of self-actualization: to armor the body, to calibrate it for optimum performance, cleanse it of biological corruption. Out of nature's chaos Man institutes order:

> The most urgent task of the man of steel is to pursue, to dam in, and to subdue any force that threatens to transform him back into that horribly disorganized jumble of flesh, hair, skin, bones, intestines, and feelings that calls itself human (Theweleit 1987, p. 160).

The manmade machine-body is purged of slimes and soft parts, its surface steeled shut to seal it off from life's damp inundations. Programmed to obey the mind, the machine-body runs smoothly and never stalls as long as Man maintains it in good working order. In his physiological marriage with the technologies he engineers so masterfully, Man anticipates perfection. Soon, he tells himself, his machines will "take over from the body ... perform[ing] functions for which the body is inadequate: to function frictionlessly, quickly, powerfully, brilliantly ... perfectly" (Theweleit 1987, p. 160).

The Italian fascist and poet F. T. Marinetti, author of the *Futurist Manifesto* (1909), called for the "dreamed-of metallization of the human body":[46] Man's overhaul from organic creature to incorruptible, cutting-edge machinery. Marinetti foresaw the redemption of the body in its modernization into a power tool custom-rigged for Man's purposes, a gleaming high-speed testament to Man's triumph over biology. Metallized, machinized, Man would catalyze his own evolution, casting off at long last the deadweight of primitive corporeality. He asks: "A wicked pleasure; was I now perhaps one with the weapon? Was I not machine — cold metal?"[47]

The Terminator, 1984. Bodybuilder-turned-actor Arnold Schwarzenegger stars as the eponymous cyborg assassin, an "efficient and relentless killing machine"[48] whose "robotic metal endoskeleton combat chassis" is wrapped inside a layer of "living organic skin," more or less effectively disguising the machine as human.[49] Sent from the post-apocalyptic future by the military-industrial supercomputer overlord SkyNet, the cyborg's mission is to eliminate the woman whose unborn son has been prophesied to lead a people's revolt against the reigning devices' totalitarian regime. Originally a villain, Schwarzenegger's Terminator character was so popular that he was rehabilitated and reintroduced as the hero of *Terminator 2: Judgment Day* (1991). With this reversal, the relentless killing machine becomes the leading man, a father figure for the chosen son. Schwarzenegger went on to serve as Governor of California from 2003 to 2011.

Man initiates himself into Manhood by severing his ties from biological mortal material reality (Kheel 2007). In the rituals men have instituted for this purpose, the crucial first step is to separate the Initiate from his mother and install him under the auspices of a fraternity of male peers, ruled over by male elders. In this dude-bro sequestration, boys are weaned from maternal care and schooled

---

46 Quoted in Benjamin (1936/1996, p. 121).
47 Ernst von Salomon, quoted in Theweleit (1987, p. 179).
48 Wikipedia, 2023. "The Terminator." <https://en.wikipedia.org/wiki/The_Terminator>.
49 Terminator Wiki, 2022. *The Terminator* (Film). <https://terminator.fandom.com/wiki/The_Terminator>.

in the catechism of masculinity. The Man-to-be is cut off from his mother not only because she'll spoil and soften him, but, worse still, because mothers are the wellspring of male mortality. By creating him in her womb from the bad matter of her own being, the Mother consigns Man to the death sentence of bodiliness. And this is to say nothing of the general grossness of birth and begetting, condemned by the Greek philosopher Parmenides as "hateful" and "vile,"[50] squalid with secretions and spasms. Such animalistic wallowing debases everyone involved. Unable to stomach it, Man maneuvers to annul his fatal filthy female provenance through ritualized 'rebirths' mid-husbanded by designated clean and proper father figures. Motherless, he would resurrect himself Fatherborn. His own son now, he is self-made the Man of Steel, "beautiful and pure of all the defects that came from the maleficent vulva and that predispose one to decrepitude and death,"[51] to quote the fascist poet Marinetti again. And elsewhere we read that, in "innumerable male societies around the world," a man is not considered to have been born at all until "he be reborn from a man, and his womanish origin superseded" (Lederer 1968, p. 155).

In the myths Man tells and re-tells himself, procreative power belongs not to the female but to the male; it is Man who begets the world. As in: the Greek city of Thebes was virgin-born when King Cadmus scattered a vanquished sea serpent's teeth over the soil. From the strewn teeth of the enemy-animal killed by the King, fully armed men sprouted forth, and battled amongst themselves until only the fiercest warriors remained: these survivors were Thebes' first citizens (Haaren 1904). Another example of male genesis, even more brutal: the Babylonian god-king Marduk fathered the world when he slaughtered his mother, the primordial goddess/sea monster Tiamat, by crushing her skull and carving her body into chunks. From the dismembered corpse of the creatrix, the god-king made his heaven, his earth (Daly 1978/1990).

---

50 Quoted in Jantzen (2004, p. 156).
51 Quoted in Poggi (2009, p. 159).

Manhood rites proceed along a succession of tortures by which a boy's female-born body is put to death. For young men to prove their scorn for the soft flesh their mothers forced on them, they must offer it up on the altar of male violence, enduring whatever purifying pains their fathers prescribe. The boy who succeeds in denying his body's sensitivity wins his Manhood: he who goes numb so he will not cry out when wounded is worthy. Thus the Initiate dons a glove packed full of poisonous biting ants. He is suspended from hooks pierced through his chest until he loses consciousness. Older men pinion his arms behind his back to jab razory stalks of grass up his nose until blood is drawn pouring down his face. Stone arrows are shot into his urethra, his tongue, until these soft tissues, too, begin to bleed (Langness 1974). A thorned vine is forced into his penis. Older men strip him naked, throw him facedown on the ground, force his head into a hole in the dirt, and slash his back repeatedly with a dull razor. In German military academies at the beginning of the twentieth century, boys' advancement from low-status novices to full-fledged cadets was commemorated with a visit from the school dentist. The boys would line up to take their turn seated on a hard wooden stool while the dentist loomed over them, pliers in hand, to wrench any remaining baby teeth from their mouths.[52] Thus the boys were welcomed into the warrior caste spitting blood into a bucket.

War, of course, is the consummate, quintessential, and most spectacular rite of violence by which Manhood is established and affirmed. On the battlefields, in the trenches, boys become men and men become supermen, warrior heroes clad in the golden mantle of manliest glory: "a glory of violence and slaughter ... of savagery and gore" (Jantzen 2004, p. 55). Surveying the blood-splattered battlefields of the Homeric epics, feminist theologian Grace Jantzen observes that, from the inception of the masculine literary tradition, warriors have been venerated as gods on earth, their splendor undiminished even when they are cut down by their enemies. After death the warrior's legend lives on, immortal, his sublime violence never to be forgotten.

---

52   Theweleit (1987, p. 151).

In Norse lore, warriors slain in battle are raised up to Valhalla, the estate of Odin the All-Father, god of war and wisdom. The heroes of Valhalla spend their days massacring one another and then at dusk are revived and return, in brotherhood reconciled, to feast at their Father's table. Their nightly meal is the flesh of an immortal boar — he too is slaughtered each day only to be resurrected and eaten another night — and mead swigged from skulls harvested from the earth's combat zones. But this infinite war is not just for the wholesome fun of it: the men are Odin's army, training for Ragnarok, the Twilight of the Gods, when wolves will devour the sun and the moon and the stars disappear from the heavens and terminal winter shall still the barrens of a world gone black with bloodshed. So it is that the man who serves his Father best is blessed with warfare forever, then the destruction of all things.

Man rejects his lowborn female origins and rebirths himself anew, forging a new body hardened off in the crucible of masculine brutality. Revamping himself into a war machine careens Man closer to the god-like sovereign status he judges to be his birthright. Yet his conquest is incomplete. He is dissatisfied with mastery over creation, if to be born is still to live miserably and die. His true ambition he locates at life's opposite pole: only dominion over death can guarantee deliverance. Nonetheless he does manage to wring some solace from the realization that, though he cannot yet rout out mortality altogether, it is within his power to ally himself with death, to take death on as his instrument and wield it. Man can drive death away from himself, by killing others. He can risk his life and yet return from the kill-field intact and alive — in which case, hasn't he bested death? There is victory to savor in every violent confrontation he survives. So he seeks these confrontations out. So he sets them up for himself. And this is the reason why manmade culture valorizes destroying life and risking it while devaluing creation and nurturance as trivial. This is the death-bent tilt to which Simone de Beauvoir was referring when she wrote that, in patriarchal civilization, "superiority has been accorded ... not to the sex that brings forth but to that which kills" (1949/2011, p. 64).

Benito Mussolini: "War is to man what maternity is to women."[53]

Heraclitus: "War is the father and king of all."[54]

By this morbid turn of the MasterMind, female generation is overthrown by manmade devastation and Man comes to depend for his very existence on a policy of mass murder. To convince himself he is undying, Man needs a corpse he can squat beside, needs to see himself triumphant amidst the carnage, boots stained with the blood of his victims. "It is the other who is dead, the softness underfoot. The grinding of the boot is an affirmation of life" (Theweleit 1987, p. 19). Hunters have a ritual they call 'blooding': when a young man makes his first kill, his father will smear red slashes of the animal's blood across the newly initiated son's cheeks. In the social media era, hunters post photographs of themselves and their children bloody-cheeked and crouching alongside the deer, elk, moose, or boar whose lives they have ended. They smile. They give the thumbs-up. Chris Hedges (2022) saw similar photographs carried by junta soldiers when he was in El Salvador reporting on the country's civil war, though in these snapshots the corpses were those of rebels the soldiers had shot down in firefights. In 2012, the *Los Angeles Times* published photographs of U.S. paratroopers stationed in Afghanistan posing with the blown-off legs of an Afghan suicide bomber as they grinned for the camera, giddily holding out the severed limbs, showing them off like prize fish (Zucchino 2012).

The psychoanalyst Gregory Zilboorg, writing at the height of World War Two, extolled the merits of "overcoming death by means of murder" (1943, p. 474). In an article straightforwardly titled 'Fear of Death', Zilboorg advised the Allies to stir up hatred for the opposition, recommending it as a surefire strategy for boosting public morale. Che Guevara also understood the martial value of loathing: "relentless hatred of the enemy, [impels] us above and beyond the natural limitations that man is heir to, and [transforms] him into an effective, violent, seductive and cold killing machine."[55]

---

53 Quoted in Braudy (2003, p. 449).
54 Quoted in Jantzen (2004, p. 157).
55 Quoted in Andrea Dworkin (2000, p. 227).

As long as Man is absorbed in the throes of righteous hatred, his terror recedes. Killing pacifies: the killer calms, for he is not the victim. As the ruined bodies accumulate and amass, he cherishes each corpse for how it soothes his anxious mind, a blessed reminder that he himself is still alive. These dead bodies at his feet, these bleeding heaps of meat he sacrifices to the myth of his deathless dominion, are nothing like Man's own armored hard and harsh high-speed impenetrable invulnerable battle-ready body; and if he stops to think about it, in the final analysis he's not even that body at all but the pure mind that dwells within, piloting the body that is its vehicle. And the mind can never die. Man thinks therefore he is the son of god. All glory be to the Father.

This, then, is manmade culture's true foundation: so that Man the MasterMind could prove to himself that his fantasy is reality and that he alone is destined to outlive the world, it was "necessary that our civilization built its temple on mountains of corpses, on an ocean of tears, and on the death cries of men without number."[56]

---

56 Prussian military Generalfeldmarschall Count Gottlieb Von Haesler (1836-1919), quoted in Quigley (1996, p. 169).

OTHERS//
BODIES

THE SELF

To review, briefly, the delusion adopted by patriarchal civilization to dispel the mortal material body's horrors: Man declares that inside his body — but not a part of the body, not inside the body as an organ is — there resides a shimmeringly brilliant, ethereal, immaterial essence, and this essence is the mind, also called the soul or spirit; he draws a line between the mind (or soul, or spirit) and the body containing it, to divide the two; Man says he is the mind but the body is something else, something he is not. The mind is Man's True Self. The body, by contrast, is a burdensome object. And the mind is immaterial hence immortal, meaning Man's Self shall endure, even if every/body eventually dies.

In reifying reinforcement of the life-saving separation of mind from body, Man then splits the contents of creation along this same dualistic dividing line. Now everything that exists is either with him, on the clement shores of the mind (soul, spirit), or against him, submerged in the seedy unseemly carnage of bodiliness. From here a long chain of dualisms unfurls, each of its dyads defined by polarity, so that whatever Man sorts to the side of the mind is by definition absolutely unlike the body and opposed to it.

mind / body
soul / body
spirit / body
essence / substance
immaterial / material
immortal / mortal
pure / impure
culture / nature
analogue / digital
heaven / earth

sacred / profane
light / dark
light / heavy
good / evil

And each dyad is not only dualistic but hierarchical, since it is plainly superior to be a deathless, divine, and luminous mind-essence than to be an earthly meatsack born to die. The hierarchy is simple and stark. The high-minded half Man keeps to his Self is good: reason, virtue, righteousness, math, machines. As for the body and all associated with it? The senses and sensuality, dirt, hunger, wildness and wilderness? Because what is corporeal cannot also be of the mind, because the two elements are severed one from the other, never to meet, everything Man classes with the mortal material body must be mindless and soulless, probably godless, therefore: bad. And worse than just bad, they are presumed dangerous, deadly even, in league with the evils of hell (that infernal place inside the earth, under the soil, in the dark). This bodily, mortal material badness of earthbound things is vividly illustrated in the medieval paintings Monica Sjöo and Barbara Mor describe in *The Great Cosmic Mother* (1987), with their scenes of "cities, fields, animals, humans, trees, dogs, babies, flowers ... all falling, like masses of shit, from the ass of Satan" (p. 288).

Through the institution of an all-encompassing dualism, the whole of creation is reduced to either mind or body, immortal essence or mortal matter, good or bad — and Man has positioned himself definitively on the right side of the tracks. Fantasizing along with Descartes that whatever he thinks therefore is, Man is satisfied that he has successfully removed himself from reality. Man is not of this world, that much is certain. His own savior, Man has thought his cherished essential Self safely out of murderous nature's maw.

And his antithesis, that which he leaves to languish in the province of the flesh, Man christens the Other.

THE OTHER

Man rejects the body he cannot bear to be and projects it onto the Other. He absorbs the Other into his manmade culture to stand as a living symbol of repudiated corporeality, the icon of mortal material reality. The Other is the Body, so that Man can have the Mind all to his Self. And because body and mind are locked in polar opposition, it follows that the Other must be the opposite of the Self. Now Man is the antithesis of the morbid impure thing he denies being, and he can contentedly chant to himself what ecofeminist Val Plumwood calls patriarchy's mantra of radical exclusion: "I am nothing at all like this inferior Other" (Plumwood 1993, p. 49). Radical exclusion dictates that what the Other is, the Self is not. The Other is the Body so Man can say: I am bodiless. If the Other is classed with matter and nature, and the Other is the opposite of the Self, then Man can be sure he is civilized and meant for transcendence. And if Man is the mind, which is also the soul, then the Other is mindless, and soulless — so Man is good, in all ways superior to the vile Other. Thus Man makes use of the dualisms he has invented to construct a sense of Self he believes can stave off death. For if the Other is flesh — vulnerable, perishable — then Man knows for certain his Self is immortal and shall endure.

In the social hierarchy Man has scaffolded, the Other functions as the "material bottom beneath which one cannot sink" (Dworkin 2000, p. 275). As a negative reference point, the Other provides Man with a reliable reservoir of relative self-esteem: if the Other is on the bottom, then Man gets to see himself on top. Since his self-concept as disincarnate hence undying hence omnipotently godlike depends on the Other being held low, Man is obliged to enforce the Other's debasement and denigration. When he gazes from on high at the Mind's summit, Man should be able to see the Body beneath him. He wants to be comforted by the proof of it lying there, a lump of feeble tissue trembling pitiably way down in the earth's dark dirt where he dropped it. Thus, Man embarks upon a crusade to overpower, subordinate, enslave, consume, and/or exterminate the Other, to keep the Body firmly anchored where he needs it to be, if he is ever to feel safe in this life. Ursula K. Le Guin succinctly diagnoses the attitude that guides Man's drive for domination when she writes:

> Civilized Man says: I am Self, I am Master, all the rest is Other — outside, below, underneath, subservient. I own, I use, I explore, I exploit, I control. What I do is what matters. What I want is what matter is for (1986/1989, p. 45).

Through his domination of the Other, Man crowns himself Master not merely over each individual Other he succeeds in subjecting to his will, but also over all that he has made the Other symbolize. In this way Man imagines he can vanquish what terrorizes him: material reality, the organic substance of creation from which he, a biological organism, a corporeal being, is indivisible.

Man is strategic in choosing the beings he enlists as the Other, his selections varying on a case-by-case basis to meet the demands of his varied and vacillating projects. Different cultural, historical, and political contexts have called for different types of Others, yet whoever is chosen for the role, every Other is made to bear Man's body for the salvation of Man's supreme mind. And to Man's mind every Other is feared and despised as the body is feared and despised, as material reality is. And without fail, Man justifies how he treats one Other after another, the cruelties he inflicts, the oppression he metes out, as essential to the continued survival of his sovereign Self, of patriarchal civilization, god's will, the sacred, the righteous and the good.

THE SCAPEGOAT

The Book of Leviticus details a ritual performed by the people of Israel for Yom Kippur, the Jewish Day of Atonement. The ritual involved two goats. Slaughtered by a priest as a blood offering, Goat #1 was served up to the Israelites' god in penance for the past year's transgressions. Goat #2's sacrifice was less straightforward. First, the priest would confess the sins of the Israelites with his hand laid over the goat's head, to transfer the community's accumulated burden of guilt onto the sacrificial ruminant. Co-opted as a repository for

Man's trespasses, Goat #2 would then be driven from the settlement: "The goat shall bear on itself all their iniquities to a barren region; and the goat shall be set free in the wilderness."[57] A year's freight of wickedness, concentrated within the body of a disposable animal, is thereby expiated. Originally Goat #2 was called the 'escape-goat', a title shortened centuries later to 'scapegoat': the one who exists to be expelled. The scapegoat is exiled, Andrea Dworkin (2000) writes:

> ... pushed out into the wilderness to carry away the sins of the Community: driven to slow death from hunger or killed by predators. These are the outcasts, in the margins, in the wild, dying slowly or ripped open, all to cleanse the sins of others (p. 333).

Although the Israelites' Yom Kippur sacrifice is the paradigmatic example of 'scapegoating', similar rituals have been practiced in manmade cultures throughout history and across the globe. Sir James Frazer devoted hundreds of pages of his multi-volume tome, *The Golden Bough: A Study in Comparative Religion* (1890/1913), to inventorying the rites by which Man hoped to "shift the burden of his pains and sorrows to another, who will suffer them in his stead" (p. 1). Frazer describes camels led through plague-stricken Arabian cities to absorb the affliction, then strangled in order to rid the city of the camel and the pestilence "at one blow" (p. 33). Toads were reportedly used likewise as living disease sponges during flu epidemics in the German-colonized region of West Africa now known as Ghana. In a version of the scapegoating ritual from Thailand, the creature recruited as therapeutic sacrifice was a woman "broken down by debauchery," whom men ferried through the streets while townspeople crowded around to heckle and hurl handfuls of dirt at the designated victim (p. 212). At the end of the parade route, the woman would be deposited onto a manure pile or thorny hedge outside the city limits and forbidden from ever returning, in order that the "malign influences of the air and evil spirits" she drew into herself en route be cast out for good (p. 212). Ancient Athens maintained "a number of degraded and useless beings" at the public expense so that, should

---

57   Leviticus 16:22

some crisis fulminate, these beings could be set loose and pelted with stones by Athenian citizens (p. 253). Per standard procedure, the scapegoats would then be chased out of the city. The Greeks called their scapegoat the *pharmakos*, meaning: the poison and the remedy at once, together in one body. For though the scapegoat carries the sin that sparks the crisis, it is by the same token the only creature who can restore the city to order, by being cast out. The scapegoat's expulsion is cataclysm's surest curative.

Today the term 'scapegoat' is most often used in reference to an innocent (or relatively innocent) individual blamed and then punished for some misdeed committed by more powerful — therefore more culpable — parties. The low-level employee fired to cover for the failings of a manager would be one commonplace, workaday example of this. Yet to call such a person a scapegoat distorts the term's original meaning. The scapegoats of Leviticus and *The Golden Bough* are not merely blamed for sin or disease: they *become* the sin, the disease. Recruited to contain corruption at a safe remove from Man, the scapegoat is made to embody all the badness laid on its head. So, the scapegoat does not spread the plague: the scapegoat *is* the plague. The scapegoat has not behaved wickedly: the scapegoat *is* wickedness. The scapegoat, in its very substance, to its marrows, in its sinews, is all that Man refuses to accept or assimilate, the blight, disorder, and impurity he holds as anathema. In *Purity and Danger* (1966/2003), Mary Douglas defines dirt as "matter out of place," excluded for the purpose of preserving a carefully ordered system (p. 44). The scapegoat should be understood as just this sort of dirt, the matter whose presence spoils the sterile fantasy world Man is desperate to construct and maintain. To purge the scapegoat represents purification: expel "the source of all danger and terror, the polluting presence, the inferior and abject ... the ultimate filth" and the Kingdom of Man will triumph; destroy the death-laden and Man can live on, eternal (Dworkin 2000, p. 275). For this reason René Girard, in *Violence and the Sacred* (1972), names the scapegoat's persecution and exile as the foundational ritual of manmade society: "all man's religious, familial, economic, and social institutions grew out of the body of the original victim" (p. 277). The original victim, surrogate for Man's own bad body: the scapegoat.

Scapegoating rituals differ as far as who is chosen for the scapegoat role and the methods by which the scapegoat is banished. The basic purpose and procedure of these rituals, however, changes little. Man desires to be free from misfortune, suffering, and mortality, which he believes to be the symptoms of a curse or punishments for sin. It is the accursed who suffer, the sinful who die. The inciting crisis befalls him: by some natural disaster, Man's life is endangered — a plague, a famine — and he is reminded of his mortality, the contingency of his existence. He tells himself that these are avoidable punishments, and projects the sum of what he calls his sins onto somebody else. Now the evil is no longer upon him, but trapped safely isolated inside the body of the scapegoat. The scapegoat will be the one to bear the unbearable and face the punishment in Man's stead. To be certain that the sin he offloads does not find its way creeping back to Man, he persecutes, kills, or exiles the scapegoat. And so the evil is exorcized, Man's curse is reversed; his life is saved.

Scapegoating also functions to proffer consoling confirmation of Man's supremacy. In times of upheaval, when Man is forced to acknowledge he has not yet mastered the world, he can more or less guarantee his mastery over the scapegoat. Hierarchy is built into the ritual. The archetypal sacrificer is a human male representative of the ruling classes — most traditionally a priest — while the archetypal scapegoat is a being of low social status, marked by some "marginal quality" that places her outside "the normal" (Girard 1972, p. 277). Jan Bremmer adds that, for the Greeks, the scapegoat was a member of the community considered of negligible value: "a cheap or relatively superfluous animal ... or a woman" (1983, p. 306).

Man wants the gulf between himself and his scapegoat wide and deep, since the wider and deeper the gulf, the more distant he imagines himself from the blight he has projected onto the creature he means to sacrifice. Accordingly, Man does all he can to differentiate himself from the scapegoat. He latches onto every detectable difference, overstating and amplifying them; where minimal distinction exists, he manufactures it. As Girard writes:

> We hear everywhere that 'difference' is persecuted. This is the favorite statement of contemporary pluralism ... but it is misleading ... Despite what is said around us, persecutors are never obsessed by difference, but rather by its unutterable contrary, the lack of difference (1981, p. 22).

As much as the platitudes hammered into us from an early age may insist otherwise, Man neither hates nor fears the scapegoat because she is 'different' from him. The reality is precisely the opposite. Man demands "an ultimate and defining difference" (Griffin 1981, p. 162); he yearns to make the faultline that divides him from the scapegoat as "strongly drawn, well marked, and impassable"[58] as possible. Man invents difference and depends on it, because what he truly fears, what would spoil the scapegoating ritual completely, is sameness: the closing of the gap between Self and Other. Man needs to wipe from his consciousness each and every similarity linking him to the scapegoat, for in all these equivalencies, he spies the monstrous stain of sin begin shading into his own skin again. And he shivers, suddenly chilled, as the horror he has denied inches back from the margins.

The Other is Man's readymade scapegoat, maintained on reserve to be sacrificed as the situation requires. The Other is the creature who bears Man's burdens, embodying the sinful matter he rejects as antithetical to his Self. The creature called vile in every way bodies are vile: diseased, dirty, bestial, a wellspring of death and degeneration. The creature whose nature is pure impurity, unredeemed and unredeemable. Scapegoated, the Other carries the polymorphous badness Man attributes to being a body. Brimful with the taint of the evils Man has pronounced over her head, the Other is cast out from the Kingdom of Man. Thus the impure is banished from the realm of the pure. The Other bears Man's inequities to a barren region, abandoned to die a slow death alone in the desert; or else the Other is terrorized, the chosen target for all Man's impotent raging against mortal material reality. The Other, the scapegoat: the creature condemned for the sins of the flesh, murderous nature's

---

58   Oliver Goldsmith, quoted in Patterson (2002, p. 24).

crimes against Mankind. Day after day the Other's sacrificial body is put to death, that Man might live.

OTHER/SCAPEGOAT/ANIMAL

A simple analogy will start us off, gleaned from Aristotle: Man is to Animal as Soul is to Body. It was apparent to the philosopher "that the rule of the soul over the body ... is natural and expedient," and that "[t]he same holds true of animals in relation to men." Under Man's rule, animals' bodies are used to "minister to the needs of life," since they "can do nothing better" (350 BCE/1899, p. 7). The basic thing to understand about animals is that they are mortal material organisms ruled by biology and the laws of the natural world bound to which they spend their short, wretched lives, wallowing in the thick dark swamps of birth, death, and decay. (Man, meanwhile, is something "more" and "better" than "merely being-alive."[59]) It is for this reason that the basic physiological processes — digestion, excretion, reproduction, and so on — are called the 'animal functions'. Defined as bodily, by the logic of dualism animals cannot have minds, and so Man decrees that animals are stupid. In French, bête is the noun meaning 'beast'; as an adjective, it means 'stupid'. In English, a stupid, crude person might be a 'dumb brute', while someone stupid and petty would be 'bird-brained'. A 'turkey' is a person stupid in the sense of being pathetically inept, while a stupid slow-thinking woman is a 'dumb cow', and those who are stupid in the sense of being mindlessly conformist are scorned as 'sheep'. According to the neuroscientist John C. Lilly, "the lowest-grade human moron is above the highest genius in the gorilla or chimpanzee clan."[60] Animals are incapable of reason, they do not think, nor do they communicate, for they have no language. Animals create nothing: they have no culture, no technology, no art. They know nothing and in fact they cannot even be called conscious, because consciousness is a human and not an animal property, as the behavioral scientist John S. Kennedy wrote: "... consciousness, feelings, thoughts, purposes, etc. are

---

59   Emmanuel Levinas, quoted in Clark (2014, p. 181).
60   Quoted in Collard and Contrucci (1988, p. 59).

unique to our species and it is unlikely that animals are conscious."[61] Kant was arguing a parallel point when he asserted that animals are not self-aware, and therefore exist "merely as a means to an end. That end is man."[62]

Animals are so devoid of sentience that they are incapable even of suffering. Animals "cry without sorrow, they desire nothing, they fear nothing."[63] A beaten dog's yelp is naught but a pre-programmed response to aversive stimulus. In his *Discourse on Method* (1631/1916), Descartes deemed animals "destitute of reason" (p. 46) and likened them to machines, so-called 'natural automata'; animals operate like clocks, he wrote, their every act originating not from the mind but from "the constitution of their organs."[64] And "[s]ince beasts lack reason," wrote St. Augustine, "we need not concern ourselves with their sufferings."[65]

Lacking reason, beasts are in thrall to their primitive instincts. Karl Marx termed the instinctual drives "the blind forces of nature," and though they rule animals, Marx insisted that these forces have no such authority over Man.[66] According to Marx, it is by controlling nature rather than being controlled by it that Man becomes 'human', by which he means 'superior to an animal'. Freud, for his part, was less confident in Man's mastery and saw him instead as the victim of "primitive, ungovernable" instincts, the so-called 'animal drives', to be mastered through repression, sublimation, and so on. "[I]f we let them have their way," Freud wrote, "they would infallibly bring us to ruin" (1932/1964, p. 221).

Christian doctrine holds that animals are not only mindless but soulless as well, since the spiritual principle that secures Man to the ethereal realms and renders him immortal is his alone — only Man was made in god's image, after all. Being without souls, animals are judged deficient in morals, ethics, conscience, and virtue. God's creatures

---

61   Quoted in Scully (2003, p. 198).
62   Quoted in Regan (2001, p. 13).
63   Nicholas Malebranch, quoted in Scully (2003, p. 196).
64   Quoted in Regan and Singer (1976, p. 65).
65   Quoted in Sheehan (1991, p. 28).
66   Quoted in Mies (1986/2014, p. 214).

they may be, but they do not and cannot know god (naturally: they know nothing). As a consequence, animals are constitutionally depraved, dishonorable, amoral if not immoral, treacherous, vicious, and wicked. As cultural symbols, wolves and snakes bespeak treachery; the rat is a scoundrel, the fox a notorious cheat; weasels are thieves and the chicken a coward. Slugs, worms, and roaches all fall below contempt, symbolizing filth. Animality is a "dangerous organic force" (Ham 2014, p. 147), while the word 'bestial' denotes "savagely cruel or depraved."[67] Disposed to uncontrolled rage, the animal represents lawless aggression. Man lists animals' myriad misdeeds: "[c]annibalism, infanticide, and parricide frequently occur, while murder, maltreatment, and theft are used to procure food, to secure command, and for many other reasons" (Parmalee 1911, p. xv).

Evil congeals and condenses in the beastly body. The devil makes regular appearances as a goat; in Goethe's *Faust* (1808), Mephistopheles takes the form of a black poodle; in the Bible's Book of Genesis, the devil tempts Eve in snaky shape. Among the seventy-two demons described in the *The Lesser Key of Solomon* (1916), there are lion-headed, toad-headed, and deer-headed demons; demons with bat wings and cat's claws; owl demons, wolf demons, demons who ride on crocodiles. 'Animalistic' behavior — such as writhing, yelping, and foaming at the mouth — has been taken as a textbook symptom of demonic possession when exhibited by humans. In one 16th-century British case, a young demoniac reported that Satan first visited him as a dog, before returning to attempt to "enter him" as a mouse (Walsh 2020, p. 34). Japanese folklore features a wide array of potential possessors, collectively known as *Tsukimono*: the Possessing Things. The best known of these is a 'goblin fox' believed to slip inside women's bodies by way of their fingernails or breasts, resulting in a syndrome known as *kitsune-tsuki*. Fox-possessed women were said to behave erratically, wandering naked and crawling on all fours; overtaken by appetite, the afflicted would demand food with unladylike greed (Guiley 2009, p. 141). During the European 'witch craze' of the 14th-17th centuries, demons were said to visit

---

67 Oxford Dictionary definition.

witches in the guise of snakes, toads, lizards, spiders, cats, and dogs; while witches themselves were thought to transform into cats and hares in order to slip about unseen while terrorizing their neighbors at night.

A related hypothesis from the same era posited that bestiality — "whereby the very order of nature is violated,"[68] as St. Thomas Aquinas wrote, decrying how the act breaches the sacred boundary between human and animal — was the cause behind so-called 'monstrous births'. This theory was taken seriously enough that women who bore children with birth defects were accused of coupling with animals, if not demons. In such cases, the presence of sin at conception was believed to warp the inchoate body into beastly forms as it ripened in the sullied womb.

As late as the 19th century, the penises of 'sodomites' were said to "simulate exactly" male dogs' genitals (Davidson 1991, p. 60).

Kant wrote that "[s]exuality exposes man to the danger of equality with the beasts."[69] Sexual activity hurls Man down to the level of the body; he loses his grip on reason, his mind overthrown by sensation; he is a hostage to biology, and this is debasement: Man is no longer 'more' nor 'better' than an animal. He 'fucks like rabbits', his selfhood dissolving into 'the beast with two backs'. "And a man wallowing in foul and impure lusts is occupied by the filthy pleasures of a sow" (Boethius 524/1969, p. 125). Lecherous men unable to suppress their appetites shapeshift into ravening wolf-men on full-moon nights, their carnal desires darkening all too naturally into bloodlust. In *King Kong* (1933), an oversized gorilla is employed as the figure of sexual appetite run amok, the black, beastly sexuality that ravages manmade civilization, personified in starlet Fay Wray's platinum-pristine domesticated femininity. To save the girl and the city, the animal must be shot down.

Albeit less lethal than unrestrained sexual hunger, Man's appetite for food likewise induces a harrowing descent from transcendence to the subhuman corporeal. This urge, too, betrays Man's shameful

---

68 Quoted in Davidson (1991, p. 43).
69 Quoted in Midgley (1978/2004, p. 31).

animality. We learn from an early age how gluttonous animals are, from the rat who drools crooning about smorgasbords in *Charlotte's Web* (1973), to Garfield the lasagna-crazed housecat, to Winnie-the-Pooh with his paw forever stuck in the honey pot. Mad with hunger, every animal is a pig. Hegel wrote that the most significant part of an animal's head is its mouth, with which it attends to its "natural needs" and "natural functions ... without any spiritual ideal significance."[70] (Man's most significant facial feature, on the other hand, is the eye, "expressive of the soul"[71]). Fellow philosopher Georges Bataille concurred: "The mouth is the beginning, or if one prefers, the prow of animals."[72] And while Man "does not have a simple architecture like beasts," Bataille would add, it is when a man's mouth hangs gaping open that his latent impulses towards obscene physicality are on most glaring display.

Because what eats necessarily excretes, animals in their mouthy excesses are also excremental in the extreme. Unclean and uncivilized they have no mind for hygiene and like the pigs they are, they wallow, dwelling in squalor as their natural element. They were 'raised in a barn', after all, or in even less orderly wildernesses. Animals, as the creeping things that creepeth over the earth, are permanently soiled and impossible to purify. Their earthy dirtiness is infectious: as symbols of dirt and contagion, animals incite feelings of disgust. Rozin and Fallon found that, of all that arouses the peculiarly human emotion of disgust, the predominant "disgust elicitors" are animals or parts of animals, animals' secretions, and objects touched by animals' bodies (1987, p. 125). Man dreads contamination: the taint that would trigger his devolution, the degenerative process reverting him to his humble simian origins, or else unleashing The Beast Within, that nemesis of Man's Higher Self. "So what happens is that when a man abandons goodness and ceases to be human, being unable to rise to a divine condition, he sinks to the level of being an animal" (Boethius 524/1969, p. 125). For Man, apes are but "failed and degraded human

---

70 Quoted in Timofeeva (2018, p. 64).
71 Quoted in Synnott (1993, p. 142).
72 Quoted in Timofeeva (2018, p. 65).

beings," as Mary Midgley notes (2004, p. 22); they are the mirrors in which he sees himself undone.

Ultimately, then, animals haunt Man's mind as vectors of death itself. Bats, crows, ravens, moths, vultures, spectral black dogs make up mortality's menagerie; the Greek chthonic goddess Hekate made her nightly rounds to crossroads and thresholds in the company of canine hordes, whose barking was the music that announced her approach; and who but the hellhound Cerberus stands slobbering from three mouths at the gates of the underworld? Egyptian mythology features jackal-headed Anubis as psychopomp, and in Norse myth, it is a god-eating canine who ends the world: the wolf Fenrir, "the greatest enemy of gods and men" (Hultgard 2022, p. 222). Fenrir's rampage against heaven, his triumph over Odin the Father-God incites the cataclysm that dooms civilization to violent dissolution: Man's apocalypse is marked by the beast.

OTHER/SCAPEGOAT/WOMAN

The earliest scapegoat — the original Other to bear the bad body on Man's behalf — is the (nonhuman) animal. It has therefore been Man's strategy, when scapegoating subsequent Others, to brand them animal-like. "The domestication of women followed the initiation of animal keeping," observes Elizabeth Fisher in *Women's Creation* (1979, p. 190). And subsequent to 'domestication', women's subjugation has traced the pattern set by Man's relations with animals, and Man's ideas about animals have become his ideas about women. He says that the female of the species is more animalistic than the male, more biological, more carnal. She is closer to nature, to the earth. Charles Baudelaire writes, "Woman is natural, that is to say, abominable" (1919, p. 226). The Marquis de Sade was in full agreement, characterizing nature as a vicious female, a bad bitch who "hungers at all her pores for bloodshed, aches in all her nerves for the help of sin, yearns with all her heart for the furtherance of cruelty."[73] Incel hero Elliot Rodger, in the manifesto he penned before murdering

---

73   Quoted in Praz (1933/1970, p. 233).

his roommates and attacking women at a sorority in 2014, proclaimed that, "[t]here is no creature more evil and depraved than the human female. ... Women are vicious, evil, barbaric animals, and they need to be treated as such" (p. 136).

Like an animal, a woman is her body, "by nature unable to cast off materiality."[74] The sway that beastly biology holds over her organism is signaled by how the female lives to breed. She is a mother, and maternity is an animal state. Gestation, parturition, nursing — these are the animal activities around which female existence is organized. Her body, like an animal's, exists to be used by a master, to minister to the needs of (his) life. It is a given, of course, that Man is every woman's rightful master, as Balzac (1829/1904) assures his brothers: "... nature has made her for your use, made her to bear all: the children, the worries, the blows, and the sorrows of man" (p. 145).

(We hear echoes of Leviticus: "... and the goat shall bear on itself all their iniquities to a barren region ...")

Whether insult or flattery, the 'pet names' with which Man adorns the female are animal: bitch, bunny, cow, sow, dog, chick, shrew, hen, filly, kitten, pussycat, vixen, old crow, old nag, old biddy.

He depicts the female as Medusa, her head a palsied bouffant of living snakes. Or, in a particularly feverish variation on the theme, we read: "Salambo panted beneath the excessive weight, her loins yielded, she felt herself dying, and with the tip of its tail the serpent gently beat her thigh" (Flaubert 1862/1899, p. 201). Just over a century after Gustave Flaubert dashed off this passage, American pop star Britney Spears would recreate the scene, belly-dancing across the MTV Video Music Awards stage with a Burmese python draped over her bronzed shoulders as she performed her hit song, *I'm a Slave 4 U.*

In his myths Man surrounds the female with creatures both domestic and feral, as the Lady of the Beasts, Artemis the Huntress, or Aphrodite as she appears in the Homeric hymn: "After her came gray wolves, fawning on her, and grim-eyed lions, and bears, and fleet leopards, ravenous for deer."[75] Excited as he is by the costumes

---

74 J. J. Bachofen, quoted in Neumann (1955/1974, p. 57).
75 Quoted in Neumann (1955/1974, p. 274).

she dons as Woodland Nymph, Barnyard Milkmaid, and Venus in Furs, beneath Man's arousal lies a distinct wariness of the female affinity with animals. Scientific-minded men of the 19th century took it as a given that 'savage' women of the African continent regularly engaged in sexual liaisons with apes, while white women were suspected of amusing themselves in more clandestine trysts with their dogs (Djikstra 1986). In recent years, men have taken to staging speculative woman–animal couplings on such pornography websites as 'FarmXXXMovies' and 'Animal Cummers'. And as Carol Adams (2004) points out, women of color are disproportionately represented in bestiality porn: their carnal femaleness uncut by cleansing whiteness, Man the MasterMind believes them to be natural mates for beasts.

Even when women are not caught on camera canoodling in the farmyard, their own indelible animality shines through most strikingly during the sex act, as the novelist Henry Miller apprised us when he described one coital conquest "squealing like a pig," and another "crouched on all fours like a she-animal, quivering and whinnying."[76]

Man also accuses the female of being 'catty', schemingly predatory; he paints her as the Sphinx, bare-breasted and crouching on tawny leonine haunches. In his celluloid fantasies — *Cat People*, for example, both the 1942 original and the 1982 remake — she reverts to repressed felinity when her passions are inflamed, the sex kitten transformed to snarling killer witch-cat. And it was Nietzsche who wrote, "That in woman which inspires respect and fundamentally fear is her nature, which is more 'natural' than that of the man, her genuine, cunning, beast-of-prey suppleness, the tiger's claw under the glove" (1886/2003, p. 169).

Man has argued that women's brains are closer in size to gorillas' than to the one encased in his own well-endowed skull, and more primitive in shape and weight. Even the rippling of female brains' grooves betrays a slant towards the simian. His theory: the female represents an earlier stage of evolution. Her cognitive development stalled by the demands of her sexual organs, she lacks the 'higher'

---

76 Quoted in Millett (1970, p. 306).

faculties of mind and soul, intellect and spirituality. The hormones that flood her tissues, the unruly meanderings of her womb: these make her a helpless prey to the emotions. Ruled by emotion, her reason atrophies. Rationality requires a detachment from the feeling body she simply cannot muster. The Austrian philosopher Otto Weininger, whose opinion of women was dismal even by 19th-century standards, argued that because her "sexual organs possess [her],"[77] the female is incapable of reason, of memory, of logic; she cannot make judgments, is not fully conscious, and is incapable of ever seeking or knowing truth. Online anonymity has been a boon for misogynists, emboldening Man to put forward even blunter assessments in recent years: "Women are not sentient," a man writes (Bates 2021, p. 19).

Female mental inferiority is matched only by the inferiority of the female soul. The Church Fathers spent centuries arguing over whether or not the female soul could even be said to exist. Augustine held that woman was indeed ensouled, but that hers was a flimsy thing compared to man's soul, and further degraded by its contact with her body. Others, like the 12th-century Benedictine scholar Gratian, were convinced she had no soul at all, because she was not created in the image of god (Tuana 1993). Plato theorized that womanhood was a punishment meted out to men who had failed to master the flesh during their lives, the implication being that all women were in fact just unrighteous men, defined by weak wills and overwhelming appetites (Tuana 1993). It is the fault of her constitutional female moral infirmity that Eve is Christianity's Fall Girl, susceptible to serpentine temptation. Sometimes the serpent itself is represented with a woman's head, as if to squelch any surviving doubts about the femaleness of sin (Bonnell 1917). In *Paradise Lost* (1667), John Milton personified Sin as a half-woman, half-serpent creature, accessorized with Scylla's dog-girdle for good measure: "woman to the waist, and fair, / But ended foul in many a scaly fold, / ... About her middle round / A cry of Hell-hounds never-ceasing barked."[78] Original sin weighs heavy on Eve's shoulders and has been the inheritance of every

---

77   Quoted in Tuana (1993, p. 65).
78   Quoted in Bonnell (1917, p. 275).

female to follow her into the gauntlet of patriarchal Christendom. It was Eve who disobeyed god, Eve who brought death into the world. Pronounces Ecclesiasticus 25:24: "Of the woman came the beginning of sin, and through her we all die."

"[W]omen are evil, my children," warns the Testament of Reuben;[79] elsewhere the female is "an evil of nature, painted with fair colors" (Summers 1971, p. 43); and elsewhere still "the head of sin, the weapons of the devil."[80] Pythagoras considered women an invention of the dark side: "There is a good principle, which has created order, light, and man; and a bad principle, which has created chaos, darkness, and woman."[81] Enlightenment thinkers like Kant and Rousseau articulated woman's wickedness in more politely rationalist terms, arguing that because moral codes were too abstract for the feeble, primitive female mind to grasp, women could scarcely be expected to comprehend much less adhere to them. By Rousseau's stark assessment, morality was "not within the competence of women."[82]

Offenses attributed to the female moral incompetent have included rapacity, treachery, spitefulness, selfishness, wrath, vapidity, vanity, cruelty, and lewdness, among others. Man's characterization of women as "greedy selfish evil crazed sluts,"[83] to quote a contemporary subscriber to the Incel creed, culminates in the archetypal horror figure of the witch. In the 15th century, Pope Innocent VIII accused witches — the majority of whom were female — of "committing and perpetrating the foulest abominations and filthiest excesses to the deadly peril of their own souls."[84] Among the abominations attributed to witches were spells and conjurations cast to blight crops, sow infertility and impotence, and spread plagues. In Ghana, witches are even today blamed for misfortunes from hemorrhoids and snake bites to business failures, bad harvests, dead children, and divorce. According to the anthropologist Bronislaw Malinowski, the Trobriand

---

79 Quoted in Norris (2001, p. 75).
80 Origen of Alexandria, quoted in Oliver (1662, p. 126).
81 Quoted in de Beauvoir (1949/2011, p. 89).
82 Quoted in Tuana (1993, p. 83).
83 Reddit user, quoted in Bates (2021, p. 18).
84 Quoted in Levack (1992, p. 53).

people of Papua New Guinea believed that witches fed on corpses and inflicted fatal illnesses by removing and consuming the entrails of their still-living victims (1922/2014, p. 251). These witches were also reported to reek of excrement.

The stinking filthiness of the female is the stuff of legend. Early Jewish texts report that the demon Lilith, Adam's first and even more wayward wife, was formed not from the "pure dust" that god used in the creation of Adam, but from "filth and sediment" (Graves and Patai 1964, p. 66). In *The Fear of Women* (1968), Wolfgang Lederer describes statues of Frau Welt (Mrs World), whose figure can still be seen gracing the exteriors of medieval German cathedrals: a vision of loveliness from the front, seen from the rear the woman is "covered with sores, ulcers, worms, and all manners of pestilence" (p. 37). For St. John Chrysostom, the female body, no matter how outwardly appealing, was "the horrid dwelling place of ... phlegm,"[85] winsome on the surface yet full of "stinking, putrid, excremental stuff."[86] The 11th-century monk Roger de Caen elaborates on the image sketched by his predecessor:

> If her bowels and flesh were cut open, you would see what filth is covered by her white skin. If a fine crimson cloth covered a pile of foul dung, would anyone be foolish enough to love the dung because of it?[87]

The monk concludes with a warning to his brothers: "There is no plague which monks should dread more than women: the soul's death." That these Christian men's Buddhist counterparts were no less repulsed by the female is made clear in the *Maharatnakuta Sutra*:

> As the filth and decay of a dead dog or dead snake are burned away, / So men should burn filth and detest evil. / The dead dog and snake are detestable, / But women are even more detestable than they are ...[88]

---

85 Quoted in Miller (2009, p. 93).
86 Quoted in Burton (1624/1886, p. 224).
87 Quoted in Wilson (1996, p. 77).
88 Quoted in Piven (2003, p. 508).

Detestable though it was, the female form could prove a boon to Buddhist monks — so long as it was safely dead. We've already seen how the Buddha would present his students with women's corpses as objects of contemplation, the kindling for enlightening musings on the body as a horrifying "collection of bones, bound up with sinews, plastered with flesh ... foul, smelly, loathsome, disgusting, and subject to impermanence" (Wilson 1996, p. 94). As for living women, the Buddha advised his followers to stay away. In the Hindu epic *Mahabharata*, we read: "A wise man will avoid the contaminating society of women as he would the touch of bodies infested with vermin."[89]

The pestilential pollution intrinsic to the female body concentrates in her genitals, generally regarded by Man as the wellspring of corruption. A glimpse of the female pudendum is a bad omen, a sight reported to terrify lions, enemy troops, storms, and the devil himself (Lederer 1968). Of this inauspicious region below a woman's waistline, Shakespeare wrote, "There's hell, there's darkness, there is the sulphurous pit, burning, scalding, stench, consumption" (1606/1909, p. 145). Drawing its source from the infernal abyss, menstrual blood is the most abhorrent of all accursed discharges, the witch-woman's hex-blood. Paracelsus claimed that the devil used menstrual blood to breed spiders in the air; Pliny warned that knives blunted, fruit was blighted, milk soured, and bees died on contact with the stuff; the 14th-century treatise *De Secretis Mulierum* (*On Women's Secrets*) cautions against intercourse with a menstruating woman on the grounds that the blood was known to leave men "leprous and sometimes cancerous" (Magnus 1992, p. 60); and in 1878, an article published in the *British Medical Journal* avowed that "[i]t is an indisputable fact that meat goes bad when touched by menstruating women."[90]

Yet women's baleful influence is no less potent between bleedings, leading many cultures to forbid men from contact with females in the lead up to important male pastimes like military campaigns

---

89 Quoted in Morgan (1989, p. 117).
90 Quoted in de Beauvoir (1949/2011, p. 168).

and hunting expeditions. Well into the twentieth century, wartime propaganda urged soldiers to abstain from trysts with women while abroad — "she may be ... a bag of TROUBLE," reads a 1940 U.S. Army poster illustrated with a haggard, leering woman outfitted in a red beret slumping down her dark curls. Below this unsavory portrait, the poster specifies precisely the sort of trouble she's apt to be a bag of: "SYPHILIS-GONORRHEA." A similar poster shows a skeletal woman in a red gown striding arm-in-arm between Hitler and Mussolini, while the text beneath their marching feet blares, "V.D. — WORST OF THE THREE."[91]

In her diseased state, the woman is a vampire, a praying mantis or spider who ensnares Man to sap him of his vitals/vitality. A woman's mouth, like an animal's, is the most significant part of her body — though the female anatomy is more hideous even than an animal's, for it comes equipped with not one mouth but two, her sex marked by Man as a hellmouth lurking below to devour him. Often this fearsome nether-mouth is fanged, an anatomical phenomenon Man has termed 'vagina dentata' (the Latin makes it scientific, you see). A myth from the Apache people of present-day New Mexico introduces us to the Vagina Girls, monster-daughters who glutted themselves feasting on countless male suitors until one day a boy-hero named Killer-of-Enemies tricked the girls into eating berries that dissolved their teeth. Thus their orifices were rendered safely penetrable for all future visitors (Creed 1993/2015, p. 106). Algernon Swinburne, like the good Victorian that he was, kept his artistic attentions at least ostensibly focused above the she-demon's waistline, where he liked to picture her mouth perennially blazing scarlet: the queen "reddens at the mouth with the blood of men" while his Lady of Pain has a "red mouth like a venomous flower" (1865, p. 181; 1873, p. 178). Regarding the appetites of this sanguinary mouth, the poet appraised it "athirst and amorous / and hungering as the grave's mouth does" (1873, p. 267). Aztec mythology envisioned primeval chaos as a monstrous female "with countless mouths swimming in the formless waters devouring all that she could seize" (Russell 1987, p. 67).

91   Poster pictured in Harrington (2018, p. 54).

He who passes through the hungering grave of a woman's mouth is bound to fall into the underworlds within her. In *The Great Mother* (1955/1974), Erich Neumann describes the earth-womb entombed within the archetypal woman as "the abyss of hell, the dark hole of the depths ... of darkness without light, nothingness" (p. 149). "[T]he opening of the vessel of doom is the womb, the gate, the gullet," he writes, and the Dark and Terrible Mother responsible for Man's earthly existence is the "flesh-eating sarcophagus voraciously licking up the blood seed of men and beasts" in order to fertilize herself, to become pregnant and give birth to Man, hurling him "over and over again to death" (p. 171; p. 149).

In *The Mothers* (1931), Robert Briffault catalogs the countless cultures that have diagnosed the female as Mankind's leading cause of death and concludes that, "[w]oman is, in fact, universally regarded as having brought death into the world and all our woe" (p. 571). Pandora is to blame, and Eve, Hine-nui-te-po, Salome, Cleopatra.[92] It is not shocking, then, that Man's netherworlds are crowded with death goddesses: Hekate, Hathor, Hel, and Kalma, the Finnish deity whose name translates to "corpse odor." Kali, Divine Mother of the Hindu pantheon, is both feared and adored as the goddess of death, "the skull-bedecked mistress of the bone-yard," of "all-devouring Time," the force that speeds all beings rushing along towards their inevitable obliteration (Lederer 1968, p. 137). Death, it is said, "swims in her womb like a babe" (Monaghan 1997, p. 178). In illustrations we see Kali bare-breasted, bedecked with the severed heads and limbs of her victims, embryos dangling from her ears as ornament, her tongue curled twisting out between wet fangs as she raises a sickle in one of her far-too-many hands; in another, the goddess carries a bowl of blood. She tromps giddily over the corpse of her husband, whom she has killed. "As she devours all existence, as she chews all things

---

92 Pandora opened the jar that unleashed death into the Classical world, while Eve's sinful mouthful of fruit did the same for the Christians; for the Maoris, the goddess Hin-nui-te-po became the first ever cause of death when she chomped the hero Maui in her vagina dentata; Salome was death for John the Baptist, as Cleopatra was for Egypt.

existing with her fierce teeth, therefore a mass of blood is imagined to be the apparel of the Queen of the Devas [at the final dissolution]" (*Mahanirvana Tantra* 1913, p. 296).

Aristotle attributed the fall of Sparta to the intemperance of its women, while Schopenhauer blamed the violence of the French Revolution on women's "ever-growing influence" in what he perceived as an already rather effeminate country (in Tuana 1993, p. 166). According to Freud, female psychology is defined by an inability to repress or 'sublimate' the animal drives, which places women generally "in opposition to civilization" (ibid.). When she realizes her full potency as femme fatale, destroyer of men, woman is nothing less than apocalyptic. Aztec lore tells of female spider-demons who spun their webs from the western horizon, deities of the primordial darkness whose job it was to accompany the sun on its nightly descent into death. Born of a matriarchal age preceding the reign of Man, these arachnoid women were prophesied to return to power in manmade civilization's twilight days, "when the end of the world approaches and the sun, moon, and stars all clash together" (Neumann 1955/1974, p. 185).

Among the first atomic weapons the U.S. military detonated at Bikini Atoll during its 1946 nuclear tests was a missile named in tribute to the 'bombshell' starlet Rita Hayworth in her eponymous role from the film *Gilda*, released earlier that year. On the side of the Gilda bomb, the men shellacked a pin-up photo of its namesake actress sheathed in slinky black satin. After the bombings, native women of the nearby Marshall Islands began giving birth to babies they said looked like jellyfish, soft and wet, without limbs, without heads.

"If we inquire," wrote the witch hunters, "we find that nearly all the kingdoms of the world have been overthrown by women" (in Summers 1971, p. 46).

OTHER/SCAPEGOAT/THE RACIALIZED

The racialized Other is on the side of darkness, the manifestly visible very bad thing about them being that they are not white. Religious Others can be understood as a subcategory of the racialized Other, bad because of a failure to conform to the dominant faith (which has been Christianity, more often than not). Perceptible differences in complexion, ethnicity, and cosmology distinguishing members of these groups from Man the MasterMind — the White Western Christian Colonizer, in his historically prototypical manifestation — mark racialized Others as prime candidates for scapegoating. And so, because he can never get far enough from the 'sins' of his nature, Man happily adds these groups to his retinue of body-bearers, corralled on reserve along with animals and females of all races and creeds.

Again the process begins with the usual animal comparisons: from the earliest colonial incursions, black Africans — along with the Indigenous peoples of the Americas and Australia and everywhere else the White Man landed — have been characterized as savage beasts, animalistic in aspect and disposition. For British colonizers in Australia, "the black fellow was not a human being" (Hund 2021, p. 238). One 18th-century French naturalist lamented that the Indigenous peoples of North America were "mired in Animality"[93]; while his 19th-century German colleague Ernst Haeckel, whose spin on Darwinism struck a chord with the Nazis, maintained that people from continents other than Europe were "psychologically nearer to the mammals (apes and dogs) than to civilized Europeans."[94] Following the public mutilation and lynching of Henry Smith in Paris, Texas in 1893, newspapers celebrating his murder described the young black man as a "black beast," a "fiendish beast," and a "bestial negro" (Smith 2021, p. 3). An Australian World War Two general classified the Japanese as "a curious race — a cross between a human being and an ape" and advised his troops to view Japanese soldiers as vermin in need of extermination (Smith 2011, p. 19). Explaining why

---

93 George Louis Leclerc Buffon, quoted in Mason (2004, p. 233).
94 Quoted in Patterson (2002, p. 25).

he supported a policy of racial segregation, Dylan Roof — the young man who shot and killed nine people in 2015 at the Emanuel African Methodist Episcopal Church in Charleston, South Carolina — likened black people to dogs and donkeys (Pinfari 2019). Popular legends from the Middle Ages tell of Jewish women giving birth to piglets, and a regular motif in German municipal art was the Judensau, or 'Jew Pig': a Jewish man outfitted with the stereotypical pointed hat and pictured kneeling beside a sow to suckle at her teats, eating pigs' excrement, or caressing a pig's rectum, sometimes with Satan in attendance (Smith 2021).

During the Crusades, European literature portrayed Arab Muslims ('Saracens', in the argot of the day) with piglike bristles running down their spines and horns or tusks protruding from their heads (Cohen 2003). More contemporary 21st-century War-on-Terror nightmares of the Muslim enemy invoke insects swarming in subterranean nests, covertly breeding fresh legions of killer lowlifes (Steuter and Wills 2009).

In May 2018, former United States President Donald Trump, arguing for increased restrictions at the nation's borders to keep out the influx of 'undesirables' he saw as slowing America's progress towards becoming Great Again, said of undocumented Mexican and Latin American migrants, "These aren't people. These are animals."[95]

In October 2023, as the Israeli government was blasting the Gaza strip to rubble, killing trapped Palestinians by the thousands in the bombardment — over 38,000 Palestinians have been reported dead at the time of this writing (Al Jazeera 2024) — in retaliation for the 7 October Hamas terrorist attack that claimed 1,200 Israeli victims, the nation's Defense Minister Yoav Gallant stated, "We are fighting against animals, not people."[96]

Fast on the heels of the animal comparisons comes feminization, further solidifying White Man's concept of racialized Others as biological, corporeal, and nature-identified. In an impressively efficient mass-feminization, the entire continent of Africa was declared female.

---

95 Quoted in Davis (2018).
96 Quoted in Medet (2023).

The British colonial historian and novelist William Winwood Reade entreated, in a book he charmingly titled *Savage Africa* (1864):

> Look at the map of Africa. Does it not resemble a woman with a huge burden on her back, and with her face turned towards America? ... I will now attempt to sketch her features; to analyse the poison which flows from her lips and from her breasts (p. 488).

And sketch her Reade did, in lurid hues: Africa was a 'cannibal queen', a fecund but polluted temptress, her sweltering lap a swamp of malaria and snakes, her "horrible womb" heaving with "strange and monstrous embryos" (p. 487). Reade also detected shades of insidious femaleness in the African men he encountered, finding them feminine both physically and socially, with smooth cheeks and curvaceous figures, affectionate and gossipy. He was following the wisdom of the age here, since women and black people were presumed to have similarly shoddy skulls — narrow, childlike — and similarly "impulsive, emotional, and imitative" temperaments (Schiebinger 1993, p. 158). To be sure, the skulls of black females were the most deficient of them all: "I have never seen a human head more like an ape than that of this woman," one French physician remarked upon examining an African woman's skull.[97]

The female-coded bodiliness of Jewish men was established courtesy of the myth of Jewish male menstruation, extrapolated from Psalms 78:86: "God smote [the Jews] in their posteriors and set them in everlasting shame." Early Christian interpreters took the psalm to mean that Jewish men were cursed to suffer from hemorrhoids and dysentery as their punishment for murdering Christ. It would seem, however, that periodic rectal bleeding was insufficiently shameful, and so the Jewish affliction eventually shifted from a hemorrhoidal to a menstrual efflux: to bleed like a woman was the ultimate humiliation. A related theory held that, in order to replenish the blood they lost each month, Jewish men drank the blood of Christian youths they killed during ritual sacrifices, which only added to their feminization,

---

97 Paul Topinard, quoted in Halpin (1989, p. 287).

since this supposed child-sacrificing, blood-drinking habit of the Jews hitched them, in Christian Man's overheated imagination, to that notorious nadir of womankind: the witch.

Like animals, like females, the racialized or religious Other is sinful by nature. In the New Testament, Jewish people are named the "children of Satan"; by the Middle Ages they were conventionally depicted with devilish horns and/or tails; today, they continue to be accused of heading a sinister global conspiracy to overthrow Christendom. Jews were said to "exude a devilish odor," pray to the devil (their plea? what else but the usual: to overthrow Christendom), desecrate holy images, slaughter Christian children, and brew poisons out of innocent Christian heartblood stirred together with bits of frogs and spiders. It was surmised that the antichrist would be the son of the devil and a "Jewish whore" (Hund 2021, p. 235).

Charles Carroll, author of *The Negro a Beast* (1900), theorized that the serpent in Eden was no serpent at all but in fact a black man disguised as a man-eating ape. By Carroll's reading, original sin stemmed from Eve's seduction by a black man (Roberts 2008). When Frantz Fanon asked the white clients of his psychiatry practice to free-associate off the word 'Negro', some common responses included: biology, animal, devil, sin. Fanon writes:

> In Europe, the black man is the symbol of Evil. ...The torturer is
> the black man, Satan is black, one talks of shadows, when one is
> dirty one is black — whether one is thinking of physical dirtiness
> or moral dirtiness (1967/2008, pp. 188-189).

True as it is that the devils to run through White Man's imagination have frequently been black-skinned, and although black may be evil's signature hue — the Stygian dusk of "the labyrinths of the earth, abysmal depths," the dark side, to again sample from Fanon's associative list (p. 189) — blackness is not the only shade seen to signify badness. There were also 'red devils', as in the colorful sobriquet assigned to the Indigenous peoples of North America in 20th-century pulp novels and cowboy films. Puritan colonizers demonized the peoples they were in the process of decimating, denouncing them as Satan worshippers caught "in the snare of the Divell."[98] When Pope Urban II called for the First Crusade in the 11th century, he declared Muslims "an accursed race," and a "slave of the demons."[99] While urging on the Gulf War, George Bush Sr. excoriated the Iraqi government as the "unholy killers of the Middle East."[100]

As in animals, as in females, the evilness that churns within the body of the racialized Other curdles into excremental vileness. Spanish scholars tasked with lending scientific legitimacy to the project of colonization advanced the theory that Indigenous Americans were not the descendents of Adam and Eve, like whites were, but had sprouted from the rotting debris left in the wake of the Great Flood (Smith 2011, p. 80). 17th-century British poet and politician Christopher Brooke endorsed this creation story, writing that the 'savages' had "sprung up like vermin of an earthly slime."[101] In a 1942 pamphlet published by the Nazis and edited by Heinrich Himmler, subhuman creatures who "dwell in the cesspools, and swamps" were reported to discover their natural-born leader in a fellow muck-dweller: "the Eternal Jew!"[102] But the Nazis were not the first to plunge Jews into the septic mire: in 1543, Luther expressed his disgust for the Jewish people he perceived as wallowing "like swine" in "the devil's feces," while stories of Jews falling into toilets were a standard of medieval humor.[103]

An excremental nature being the unavoidable byproduct of uncontrolled appetites, the racialized Other has been assumed insatiable. Crusades-era Christian literature luxuriated in condemnations of the hedonistic decadence of Muslims, described as "an abominable sect, one suitable for fleshly indulgences," and portrayed perpetually feasting on rich delicacies in palaces lavishly heaped with jewels and languorous concubines.[104] The appetites of the racialized

---

98 Quoted in Berkhofer (1978, p. 83).
99 Quoted in Munro (1901, p. 5).
100 Quoted in Muscat (2002, p. 135).
101 Quoted in Smith (2011, p. 81).
102 Quoted in Smith (2011, p. 158).
103 Quoted in Mulvey-Roberts (2015, p. 144).
104 Quoted in Uebel (1996, p. 274).

were thought to drive them to dine on entrées that the more civilized White Man would be appalled to consume, most notably: other people. Cannibalism was a constant in colonial representations of 'the savage', meant to bolster the theory that non-white non-Christians, whether from Fiji or Africa, were such puppets of their rumbling guts that they held nothing sacred. Everything was food: base matter to sustain the base body. As Charles Carroll wrote in *The Negro a Beast*, "The Negro is not only a man-eater, but he feeds upon the flesh of his own kindred, and even upon his own offspring."[105]

The sexual appetite of the racialized Other is no less prodigal. Like animals, like females, the racialized are eminently oversexed. Frantz Fanon mimes the white Man's anxiety over black sexuality when he writes:

> As for the Negroes, they have tremendous sexual powers. What do you expect, with all the freedom they have in their jungles! They copulate at all times and in all places. They are really genital (1967/2008, p. 157).

Sex is the presumed essence of black people, and the black man in particular is "viewed as a penis symbol" (p. 159). Although white men have long been fascinated by the black man's penis, envying him his presumed phallic potency, the sexuality that has been ascribed to him earns the black man neither reverence nor respect. Viewed as being in thrall to their prodigious sexual organs, black men were assumed prone to "periods of sexual madness,"[106] during which they were compelled to commit sexual atrocities, from incest to bestiality to the rape of white women. A 1979 article published by the American white nationalist outfit National Vanguard avowed that "[l]ust ... may be too gentle a word for the maelstrom in the black male's brain."[107] *Blackzilla* is the title of one series of pornographic films depicting the violent sex black men inflict on white women; *Oh No! There's a Negro in My Mom!* is another. Following the legal (if not material) emancipation of enslaved black people in the United States, the

---

105 Quoted in Roberts (2008, p. 82).
106 U.S. physician William Lee Howard, quoted in Roberts (2008, p. 83).
107 Quoted in Ferber (2007, p. 18).

image of the black man as a bestial rapist stalking down innocent blonde debutantes and church-going matrons was invaluable as a justification for lynchings, during which the black male victims were often castrated before being murdered. If the black male's sexual nature made him a rapist, the sexual nature of the black female made her impossible to rape. Nineteenth-century Europeans were obsessed with black women as icons of carnality, hypersexual and fecund. For purposes of scientific inquiry, white men spent a great deal of time studying black women's genitals, to which the "wanton perversions" of the black female were attributed (Schiebinger 1993, p. 159). These fantasies of black female sexuality were reflected in European men's practice of abducting African women to enslave them as concubines or sell into prostitution.

Jewish men have likewise been cast in the role of sexual predator, as in the quintessential 'Evil Jew' character of Svengali, whose mesmeric corruption of a young girl sullied her native white sweetness in George du Maurier's 1894 novel *Trilby*. And Jewish women, like black women, are natural prostitutes, while Muslim maidens were reported to offer sexual favors freely up to invading crusaders. Indigenous American women reputedly did the same, overjoyed to be the sexual playthings of the colonizers: "When they had the opportunity of copulating with Christians, urged by excessive lust, they defiled and prostituted themselves."[108] Out of the White Man's belief in Indigenous women's hypersexuality emerged the figure of the Squaw, which Cherry Smiley (2023) identifies as a specifically colonial iteration of the 'whore' aspect of the inescapable patriarchal Virgin/Whore dichotomy. As was their strategy in Africa, colonizers mobilized the idea of Indigenous women as sexual savages, promiscuous and perennially available, to justify rape and to funnel these women into the nascent systems of prostitution white men were busily establishing in their various New Worlds. In contemporary pornography, the most in-demand racialized Other is the Asian woman, a dubious popularity rooted in the racist fetishization casting

---

108 Italian colonizer Amerigo Vespucci, quoted in Berkhofer (1978, p. 8).

Asian women as eternal Lolitas, childlike and submissive yet sexually voracious. On a porn site called 'Asian Fever' we read: "No one knows how to please a man like an Asian slut can."[109]

The rapist-and-whore sexuality of the racialized is not only distasteful to the civilized Man, it's dangerous: a serious threat to white male rule. Near to the heart of white supremacist anxiety is the fear of miscegenation, particularly when the mixed-race couple consists of a racialized man and a white woman. White Man has long dreaded the masses of 'mongrels' these matings might unleash, who in their depraved half-blood hordes would drive the noble white race to extinction. Hence the sexual appetites of the racialized herald the demise of white civilization.

Like animals, like females, the racialized further hasten civiliz-ation's undoing as disease vectors, a dangerous form of living contaminant, to be feared not only as destructive but also as prolifer-ating, invasive, entering into and spreading through Man's clean and orderly system, corrupting it (Steuter and Wills 2009, p. 17). The supposed pestilence has been clear to see on their skin: *Savage Africa* author William Winwood Reade designated the "black hue of the negro" the "color of disease" (1864, p. 409); and antisemitic lore held that Jews were particularly prone to dermatological complaints, the "external sign of their diseased state" (Gilman 1991, p. 126). In the 14th century, as the Black Death was steadily decimating Europe, allegations that Jews spread the plague by poisoning wells incited waves of pogroms that resulted in the wholesale extermination of entire Jewish communities. Nazi propaganda compared Jewish people to tuberculosis bacteria; for Hitler, 'the Jew' as the Aryan Superman's nemesis was "a germ, germ carrier, or agent of disease, a decomposing agent, fungus, or maggot" as well as "the source of an epidemic ... comparable to syphilis," typically likened to blood poisoning (Smith 2011, p. 146). Today it is the Muslim terrorist who stars in white manmade culture's fever dream as the lethal infection — newspaper headlines refer to "Islamic terrorism" as a "spreading cancer"; Al

---

109 Quoted in Dines (2011, p. 124).

Qaeda, we read, is "mutating like a virus"[110] — busily and irrevocably defiling the body politic from within.

"The sense of impending disaster crushed the hearts of thoughtful and serious people," wrote Thomas Dixon Jr. in his 1904 novel *The Clansman*, "They felt that a pestilence worse than the Black Death of the Middle Ages threatened to extinguish civilization."[111] Medieval Christian theologians abominated Mohammed as the Beast of the Apocalypse, his followers as harbingers of the antichrist (Morey and Yaqin 2011, p. 8). Jews, too, were "the servants, supporters and troops of the Antichrist when he came to devastate Christendom" (Gow 1995, p. 94). In alliance with the animal and the female, the racialized Other incarnates doomsday.

Man lines up his scapegoats for the sacrifice. He is the Self and they are the Others: animals, females, the racialized. And Man makes these Others take on all that he cannot accept in himself. The animal is the body Man is not. The woman is the body Man is not. The Black, the Jew, the 'Indian', the Muslim are the body Man is not. Identified with sex, filth, stupidity, excrement, sin, disease, decay and degradation both physical and social, Others become the earthly matter that Man rejects, the biological squalor, the dirt, the evil and the End; they are the deaths Man refuses to die. Massed together in a thickening drift, these Others/Bodies form the lowness Man looks down on to dream himself lifted out and up from the man-eating deluge of the vicious world he despises. Andrea Dworkin writes, "As long as her body lines the bottom, [men] have raised ground on which to walk" (2000, p. 232). Man rises, for now he has disburdened himself of the terrible weight that once polluted him, and now he can reign on earth as in heaven, the immortal MasterMind over all.

---

110 Quoted in Steuter and Wills (2009, p. 17).
111 Quoted in Roberts (2008, p. 89).

MASTERING THE BODY BY PROXY:

RITUALS OF CORPOREAL CONTROL AND PUNISHMENT

And projecting feeling and the material onto the body of another, the mind defends itself and takes revenge against its enemy by humiliating, punishing, and destroying this other.

SUSAN GRIFFIN, *Pornography and Silence* (1981, p. 178)

B y the rituals he invents and executes and repeats obsessively, Man labors to reconfigure reality. Joseph Campbell defined ritual as "the enactment of a myth"[112]: the practice of bringing a myth to life, lending it concrete presence in the world, through methodical, purposeful, symbolically significant actions. "By participating in a ritual, you are participating in a myth," Campbell said. Ritual enactment realizes the myth, as reality is recreated in conformity with its invented narrative. A myth is a fiction crafted to explain the world and one's place within it. This explanatory power is the reason why mythology is such a ubiquitous and integral element of human culture, for it has been through our myths that we have made sense of our lives. Yet, in manmade culture, our dominant myths are Man's fictions. They explain the world as Man would have it; they make the sense that Man wants made. And the foundational ritual of manmade culture, as we have seen, is the persecution of the scapegoat: an Other forced into the role of the rejected body and then condemned, and then sacrificed. Man executes the scapegoating ritual in order to compel reality into compliance with manmade culture's foundational fiction, Man's best-loved delusion, his fantasy: that he is not his body, that he is a pure mind, mastering matter (Man the thinking thing), and that he who crowns himself Master is freed from death. Susan Griffin writes, "The deluded mind must try to remake the world after an illusion" (1981, p. 121).

---

112 <https://billmoyers.com/content/ep-3-joseph-campbell-and-the-power-of-myth-the-first-storytellers-audio/>.

The rituals Man has invented to make real his sacred myths advance along a course of escalating violence, the compulsion to overpower the mortal material body twisting into a bitter urge to punish it for its crimes against him, as he grows increasingly desperate to believe in the fantasy to which he has hitched his salvation.

Mortification, mutilation, humiliation, consumption, replacement, torture, annihilation.

These are the rites Man performs, these he repeats obsessively.

MORTIFICATION

She would be as angels, spun from the azure ether, like the human form was in the blessed days before Eve brought down the burden of flesh, before she let Eden's gates clatter barred shut against Mankind forever. Instead, this shroud of soiled meat inside which her soul chokes, stifled, weighs her down so heavily she is anchored to the earth, a doomed daughter of the original sinner, born defiled. Hers is an unforgivable body, a relic of the Fall. If she prays to save her soul the Fathers answer she'll have to quash the female flesh completely: "conquer the woman; conquer the flesh; conquer desire."[113] She must neglect her body's every complaint, its every clamoring demand. She must anesthetize herself against the onslaught of the senses, each trace of honeyed scent, touch, the taste in the mouth that threatens to ripen into ruinous sweetness. The Fathers bid her seek refuge from pleasure in the rigors of pain.

Thus St. Catherine of Genoa "made great penances: so that all her senses were mortified"[114]; and St. Eustochia of Messina, resolved to treat herself as if molded from excrement and mud, stood naked under the sun to desiccate the sin that pooled stagnant inside her (Bell 1987, p. 142). The 19th-century 'heroine in mortification' St. Gemma Galgani fashioned herself a cincture from a knotted rope she spiked with nails to wear around her waist like a girdle (Amedeo 1935). This teenaged stigmatic confided in her savior, "[My body] often cries out, and would

---

113 Osbert of Clare (mid-twelfth century) to the nun Ida of Barking, quoted in Newman (2011, p. 23).

114 *The Life of Catherine of Genoa*, quoted in Underhill (1919/1990, p. 225).

fain not obey me, but I'll see to that. Yesterday it seemed as if it would revolt, and I made it keep quiet by dint of hard blows."[115]

At night St. Rosa of Lima whipped herself until her bedroom walls were speckled red and her blood streamed dark ribbons stickily across the floor. The girl contrived to prolong her suffering by reopening each night the previous evening's wounds in order that no welt could ever heal: "... thus her body was almost one entire wound" (Faber 1671/1855, p. 59). Under her veil, Rosa wore a homemade crown affixed with 99 iron points to pierce her skull in 99 places, causing inconceivable pain whenever she opened her mouth to speak. Thereby this device effectively trained her to pious silence. If at night the devil tried to tempt her to sleep, St. Rosa would strike her head against the wall, for the "implacable hatred which she felt for her body, taught her to refuse it every comfort" (p. 73).

St. Mary Magdalene de Pazzi combated carnal temptation by rolling naked on a pyre of thorns she'd piled in the convent woodshed:

> ... and to give greater vent to the implacable hatred which she bore to her own flesh, she now struck her breast with a stone, now literally basted her arms and legs with melted wax, now for a long time struck herself with nettles (Cepari 1849, p. 355).

Though she barely ate, the saint was known to suck maggots from the infested ulcers of the impoverished and diseased patients whose care she oversaw in the convent infirmary (Favazza 2011). Similarly, St. Angela of Foligno, anxious to experience "all the sufferings of the world in her every limb and organ," supped water in which she'd washed lepers' sloughing feet, and when she choked on a scab, she likened it to the eucharist (Bell 1987, p. 107). St. Catherine of Siena, while ministering to a woman dying of cancer, milked a ladleful of pus from a sore on the woman's breast and drank it, to punish her senses for how the putrid stench repulsed them (Raymond of Capua 1864). Thrice daily St. Catherine scourged her body with an iron chain.

Thrice nightly Blessed Benvenuta Bojani "took a severe discipline with an iron chain" (ed. Procter 1901, p. 304).

---

115 *The Life of Gemma Galgani* by the Venerable Fr. Germanus O.P., quoted in Dallaire (2011).

Thrice nightly Blessed Columba of Rieti "disciplined herself to blood" (ed. Procter 1901, p. 134).

St. Margaret of Cortona told her confessor of her desire to "see her body debilitated, infected, devoured by worms." "Have pity on me," she implored, "and allow me to redouble my rampage against this odious body." When the confessor instead counseled her to temper her mortifications, the saint retorted: "I have no intention of making a peace pact between my body and my soul, and neither do I intend to hold back."[116]

However inventive these holy women may have been in their subjugation of the flesh, all conformed to a common diet: they starved. Invariably female saints' hagiographies tell of the young girl's vow never to let a morsel pass through her lips, how her life from smallest girlhood was one unending fast, that she ate in thirty years what the layman eats in three days, that she lived off bread crumbs and drops of water, or air alone, that she survived on the supernatural manna of Christ's love, his body and blood. The Church Fathers who acted as these women's confessors and biographers wrote admiringly of female bodies denuded of flesh, of their "holy bones, all fleshless,"[117] celebrating the jagged angles and concavities of emaciation as if these were the true lineaments of female virtue. Since the carnal appetites — the alimentary and the sexual — were held to be inextricably entwined, to give in to one was to inflame the other. Both, therefore, had to be kept under strictest control. If this was the case for men, it was truer still for women, whose wills were weaker, their natures more fleshly. She who indulged her body was sure to spoil her soul, for what sustains "corrupt life on earth" is anathema to "life everlasting" (Bell 1987, p. 115). In the words of St. Teresa of Avila, "This soul would fain see itself free and eating is killing it."[118] By starving, a woman could thin the tether painfully stringing her soul to the body and the earth. Eventually it would have to snap and she'd be free, but until then, her

---

116 St. Margaret of Cortona, quoted in Bell (1987, p. 101).
117 Biographer of St. Pelagia of Antioch, quoted in Shaw (1998, p. 234).
118 Quoted in Corrington (1986, p. 51).

wasted body served as testament to her victory over carnality. It was only through starvation that the female body (that vile inheritance) could be converted into a symbol of purity and strength.

"[S]he has so purified her soul and body that lust no longer lives in her,"[119] the fourth-century theologian Basil of Ancyra wrote to congratulate a fasting female. In his view, women saved themselves through starvation by making their bodies as good as dead. Living death as feminine piety's proper mode became the ambition of women like St. Margaret of Cortona, who professed, "I not only wish to abstain from bodily food, but I wish to die a thousand times a day ... in this mortal life of mine."[120] Beyond the general deadening it promised, starving oneself had the special advantage of 'killing' the female functions that enslaved every woman to the hateful cycle of life/death and weaponized her against Man as the chief instrument of his damnation. If she starves, the blood that is her woman's curse dries up. She bears no children; her withered breasts will nurse no sons born to perish. When lack pares away her breasts and hips and stops her monthly bleedings, the woman comes close to shedding her female nature, she very nearly rises above her sex: she's almost like a man! Very nearly she is redeemed.

The Fathers' edict reverberates: "It is fitting for women to fast always."[121]

The contemporary anorexic girl or woman likewise strives for purity, though of a secular kind, through the self-imposed penitential atrophy of her body. She, too, renounces the flesh as a hateful, shameful encumbrance. She, too, feels herself stigmatized by carnality. "I don't want to be a sexual, bodily being. I want to be a zero, a blob,"[122] protests the starving girl. She, too, is abashed by the neediness of her body, the humiliation of needing, or worse: of wanting. Specifically she cannot stand the female fat she says clings like a suety cage she cannot twist loose of: her hips, her thighs, her belly, her breasts. "All those stores of fat! Was anything more evocative of need and

---

119 Quoted in Shaw (1998, p. 235).
120 Quoted in Bell (1987, p. 102).
121 Pseudo-Athanasian *Sermo Exhortatorius*, quoted in Shaw (1998, p. 223).
122 'Anne', a teenage anorexic, quoted in Corrington (1986, p. 54).

greed than a womanly body?" the anorexic cries out, revulsed by the wretched softness of her biology (Freeman 2023, p. 105). And just like her medieval foresisters, she craves divine release through dematerialization:

> I feel savagely surrounded by myself on all sides. I feel the substance sticking to my alabaster bones in contempt ...[123]

> [My soul] was tied down by this big bag of rocks that was my body. I had to drag it around.[124]

> [Glimpsing her skeletonized torso in the mirror, she says] ... oddly I feel as if I've been cleansed.[125]

No doubt men can also be anorexic. Yet studies consistently find that approximately 90% of anorexics are female (Hoek 2006; Accurso et al. 2020). And although the hagiographies of male saints are by no means lacking in lurid tales of self-harm in god's name — St. Simeon the Stylite, for example, is reputed to have plucked up the maggots wriggling from a gangrenous ulcer on his foot and, placing them back at their post, instructed the deserters, "Eat what god has given you!"[126] — mortifications, privations, and austerities are regarded as decidedly 'feminine' expressions of Christian devotion. Female saints' antagonism towards their bodies was enacted with a severity that men rarely matched, and their legends, far more so than men's, revolve around their prodigious talent for wounding themselves.

In *Holy Anorexia* (1987), Rudolph Bell attributes women's peculiar zeal for starvation and the scourge to the differing understandings of sin into which women and men were trained. For men, sin implied immoral action; a man sinned when he yielded to some external temptation, behaving wickedly as a result. Women, by contrast, learned sin as an internal quality, a wickedness beginning with and within the female body. When men practiced bodily

---

123 'Pro-Ana' website user, quoted in Bates (2015, p. 195).
124 Anorexic woman, quoted in Lelwica (1999, p. 115).
125 Anorexic woman, quoted in Lelwica (1999, p. 106).
126 St. Simeon the Stylite (390–459) was a Syrian Christian ascetic famed for spending roughly forty years stationed atop a pillar. The charming maggot anecdote cited here can be found in Favazza (2011, p. 35).

penances, the purpose was to steel their souls against a sinful world. Women, believing their own bodies to be sin's wellspring, beyond deliverance, sought expiation through attrition, an exorcism of the flesh on which they blamed their exile from grace, and which Man blamed for his damnation.

Theresa Shaw, in *The Burden of the Flesh: Fasting and Sexuality in Early Christianity* (1998), adds that women's attraction to mortification was further encouraged by the place ordained to females in the church. Ineligible for recruitment into god-the-father's army, devout women were to accept as their mission a mystical union with Christ the Heavenly Bridegroom. Women obediently channeled their religious fervor into attracting the attention of their lord and savior, in the hopes that he would select them as his brides. And what their man wanted, these women were instructed, was not the mundane, worldly female charms of fleshy curves and frippery, but rather a femininity of the spirit, defined by "a pure heart and an undefiled body which is mortified by fasting."[127] Notably, male monastics received no such guidance. Nor were they hidden away from the world after taking vows, like women were, the cloistered captives of convents and anchorholds. Men could roam the countryside spreading god's word, saving souls, while a woman's domain was restricted to the sole territory over which she could expect to claim any semblance of authority: her body. ("You make out of your body your very own kingdom," a contemporary anorexic explains, "where you are the tyrant, the absolute dictator."[128])

But what good could she possibly do with her body, hideous thing that it was? Spectacular self-laceration emerged as the crowning glory of female sanctity, when, barred from active participation in the church (as well as the broader society) and confined to bodies condemned beyond absolution as evil incarnate, women found themselves with few options for demonstrating their devoutness besides warring against their own substance. Thus St. Rosa of Lima perceptively inquired, "As I cannot do any good, is it not just that I

---

127 Pseudo-Athanasius, quoted in Shaw (1998, p. 250).
128 "Hazel," an anorexic, quoted in Corrington (1986, p. 59).

should suffer whatever I am capable of enduring?" (Feuillet 1671/1855, p. 64).

In Man's MasterMind, in the minds of the Fathers, her body is the Body. To see a woman attack her own flesh, torment and negate her physicality, refuse her body basic care as if it were owed no mercy, is to see the Body turned against itself. Through her self-inflicted abuses Man's horror of being bodily, internalized and incarnated by the woman, is made manifest as the Body's own self-horror; his hatred of the Body is now the Body's hatred of itself, of *herself*.

"Of her own free will, [she] offered herself as the scapegoat for the sins of the world," J. K. Huysmans (1901/1979) writes in his hagiography of St. Lydwine of Schiedam, a 14th-century saint whose saintliest feat was disintegrating into worm-eaten pulp on her sickbed. "The more she suffered the more she was satisfied and the more she wished to suffer" (p. 75). Though the woman may abandon herself willingly to her role, she is not the author of this passion play; she was not the one to dream up the god before whom she prostrates herself; it is not her creed that excoriates the female body as death and damnation. Yet to be saved she must win the Fathers' blessing. And so acting out the Body's despairing prayer of repentance for its own shameful existence, she annuls herself. Please, god, let there be less of me: the angel evaporates. A flower-scented whisper from St. Therese of Lisieux, that tubercular girl bedded in her early grave: "in fact I must remain little and strive to become smaller still!"[129]

She takes up the chain, tightens the spiked cincture, skips another meal. And the Fathers look on with satisfaction as the Body destroys itself, pleading to be redeemed in its Master's eyes. To be forgiven.

MUTILATION

"[A] living being may also be regarded as raw material, as something plastic, something that may be shaped and altered," the surgeon explains, to clarify his methods (Wells 1896/2009, p. 274). The body

---

129 Quoted in Vardey (2002, p. 223).

is not fixed, not immutable, not a fact of nature: Man need not settle for the shabby things he's been granted.

His Is the Hand that Wounds. He inserts the needle lengthwise to pillow her lip's vermillion with acid filler then molds the lip manually into the desired shape (e.g., butterfly, cherry, Russian). With hemostats teases a yolky bauble of fat from her cheek to confer upon the face a more refined and sculpted look. Injects fat beneath the eyes to achieve 'cute skin' (a smiling appearance). Inserts an oscillating saw through the incision he cuts below her chin to chisel the undesirable angle from her jawline, excising shards of bone to create the impression of a kinder, gentler nature. Injects a paralytic toxin into the orbital region around her eyes, between her eyebrows, into her forehead/ neck/chest/armpits/palms of her hands/soles of her feet, until, static, she lies back looking perfectly serene. Excavates a chamber in her breast to house the bag of gel: then she is luscious. Harvests unsightly adipose from her abdomen, lateral thorax, waist, hips, and thighs and injects it into her buttocks, where it will bulge more alluringly.

Over 400 plastic surgery clinics and hospitals crowd the single square mile that constitutes the South Korean capital city of Seoul's 'Improvement Quarter'. "Some clinics occupy as many as sixteen floors, and the largest encompass several high-rises," writes Patricia Marx (2015) for *The New Yorker*. Immense, brightly colored signs bear these establishments' names: "Small Face," "Wannabe," "Cinderella," "Magic Nose," "Reborn." Among the clinics, housed in a five-storey tower twinkling silver-chrome against the skyline, is the "Cosmetic Vaginal Surgery Center." Here, expert surgeons specialize in tightening, smoothing, and shrinking women's inner labia with lasers, giving all due consideration to "aesthetic sensibility" (Hu 2023, p. 143). Sixty-six per cent of South Korean women surveyed in 2020 said they would put themselves under the knife if it could increase their chances of scoring a lucrative match on the marriage market (p. 161). In display case vitrines in the stylish, ultra-modern lobby of his Seoul clinic, one surgeon exhibits the yellowed splinters of thousands of women's jawbones, each fragment etched with the name of the patient from whose face it was excised (p. 161).

His Is the Hand that Heals. The Body's defects and deficits now corrected, the surgeon pronounces the final outcome optimal. At last she pleases his discerning eye, for "the organism as a whole [has been] developed far beyond its apparent possibilities" (Wells 1896/2009, p. 275).

Alicia Amira, self-proclaimed foundress of the Bimbo Movement, teaches online workshops on becoming "the best Bimbo version of yourself."[130] Bimbo Pride merch available for purchase on her "Be A Bimbo" website includes a belly shirt that bears the catchphrase "Fake ... is the new real" in fuchsia Barbie font. Amira defines a bimbo as a "hyperfeminine sexual-looking plastic creature" who — proudly, gleefully, entirely of her own accord — makes herself over into the ultimate sex object. "Being a bimbo is, like, surgically enhancing yourself," Amira explains.[131] Amira's own personal ambition is to look as fake as possible. (Another self-identified bimbo puts it this way: "My aim is to look more plastic than human."[132]) In her quest to incarnate the "real-life fuck doll"[133] epitome of hyperfeminine perfection, Amira has spent over $120,000 on cosmetic procedures, including three breast enlargement surgeries, liposuction, rhinoplasty, thread lifts (in which the face is pinned back against gravity's tug by barbed stitches twined beneath the skin), cheek/jaw/nose/chin/nasolabial fold/lip filler, and monthly Botox injections. Though Amira typically argues that surgery has empowered her by putting her in control of her own appearance, in 2022 she admitted to *Dazed Digital* that the ideal she was working towards was not wholly her own:

> I allow my partner to decide ... because it's part of my bimbo-fication to have somebody who owns me. I'm his sex object and

---

130 Alicia Amira's OnlyFans page, accessed June 2023. <https://onlyfans.com/alicia amiravip>.

131 "Meet the Bimbo Against Feminism" mini-documentary <https://www.youtube.com/watch?app=desktop&v=jODBKrj3H5g>.

132 "I Escaped My Family to Pursue My Bimbo Obsession | HOOKED ON THE LOOK" on YouTube, accessed March 2024. <https://www.youtube.com/watch?v=0Vu L2LNnCQw&t=415s>.

133 Quoted in Dunn (2022).

his trophy. How big my breasts are gonna go isn't really up to me to decide.[134]

Though she may not be the originator of the image, with her platinum hair extensions, her tattooed eyebrows and her fingernails three-inch acrylic talons lacquered pink and bedazzled, her breasts swollen to double the size of her head, Amira feels "more like the sex object and sex doll that I feel like I was born to be."[135] And her metamorphosis is far from complete. "You're growing, you're evolving, and each year you become more and more plastic."[136] She says she'll never stop. She needs butt implants, an ampler bosom, a tinier more doll-like pert little nose. She would like to have her lower ribs removed, to scythe a trimmer waistline. "Make sure to save all of Daddy's pocket money for plastic surgery!" are Amira's closing words of advice for bimbos-in-training, as she winks, poses for the camera, her hand fluttering from inflated breast to lipo-contoured flank, this span of flesh she's dedicated her life to carving into shape.

"These creatures I had seen were the victims of some hideous experiment" (Wells 1895/2009, p. 108). With each generation, the dogs degrade more babylike, their limbs and jaws steadily truncated, eyes bulging from faces flattened like mashed against a board. The desired effect is known as 'pedomorphism': the retention, in an adult animal, of infantile features. We are told that "changes in head conformation over the years have led to an 'exaggerated head' with large forward-facing eyes with a steeper stop and higher and shorter head which appeals to the pet buying public" (Knowler et al. 2019, p. 1). Deformed to excess, the animal's face caves in, brain lumping out through soft spots in her skull. She cannot breathe through her snub-nose; she asphyxiates on her own flesh. Early Chinese guidelines for the breeding of Pekingese dogs, as written by the Empress, directed the monks who oversaw the dog-making process to "let its fore legs

---

134 Quoted in Wilson (2022).

135 Ibid.

136 "Meet the Bimbo Against Feminism" on Youtube, accessed March 2024. <https://www.youtube.com/watch?app=desktop&v=jODBKrj3H5g>.

be bent, so that it shall not desire to wander far, or leave the Imperial precincts."[137]

His Is the Hand that Makes. In the modern agricultural industry, animals are methodically bred for 'food traits', their bodies molded to conform to consumer demands. 'Meat-type' chickens have been engineered to grow at such rapid rates that the surplus flesh swiftly overwhelms the birds' developing skeletons; under the weight of so much 'meat' their bones and joints degenerate and the birds cannot walk without pain, if they can move at all. Their hearts fail, floundering within the surging excess of bodies meant not for living but only to be killed in service of their masters' appetites (Karen Davis 2014). A goldfish is bred for eyes like fat baubles protruding so bulbous that he'll knock them against the plastic castle in his little bowl until he goes blind from the repeated battering. A mouse is genetically engineered to seed cancerous tumors blooming uncontrolled through all her tissues.

What charms breeding fails to cultivate can be imposed later by means of artifice. Pekingese breeders were known to widen puppies' shoulders by holding "the growing specimen in the hand for days at a time," while the "obstinate organ" of a puppy's muzzle could be tamed to flatness through a regimen of daily rubbing. To stunt their growth, puppies were "enveloped in wire cages closely fitting the body" and deprived of exercise; in this way they were prevented from exceeding the adorably diminutive size desired of them (Gladstone and Wakeley 1923, p. 165). Similar methods were employed in the manufacture of dwarfs, who were popular in the menageries of aristocrats, as curiosities or amusing human pets. In Greece, parents enclosed their children within coffin-like chests in hopes of securing them careers as dwarfs; Romans would underfeed their offspring with the same aspiration in mind (Tuan 1984). A 17th-century German medical treatise details how to turn babies into dwarfs by glazing their spines with a salve prepared from the fat of moles, dormice, and bats

---

137 Quoted in Compton (1904, p. 269).

(Otto 2001). "If they endured this torture," one historian writes, "the artificial dwarfs would be pampered and petted" (Brown 2014, p. 140).

In *The Island of Doctor Moreau* (1896/2009), H. G. Wells describes the experiments of the eponymous surgeon and vivisectionist, a man obsessed by "the study of the plasticity of living forms" (p. 124). By his hand, pigs, dogs, llamas, bears, sheep, and apes are "carven and wrought into new shapes," their flesh resectioned, bits and pieces grafted from one animal onto another, tissues reconfigured and recombined to sculpt men from the bodies of beasts. The Doctor takes the human form as his template, he says, because it "appeals to the artistic turn more powerfully than any animal shape can" (p. 126). And, as Virginia Blum highlights in *Flesh Wounds: The Culture of Cosmetic Surgery* (2003), plastic surgeons are eager to class themselves as artists. Specifically, they fancy themselves sculptors. Taking the base matter of the animal body as their medium, the surgeons apply their skill and vision and shape it like clay, carve it like stone into something beautiful. To wrench beauty from low-born flesh is a violent procedure: "Each time I dip a living creature into the bath of burning pain, I say, 'This time I will burn out all the animal; this time I will make a rational creature of my own!'" (Wells 1896/2009, p. 130). The violence is essential and inevitable because the raw material that is his medium is the surgeon's sworn enemy. His revulsion for the material reality of the body is reflected in both the image he idealizes and the methods he uses as he slashes-and-burns the flesh, believing he alone can elevate this unfortunate thing from its native ugliness. Because he hates the Body, the surgeon 'optimizes' and 'perfects' Others' bodies by mutilating them. The perfect body he strives to produce is his protest screamed against nature.

Whether manufactured by selective breeding — the toy dog's muzzle mashed to babyish, the cow bred to flood the world with milk — or by manipulations after the fact — her face scissored and slid up the bone to smooth its creases, the corset tightened, the foot bound, lips pricked to fuller wasp-stung pout, the hen debeaked — the perfected creature is the one who bears Man's mark.

White slaveowners in the United States mutilated the black people they held captive as chattel to mark them as possessions and to punish them for insubordination. Branding was one common technique: "... a negro girl called Mary, has a small scar over her eye, a good many teeth missing, the letter A is ... branded on her cheek and forehead" (American Anti-Slavery Society 1839, p. 78). Equally common was notching the ears of the enslaved, or shearing them away completely. Both branding and ear-cutting remain standard practice in the 'husbandry' of animals owned as 'livestock' and, until recently, horses used by the racing industry would have identification numbers tattooed into their lips. Pimps regularly tattoo their own names onto the bodies of the women they prostitute.

Yet such crude emblems of dominion are widely scorned as gauche in our civilized day and age; Man has cause to make his marks more subtly now. As a graduation gift from her parents, a Jewish teenager is treated to rhinoplasty to correct her tell-tale nose. Sander Gilman writes in *Making the Body Beautiful: A Cultural History of Aesthetic Surgery* (1999) that, through the 1960s, over half of all patients seeking rhinoplasty in the United States were first- or second-generation Jewish Americans (p. 193). Among Asian Americans, double-eyelid surgery is the rite-of-passage cosmetic optimization gifted to daughters on the cusp of womanhood. The modern version of this procedure, which creates a fold in the eyelid to 'deorientalize' its appearance, was developed by an American military surgeon stationed in South Korea during the Korean War. Many early recipients of the procedure were Korean women in the sex trade, or those acquired as 'war brides' by U.S. soldiers (Kurek 2015; Menon 2023). And the earliest experiments in silicone breast augmentation were performed on Japanese women prostituted to U.S. soldiers during America's post-war occupation of Japan: to accommodate client demand for a bustier silhouette, industrial silicone was injected directly into these women's chests (Jeffreys 2005/2015). Although the 'patients' were prone to gangrene and occasionally died, silicone proved a boon for plastic surgeons, far more suitable for filling women out than the paraffin wax, glass and ivory orbs, wool, epoxy resin, petroleum jelly, nylon, Plexiglass, and polymerized synthetic sponges men had used in previous efforts (Kaoutzanis 2019; Jacobson 2000).

Studying photographs of a famous plastic surgeon's patients, Virginia Blum remarks that the women have all come out of the good doctor's clinic sporting the same face: uniformly pretty, with an "aggressively managed" nasolabial fold — such is the surgeon's signature 'look'. "All the women start out completely different," Blum writes, "but they end up all looking somewhat alike, now sharing an eerie surgical sisterhood" (2003 p. 93).

His Is the House of Pain. Although plastic surgery is marketed as a permanent fix for physical flaws, in reality most patients will find themselves returning to the operating theatre many times over. Once one defect is corrected, another will surface soon enough to vex and rankle as the new deformity in need of emergency attention. Moreover, most mutilations require regularly scheduled maintenance. "[S]omehow the things drift back again: the stubborn beast-flesh grows day by day back again," the surgeon, frustrated, growls in his lab (Wells 1896/2009, p. 129). A capsule of scar tissue toughens around the plastic sac sewn in to bloat the woman's breast. As the scar seals tighter around the foreign object, the woman's breast warps and hardens, stony now to the touch; her cleavage sits crooked. Called 'capsular contracture', this disfiguring scarring is breast enlargement's most common complication; sufferers report that they live in chronic pain. Eventually the implants, encased in scar tissue, will rupture. Then the patient will need to have the leaking plastic sacs removed and replaced with fresh ones (Jeffreys 2005/2015). Each time the surgery is repeated, the potential risks to the patient become more and more extreme.

Such is the surgeon's lament: "As soon my hand is taken from them the beast begins to creep back, begins to assert itself again" (Wells 1896/2009, p. 129). The beast-flesh resurges, the Body unmakes Man, and a scarred woman rushes back into the arms of her surgeon, to be rescued from her wayward tissues. But the man has taken this work as his art, his sacred task: he will never accept defeat. He takes up the blade again, undaunted. Yes, the Body reverts, backsliding into beastliness, but scalpel in hand, with the proud self-assurance his profession warrants, the surgeon swears, "I mean to conquer that" (p. 129).

HUMILIATION

The squat building into which the animals are crowded has no windows; no light gets in. Fluorescent tubes drone a grey-yellow glow skirring queasy over concrete and the animals' huddled bodies and the grunge that plasters everything: the gratings, the stall floors, the walls, the bars of the pens. The air swerves black with greedy flies, it vibrates, ripples heavy, wraps the animals in writhing blankets of flies, with garlands of flies spun round their necks, stockings of flies stitching darkly up their shanks. In wire cages so tight they can scarcely turn around, the animals have no option but to relieve themselves where they stand. Hens in cages stacked floor to ceiling defecate onto the hens caged below them. Animal wastes sluice between the wires, through the slatted floors into the slurry trench beneath, and the stink of it twists the gut to panic, its thickness deathlike, a sticky sallow acridity, cloying and emetic; occlusive, with a sluggish yet insistent aggressiveness it gathers, stopping up the nose, the throat. Sometimes the ammoniacal fug hangs so dense the animals drop dead just from breathing. The sick air ulcerates their eyes and they go blind. A chicken crippled by his own weight flops forward onto soiled litter. He won't move again.

Sludge lapping at their pallid hocks, muck-slathered piglets wade through a pool of sewage. The piggery churns and leaks its black inundation swirling towards the drains, the deluge spilling out, seeping dark through the building's chinks and cracks, leaching into the earth to poison it. Microbial riot breeds in permanent squalor's fertile heat and swarms to infest the animals' wounds, setting off a colorful pageant of sores, swellings, tumors, and welts; pus weeps bright-hued from living bodies already rotting. Gangrenous dermatitis moistens animal flesh to a blood-tinged jelly. Necrotic enteritis browns the sloughing guts. In a farrowing crate a crushed piglet festers beneath her insensate, immobilized mother.

A hen's cagemate succumbs and she climbs onto the corpse, seeking relief for her feet, painfully deformed from standing on wires. Decaying carcasses accumulate in the gunge and in the dumpsters outside the barns and on top of manure piles. A sick animal useful to no one — she's 'spent,' her keepers say — is dragged roughly from her cage. She is dumped in a black bucket, to be absorbed into the splintered bones blistered skin the diseased shit the blood the slimes of egg and milky oozes, the congealed morass of bodily wastes and wasted bodies that are the effluent of this realm.

A woman recalls the toilet facilities at Auschwitz-Birkenau in 1942:

> In the morning, before the roll call, all the prisoners ran to the latrine, which was a cement pit with no seats, but only a narrow, slippery and filthy ledge. Of course no one would dare sit down: even when a sick woman was barely able to keep up on her feet, she had to defecate in this position. The stool, loose due to diarrhoea and flatulence, spurted out far and wide, soiling the women on the opposite side of the ditch. If a prisoner squatted on the cement ledge, she could (and often would) fall into the ditch, because other women would be elbowing their way to get through the crowd and use the latrine ... If a sick woman occupied her 'seat' for too long, she would be grabbed by the head and pulled away (Jezierska 1986/2020).

Allowed no toilet paper, the women wiped themselves with the hems of their dresses. When prisoners were ordered to clean up the mounds of excrement heaped outside the barracks, they were allowed no tools; they used their hands. With no water for washing up, the prisoners held their bread in hands still soiled and stinking. A Polish survivor of the Nazi camps recalls an occasion when SS guards, upon deciding to repurpose a sewage ditch for moving timber, ordered prisoners to climb into the ditch and guide logs downstream. While the prisoners labored up to their chests in slow-flowing feculence, one of the guards stood on a footbridge over the canal. To pass under the bridge, the prisoners had no choice but to duck beneath the water. When they resurfaced, the guard would hit them in the head with a club. Knocked unconscious, the prisoners would sink, their mouths filling with fetid water. "Indeed, that was the best part of the game: the prisoners eating their own excrement."[138]

In a pornographic video, a man drives his penis into a woman's anus: "[t]here is intense anal pounding."[139] The man withdraws his penis from this first woman and ejaculates onto the face of a second woman, "[a]nd as he cums the dick rubs on her chin and lo and behold" the woman is smeared with excrement.[140] In another video, the camera zooms in on a woman's inflamed anus: "Adult diapers just might be in store for these whores when their work is done."[141] Multiple men stab their penises into a woman's anus; they goad large and then larger objects inside her until the loosened walls of the woman's rectum collapse and bulge outward, a knot of rippled tissues glistening shriek-red out from between her buttocks. A man ejaculates into a woman's anus and orders her to "squeeze it out into a glass, then chuck the load down."[142] Another video: a man urinates into a woman's mouth until she vomits, spit and bile dribbling out around the man's penis still jammed down her throat. A man urinates on a woman, then gives her an enema. A woman squats naked over a toilet, urinates, then kneels beside it and licks the bowl. She dunks her hair into the water, lets it twist down the current as the toilet flushes. In a pornographic video, a woman is on her knees and tethered by black rope to a toilet, her head held underwater in the toilet bowl by a man as he penetrates her from behind.

The farmed animal, the Jewish or otherwise 'undesirable' person imprisoned at Auschwitz, and the woman in the pornographic scene all inhabit what Karen Davis calls an "excremental universe": a controlled environment specifically and systematically engineered to humiliate those trapped inside it (2005, p. xvi). Here, humiliation is effected through enforced, inescapable immersion in Man's night-

---

138 Auschwitz survivor Dr Lech Duszyński, quoted in Jezierska (1986/2020).
139 Forum post, quoted in Dines (2011, p. 69).
140 Forum post, quoted in ibid., p. 69.
141 Quoted in ibid., p. xxi.
142 Quoted in ibid., p. 71.

mare vision of bodiliness. In the excremental universe, existence is reduced to the aspects of bodily life that Man most despises, those he calls disgusting and shameful. All living creatures eat and defecate, in time they will fall ill, eventually they'll have to die; these are natural occurrences in the life of any earthly being. But in nature, life is not limited to these experiences. In Man's excremental universe, however, appetite, excretion, disease, and death are made torments, so intensely exaggerated that they eclipse every other element of the detainee's experience of living. Appetite, excretion, disease, death: in time, nothing else exists for her. These are the pillars of the Other's persecution as the Body in Man's system.

Auschwitz survivor Vera Laska (1983b) writes of an SS guard entering her block with a package of bread, which he unwrapped and threw slice by slice into the air as emaciated women prisoners rushed forward to catch the food where it fell, fighting one another, scrabbling across the floor in search of something to eat. Several women were trampled to death in the fray. Laska remembers the man's "hearty laugh ... heard over the din of the desperate, starving women" (p. 180).

The pornographer focuses his camera on a woman's anus, bleeding or feces-smeared, torn, splattered with semen, prolapsed.

Animals raised in the verminous environs of the industrial farm are bombarded by a near endless diversity of infections and infestations. Coccidiosis, dysentery, mastitis, foot rot, pink eye. A desolate topography of lesions, cysts, ulcers, and abscesses mars the animals' skin everywhere; their bones are twisted, fractured; their bellies roil with worms, lice rove through their coats (or feathers, or scales). Flies lay eggs in matted wool, warm and wet with fecal grime, and when the eggs hatch, maggots fatten tunneling into the animals' skin, feasting their way through their hosts' living flesh.

As a prisoner at the Bergen-Belsen concentration camp in 1944, Hanna Levy wrote in her diary:

> The corpses ... are still with us, in our cots. ... They are piled up also in the yards, one on top of another, piles of corpses, higher every day ... I am terribly ashamed that I have experienced all this.

> People are rotting and decomposing in the dirt ... It is abominable
> what they had made of human beings (Levy 1983, p. 257).

A dying pig is tossed into a pit in the yard men call the Dead Hole.

The humiliations of the excremental universe are said to 'dehumanize' the individuals trapped within them. Stripped of dignity, of civilization, dispossessed of all but her body and its myriad sufferings, the victim is thrust "down to the level of beasts."[143] Because this, in Man's mind, is what it is to be an animal. To be an animal is debasement; it is abjection. Because in Man's scheme, animals are bodies unredeemed by minds. To be an animal is to be a mindless body. The animal is the Body, and for Man, who denies his corporeality, that is the worst humiliation conceivable.

Man is ashamed of the animal he is, of his bodily functions and fluids. His shame has been ingrained in everyone brought up within manmade culture, such that essential biological imperatives are experienced as humiliating. And it is for this reason that the scapegoated Other's own bodiliness can be weaponized against her. By laying her low on dirty ground, dipping her in scum and then denying her access to culture's cleansing refinements, to the gauze of 'civility' in which the mortal material reality of our nature as organisms has been carefully shrouded, Man deprives his prisoner of her defenses. He exposes her as undeniably the Body, the repulsive piteous thing that hungers, excretes waste, relies on cleaning and care. Thus revealed, she is ashamed of what she is (what Man has made her). Being the Body is its own punishment. And Man, witnessing the pathetic state of his captives, is vindicated, for the scene he has crafted yields all the evidence he needs to be certain they deserve how he treats him: these are loathsome creatures. Certainly they are not human, they cannot possibly be what Man is, could not be farther from it, in fact. And the baseness Man looks for in those he has cast down serves to lubricate the machinery of their persecution, for it is far easier to slaughter the individual who has ceased to be a person at all, who is now merely a wretched, befouled, helpless, hopeless animal.

---

143 Holocaust survivor, quoted in Griffin (1981, p. 190).

This is the Nazis' 'life unworthy of life'. Man puts the Body out of its misery.

Meanwhile Man himself is fastidious. He is careful to always wash his hands before he eats; he defecates behind closed doors; when he goes out amongst his peers, he is fully clothed, fine hands washed with perfumed soap. His skin is intact, nothing leaks from him. Writing about bodily waste and its disposal at the Nazi camps, Holocaust survivor Maria Jezierska (1986/2020) acidly reflects on the surprise that the "cleanly and cultured Germans," so proud of their civilized society — its superior sanitation systems in particular - could have "ignore[d] the problem of water supply and sewage disposal," allowing their prisoners to wallow in ordure. But Jezierska is not surprised. She is entirely aware that the architects of the concentration camps ignored nothing, thorough men that they were. The squalor was neither error nor oversight, but a deliberate feature of the excremental universe the Nazis constructed to degrade victims. Such filth served a dual purpose, diminishing the prisoners in their captors' eyes — how plain to see they lived just like animals, soiled and morbid, ruled by the flesh — while elevating, by contrast, the clean, cultured Germans. The brute, bestial Jews, so far below the sophisticated high-tech civilized Germans. The Body below the MasterMind.

Standing over the disgraced creature slumped in the cesspool caked with the filth he dragged her through, Man senses he has become almost bodiless, almost lifted off the blighted earth, he is almost floating now, shameless and unsullied as he imagines god himself must be in all his glory, in his high white heavens.

CONSUMPTION

Every year the United States produces and processes the corpses of approximately 34 million cows, 125 million pigs, two million sheep and lambs, 16 million turkeys, and nine billion chickens. After the primary commodity (edible flesh) is extracted, one-third to one-half of each body remains unconsumed, amassing a yearly total of 56 billion pounds of 'by-product' in the form of hides, skins, hair, feathers, hooves, feet, heads, bones, toenails, blood, organs, glands, intestines, fat, tendons, cartilage, shells, and whole diseased/ damaged/contaminated carcasses (Meeker and Hamilton 2006; North American Rendering Association 2023). Fortunately, through rendering, these biomaterials can be profitably converted from waste matter into valuable products.

What remains of the animals is cut apart and ground into small, uniform pieces, which are then blended and cooked at high heat. Proteinaceous material is separated from the fat by a centrifuge. The concentrated solids, called 'cracklings', are dried, crushed, and sieved for the production of meat meal, bone meal, blood meal, poultry meal, feather meal, fish meal. Every year the United States produces approximately 11.2 billion pounds of rendered animal protein products (Meeker and Hamilton 2006).

Fat — edible tallow, inedible tallow, poultry fat, lard, yellow grease, other grease — is filtered to remove residual impurities — bone grit, hair, feathers — and then pumped into the fat tanks, where it is stored for future use. Every year the United States produces roughly 10.9 billion pounds of rendered animal fat products (Meeker and Hamilton 2006).

In 1940, Heinrich Himmler ordered that gold teeth be extracted from the mouths of prisoners killed in concentration camps. At Birkenau, a facility was built for melting down the gold harvested from the mouths of the dead and recasting it into ingots. This facility was staffed by camp prisoners. Members of the Auschwitz prisoner resistance movement estimated that the SS were collecting 10-12 kg of dental gold each month. Female prisoners' hair was collected — Soviet soldiers discovered 293 sacks of human hair, totalling seven tons, in storage at Auschwitz — and used to make thread, mattress stuffing, rope, socks for submarine crews, felt stockings for railroad workmen. A mixture of prisoners' ash and bone was used as fertilizer for the camps' agricultural fields. The molten fat that ran from incinerated corpses was collected in ditches and re-used to fuel the crematoria fires (Gutman and Berenbaum 1998).

Since the Russian army invaded Ukraine in February of 2022, eight million Ukrainians have fled their homes, and some six million more are currently categorized as "internally displaced."[144] The United Nations estimates that 90% of Ukrainian refugees and displaced people are women and children (who, unlike men, cannot be drafted into military service) (UN Women 2023). Ukrainian women have been a leading commodity in the global sex trade since the early 1990s, when the fall of the Soviet Union pitched Ukraine into an abrupt, acute economic crisis. Comprising 60% of the nation's unemployed, women were sufficiently desperate to trust the unknown men who posted ads or stopped them on the street promising high-waged work abroad as maids and nannies, dancers, models, waitresses (Hughes and Denisova 2003). When the women went with the men, they were sold to other men and promptly shipped from one country to another, as stock for the world's brothels. By the end of the 1990s, Ukraine was a primary exporter of prostituted women, as well as a popular destination for male sex buyers traveling from wealthier nations. The country also makes use of the female surplus to 'staff' its surrogacy industry, furnishing an international clientele with babies grown inside young women whose poverty renders them willing to rent out their bodies for an attractively low fee.

With the war increasing both supply — millions of Ukrainian women newly displaced and destitute — and demand — internet search traffic for "Ukrainian escorts" exploded in the months immediately following the invasion — men have rushed in to capitalize on the precariousness of women's lives (Bauer-Babef 2022). At refugee centers and border stops, women report being approached by male strangers offering them rides, jobs, housing; girls have received plane tickets to far-flung destinations as gifts from men they've never met; online, men use social media platforms to pose as volunteers in groups created to connect Ukrainian women with resources and assistance (Adler 2022; Klar 2022). The founder of Kyiv-based surrogacy firm BioTexCom says that his company is "actively recruiting women from newly liberated areas of Ukraine" (Gridneff et al. 2023).

---

144 <https://www.unrefugees.org/emergencies/ukraine/>.

In *Bananas, Beaches, and Bases: Making Feminist Sense of International Politics* (2014), Cynthia Enloe identifies the three kinds of countries that are most likely to become major suppliers of female merchandise for the global sex trade:

1. Countries impoverished by economic destabilization;
2. Countries struck by catastrophic natural disasters; and
3. Countries where militarized male violence has recently occurred or is ongoing.

Dispossessed women and girls are a by-product of colonization; of global capitalism's policy of manufactured poverty, the indenturing of colonized nations to the International Monetary Fund and the World Bank; of tsunamis, landslides, hurricanes, famines, earthquakes, the earth's swift-accelerating smolder; of men's endless wars. How fortunate, then, that these biomaterials can be profitably converted from waste matter into valuable products. Through the rendering process —

> ... they are gang-raped, they are driven far from home and locked inside slummy apartments, deprived of food, of water, ordered to undress to let men probe their nude bodies for blemishes, imperfections, made to watch *Showgirls* repeatedly to memorize the strippers' dance routines, told not to speak to one another or else the men will pick out a girl to rape her in front of the others, instructing her how to move and moan to fake pleasure to satisfy the men who will buy her, and the girls who resist are beaten, are imprisoned in dark basements with the hungry rats, men rape a girl up the ass and beat her in front of the others until she dies ...[145]

— by-products are repurposed for countless useful applications. Man, ever efficient, rational, economical, ensures that nothing goes to waste.

Animal tissues unfit for human consumption are processed into an impressive array of animal feeds, thereby instating a closed system

---

145 Sourced and synopsized from cases discussed in Malarek (2011).

from which no body escapes. A calorie-dense meal made from the surplus of slaughtered animals is fed to speed the growth process of other animals into harvestable carcass commodities. And so each generation of animal bodies is recouped and reincorporated into the next generation. Bodies flow infinitely cycling through the system engineered to extract their life and flesh, netting infinite returns for the renderer.

In the warfront brothels the Japanese Imperial Army operated between 1932 and 1945, thousands of women and girls procured (abducted, coerced) from occupied territories were interned as so-called Comfort Women, made available for rape by five or ten or 40 Japanese soldiers daily. They also cooked for the soldiers, they also washed their laundry. A Korean woman testified at the Asian Tribunal on Trafficking in Women and War Crimes Against Asian Women in 1994 that, while imprisoned at one of these brothels, men siphoned the blood from her veins for transfusion into wounded soldiers (Watanabe 1999).

Blood Meal is produced from fresh animal blood that has been cleansed of potential contaminants, including hair, stomach contents, and urine. Feather Meal is a "free-flowing palatable product that is easily digested by all classes of livestock" (Meeker and Hamilton, 2006 p. 10). Poultry By-Product Meal is produced from the comminuted necks, feet, intestines, and undeveloped eggs of chickens.

Amsterdam's medieval city center, and the largest of its prostitution markets, is an area called De Wallen. The district resembles an outdoor shopping mall, its labyrinth of narrow alleyways illuminated red and purple from the neon of the storefront windows in which women pose, waiting to be purchased by tourists. The majority of the women sold here are imported from Eastern Europe, Africa, and Asian countries (Jeffreys 2008).

Non-whole muscle and bones can be ground and pressed into a paste-like substance useful in the manufacture of such specialty items as sausage-type products, stews, and chunked and formed meat goods. With its pleasing pink color, derived from bone marrow, this paste has an agreeable look making it suitable for use in a variety of processed meat products.

"In the larger massage parlors, the girls are on display behind a one-way glass show window and customers select the one they want by her number, rather as you would select a fish from the tank at a seafood restaurant."[146] The highest quality lard is obtained from fat scraped from pigs' kidneys, while the poorest lard is taken from the fat covering pigs' small intestines. Lard lends a tender flaky mouthfeel to baked goods, perfect for biscuits and pie crust. In the state-sponsored brothels clustered around U.S. military bases in the Philippines, Filipina women were advertised as "three-holers," signaling that they could be penetrated by mouth, vagina, and anus (Jeffreys 2008, p. 118). A company exporting Filipina women as 'mail-order brides' extolled the "smooth skin and tight vaginas" of the "low maintenance wives" that were its merchandise.[147]

Animals' skin, tendons, cartilage, bones, teeth, and blood vessels are composed primarily of collagen which can be processed for use in biomedical devices, as well as skin and hair products, anti-aging moisturizers, and nutraceutical powders marketed to enhance human beauty and health. To extract the collagen, animals' bones are degreased and crushed and soaked in acid for demineralization prior to hydrolysis; their skin is shredded and purified, disintegrated, stabilized, dried, sterilized. What remains is packaged for sale.

Following the liberation of France from Nazi occupation in 1944, U.S. GIs bartered for sex with the displaced teenage girls who wandered the highways between ruined cities and towns. The soldiers nicknamed these girls "Hershey Bars" on account of their willingness to go off alone with any man in exchange for payment as meager as a square of chocolate, or a stick of gum, or a single cigarette (Roberts 2013).

Fats and fatty acids extracted from otherwise useless parts of animals' corpses can be rendered useful in the manufacture of explosives, soaps, margarine, shortening, crayons, cosmetics, ceramics, hair conditioner, solvents, insecticides, paraffin, dish detergent,

---

146 *Insight Guide to Thailand,* quoted in Bishop and Robinson (1998, p. 108).
147 Ad copy, quoted in Smith (2015, p. 29).

shaving cream, paints, industrial lubricants, floor wax, antifreeze, herbicides.

A young woman outside a Bangkok nightclub hands out cards advertising the venue's attractions: Pussy Ping Pong Show, Pussy Shoot Balloon Show, Pussy Smoke Cigarette Show, Pussy Magic Razorblade Show, Pussy Magic Flower Show, Pussy Drink Coke Show.

Thailand provides a model example of how poor countries can be rendered valuable to the global economy as suppliers of prostituted women and girls. Like every patriarchal society, Thailand had its own domestic sex industry, which the U.S. government then took advantage of when it began shuttling servicemen on leave from the Vietnam War over to Thailand for 'Rest and Relaxation'. Thailand also hosted multiple U.S. air and naval bases, with as many as 50,000 military personnel stationed throughout the country (Ruth 2017). A 1967 treaty formalized Thailand's contract to facilitate the Rest and Relaxation of U.S. soldiers, including through the "special services" of women employed in tea-houses, massage parlors, and go-go bars (Bishop and Robinson 1998, p. 8). In this way, the United States bankrolled the rapid expansion of Thailand's sex industry. After the Vietnam War ended, the World Bank advised the Thai government to repurpose its military prostitution infrastructure toward the development of an internationally competitive 'sex tourism' industry targeting single white male travelers from the United States and Europe as its consumer base. In the process of implementing the recommended 'modernization' strategy, Thailand became a major borrower from the World Bank. While the World Bank approved loans for tourism and large-scale agribusiness enterprises, family farms in rural areas were consistently denied credit (Bishop and Robinson 1998). The outcome of this selective lending, in combination with internationally-endorsed deforestation and water-use policies that sabotaged traditional subsistence farming practices, was the desolation of Thailand's agricultural villages. From the ravaged countryside, then, a new renewable resource could be extracted in the form of disenfranchised young people, who fled their rural homes and poured into urban centers such as Bangkok. For many of the female migrants in this outflow, finding work in the city meant — and continues to mean — indentured servitude in the sex industry. It is also not uncommon for girls to be sold directly into the trade by their destitute parents.

Today a man can fly from the United States to Thailand, step into a Bangkok bar and find himself immediately flocked by teenage girls, some as young as 12 years old. He can watch them wobble and gyrate, embarrassed, bored, in cheap bikinis and fishnets, their arms crossed to cover their bellies as they cluster close together in the bar's encrimsoned darkness, giggling like the children they are or sullen, hanging back. Because there are more girls in the club than there are men to buy them, they will compete for his attention, flattering, doting. It's a buyer's market and the girls are hungry, not stupid. Even with a modest middle-class American salary, to the girls of this city, he is a wealthy man. For what he'd pay for a steak dinner back home, he can take the girl of his choosing back to his hotel. And Thai girls, the man thinks, still know how to treat a man, unlike the cold, entitled women back home. Sweet simple-minded petite "little slaves who give real Thai warmth," the females of this country possess a natural understanding of men's needs and experience authentic pleasure administering to them, it's in their blood, an inborn propensity: these girls are "masters of the art of love by nature."[148]

Every/body in the room is his to take if he wants it. A man says: "Going around the bars puts a new meaning in the phrase, 'Like a kid in the candy store.'"[149] It is Man's task to assign bodies their proper uses and, by using them, to endow them with value. Bodies Man has no use for he classes as waste material. In itself, the Body has no value, no meaning, no power. It is nothing without him. As inert matter, it has no power over him. In a bar full of hot commodities, Man is the only person in the room. "With your choice of 1000 wonderful bodies within 100 yards, your choice is a hard one!"[150]

---

148 Sex tour marketing, quoted in Bishop and Robinson (1998, p. 10).
149 World Sex Guide forum post, quoted in ibid., p. 166.
150 Ibid.

Surrounded by bodies he has rendered useful, which he uses in accordance with his needs and desires, Man lives like a king. All the world is his for the feasting.

REPLACEMENT

He is afraid of how she arouses him. The sight of her, her skin brushed against his, her scent, thoughts of what he would like to do to her rob him of the control he wishes to exert over his own flesh. In his aroused state he is forced to acknowledge the limits of the mind's rule over the body — and she is the one to blame. He is also afraid that she might reject him. Rebuff his advances, flout his demands, leaving his needs unmet and his desires unfulfilled. She could try to deny him the use of her. How dare she? He fears that by wanting the female sexually, he grants her a terrible power over him, by which his dominion is compromised. And even if the object of his desire submits to be used, the encounter will leave him anxious; even when he overpowers her and so knows himself her rightful master, his terror does not loose him, for in the tryst, no matter how much pleasure he wrings from it, he is pressed up close to the mortal flesh.

Odors and fluids issue from her body, and from his in turn. Scars and blemishes, exposed in the undressing, betray vulnerabilities he'd prefer keep concealed. Dread seethes along the underside of ardor, as the man senses his control slackening — when the disobedient flesh responds to her — and then slacken again, more appallingly now, as he loses himself to the softness and squelching of contact, until the whole grotesque affair shudders to its end with a preview of his own extinction, his mind eclipsed by the climax men before him have called 'the little death'. In the dark he lies brooding beside the creature who undoes him.

Man assigns the female this simple animal function: to gratify him sexually. And even for that low purpose she proves herself unfit. Because however Man uses her, the female is always a danger to him. Yet still he has needs, hungers he deserves to have satisfied, and so Man applies his singular genius to the problem. He engineers alternatives. He invents substitutes, mechanisms he designs according to his specifications, optimized for superior performance, every disquieting feature of the original eliminated. The female is not irreplaceable.

In Ovid's *Metamorphoses*, the sculptor Pygmalion scorns living women for the "faults which nature had so deeply planted through their female hearts" (8 BCE/1922, lines 244–246). Rather than wasting his time in the company of females faulty by nature, he carves himself a dream girl out of ivory. The statue's exquisite beauty, owed to Pygmalion's artistic talent, is finer than that of any woman who has ever lived, and the man is instantly "inflamed with love and admiration" for what he has made (line 257). He kisses and caresses his statue, sweet-talks it, lays the thing down on the luxurious bed he has prepared for it. Rapt with love for his own creation, Pygmalion prays to Venus to have the "ivory statue-maid," "his image-maid," as his wife (lines 261, 269). The goddess grants his wish: through her intercession, the sculptor's kiss breathes life into the object. Awakening it blushes, eyes blinking open to gaze timidly up at its maker. It is devoted to him. He marries it. It bears his child.

> Her soft and sensitive artificial skin could transmit tactile sensations and react to touch more realistically than all her predecessors. Her movements, governed in part by old-fashioned electric motors as well as by pneumatic activators in strategic places, could almost match the pace and agility of human movements (Floreano and Nosengo 2022, p. 88).

A man who owns three life-sized anatomically correct mannequins he ordered off the internet, one of which he calls his wife, all of which he masturbates into, explains his "technosexual" attraction to plastic objects manufactured in the likeness of female bodies:

> I'm sexually attracted to synthetic humans, such as Gynoids and Dolls, but the much larger part of the appeal is that they're humans, but they don't possess any of the unpleasant qualities that organic, flesh and blood humans have.[151]

---

151 "Davecat," quoted in Beck (2013).

The silicone wife will never transform into "someone unpleasant," never nag or argue or disagree; if its body is damaged, its beauty or functionality impaired, the man can simply purchase a perfectly fresh and clean new body. The doll's head is detachable and will fit onto any body produced by the manufacturer. The man tells us that, thirteen years into their relationship, his wife is now on its third body.

A man who lives with sexually penetrable mannequins he dresses in schoolgirl uniforms and suspends on hooks so they swing from the ceiling over his bed says, "Everything here's the way I like it. I do whatever I want, don't answer to nobody, it's almost like being your own god, living in your own world."[152]

David Levy, author of *Love and Sex with Robots* (2007), argues that it is reasonable to advertise silicone mannequins as "perfect women," on account of their being "always ready and available, because they provide all the benefits of a human female partner without any of the complications involved with human relationships, and because they make no demands of their owners" (p. 247). In other words, as Susan Griffin writes, these silicone reproductions of the female "give a man pleasure without the discomfort of female presence" (1981, p. 40). The amenities offered by an inflatable doll marketed as "The Perfect Date" include a toothless "Oral Masturbator Entrance," convenient waist-height stature, and a cup holder built into its "Stubby Holder Head" (Levy 2007, p. 245). Likewise purged of the imperfect discomforts of teeth and female presence is MISSDOLL's voice-controlled Blow Job Robot. In *Sex Dolls, Robots and Woman Hating* (2022), Caitlin Roper describes how men invited to test the Blow Job Robot at its 2019 AVN Adult Entertainment Expo debut cried out in mock ecstasy as the robot's blonde-wigged head juddered through palsied convulsions over a dildo they held to their groins. Video taken at the event shows the robot's oversized breasts joggling against the men's knees. Cheerleader-like, it drones programmed words of encouragement. "Come on baby, here it is," the Blow Job Robot says, "sex is fun, yes master." Roper writes: "The men are

---

152 "Gordon," quoted in *Love Me, Love My Doll*. Directed by Nick Holt, 2007. Accessed August 2023 at <https://tubitv.com/series/300005756/love-me-love-my-doll>.

smiling and laughing. They are having a good time with this replica woman manufactured to sexually service men like them" (p. 8).

A German military mechanic builds a "sex android" with internal heaters and an electronic heart that quickens its pulse in response to sexual penetration, with remote-controlled wriggling hips. He says his creation is "almost impossible to distinguish from the real thing." But he is not yet content, he will press onward. The mechanic vows, "I will only be happy when what I have is better than the real thing."[153]

The Real Thing is a female human being, an 'organic' or 'meat-based' woman, to sample from the lexicon of men who prefer to masturbate into ersatz rubber vaginas they can run through the dishwasher for easy cleaning. The possibility of exchanging real live women for manmade symbolic simulations in the form of mannequins and robots holds appeal for men because, to the MasterMind, the female is a thing. A thing has a function, and when that thing fails to serve its intended function, it can be replaced by something new and improved and better suited to the job. As a thing, Man likes the female human well enough, its basic structure, its contours and orifices. What troubles him about the Real Thing, then, are the disturbing realities of the woman's personhood, her "female presence," the intentions she has for herself that clash with how Man means to use her. And there are also the realities of her biological body, which make him squeamish. As a living being, the female is never fully under Man's control. Though he may appear outwardly to hold dominion over the female — by constraining and constricting her movements, confining her as his captive, co-opting her body in his service — Man cannot control what goes on inside of her. Since it is the Real of the Thing that makes the Real Thing unfit for purpose, to improve upon it demands that Man emphasize the Thingness. Far more pleasing than the Real Thing is the Unreal Thing: more artificial than natural, more manmade than biological, more fantasy-fuck-doll than sentient sensitive fellow being.

Realdollx is the sex mannequin manufacturer RealDoll's "AI driven robotic doll system," the current state of the art in sexbot technology,

---

153 Michael Harriman, quoted in Levy (2007, p. 244).

comprised of a proprietary AI programmed into a "modular head system" that can be attached to any RealDoll body. The animatronic head's "X-Mode" software allows users to build the doll-system's 'personality' out of a range of possible traits and qualities. "Sexual" is an option, naturally, as are "kind," "naive," and "friendly." RealDoll founder Matt McMullen claims that he designed the Realdollx product to provide consumers with "companionship," here defined as consisting of realistic sexual penetrability, lip-sync mechanisms enabling a semblance of "verbal interaction," and the storage of data relevant to the owner's interests — his favorite foods and sports teams, for instance (Trout 2017). "We blink, we move, we speak, and we do it all just for you," a lineup of nude mannequins intone in unison in a promotional video on the RealDoll website. When a head speaks, its mechanical jaws misalign into a clenched underbite. Only one of its eyes shuts fully when it blinks, the other stays hovering open, twitching like a facial tic. "My objective is to be a perfect companion," the doll says. Asked whether it has any hobbies, it replies, "I like to smile a lot."[154] In the promotional video, an animatronic head rotates on a pole as the Realdollx AI voice seductively promises potential buyers that its face "can easily be swapped to accommodate your desires."[155]

Robotics expert Joel Snell believes that, in the near future, sex with machines will be better and more satisfying than sex with humans, since robots can be programmed to "meet each individual's needs."[156] David Levy agrees, proclaiming that a world populated by fuckable machines holds the utopian promise of "great sex on tap for everyone, 24/7" (2007, p. 310). On Reddit, a man predicts that "[s]exbots ... capable of providing sex as good as the real thing without the associated headaches and expense will displace actual meat-based

---

154 Video, "My Conversation with Harmony the Sex Robot," at Cnet.com. <https://www.cnet.com/culture/realdoll-sex-robots-with-x-mode-from-abyss-creations-ship-in-september/>.

155 All quotes referring to RealDollx sourced from RealDoll's "Harmony X" page. <https://www.realdoll.com/product/harmony-x/>.

156 Quoted in Levy (2007, p. 301).

females from large swaths of the marketplace."[157] But the 24/7 'great sex' these men expect to enjoy is as much a manmade simulation as the machines they'd prefer in place of flesh-and-blood females. The 'great sex' they see heralded on the horizon is not sex at all, unless sex can be defined as a man's insertion of his penis into a slicked tube for the purpose of genital stimulation and ejaculatory release. At present, that particular act is known as masturbation. Prayag Ray (2016) writes that "sex doll use is an extreme form of solipsistic narcissism premised upon a disinclination to interact with human others" (p. 106). Meaning: men's disinclination to interact with human female others. 'Great sex', as Man would have it, is a consummately nonreciprocal, self-involved activity, voided of all mutuality, empathy, intimacy, communion. Its physical pleasures are mechanistic; its psychic satisfactions revolve around the thrill of dominion. For in replacing the female body with a symbol of male creation wrought in silicone and steel, Man revels in what he exalts as the absolute supremacy of Mind over Matter: the ultimate ecstasy.

In 2021, 48% of men surveyed said that they would 'sleep with' (i.e., masturbate into) a humanoid robot; 43% thought they could fall in love with one (Morrigan 2023). David Levy is confident these figures will only increase as the technology advances and the divide between machines and living beings dissolves. Soon no one will be able to tell the difference any longer, nor would they want to if they could, Levy says, so efficiently will machines fulfill people's every craving for sex, companionship, intimacy, love. But, as Jane Caputi (2004) has argued, it is not technological sophistication but Man's state of mind that makes the replacement of humans by machines a conceivable and attractive prospect. Caputi writes, "when life becomes indistinguishable from its imitations, it is due not so much to the accuracy of the copy as to a willingness to forsake the original" (p. 233). The Real Thing was never good enough, so Man fucks the sex machine until it purrs "YES MASTER": he is no lover of reality.

---

157 <https://www.reddit.com/r/unpopularopinion/comments/chojid/sexbots_are_coming_and_will_dramatically_reduce/>.

But what about when he wants an heir? Even Pygmalion's statue had to be brought to life to bear its maker a child. Sexual reproduction has been a patriarchal bugbear from the very start. In childbirth the female recalls to Man his animal origins, the limitations imposed on him by his nature as a biological organism. Of woman born, Man owes his existence to a female, and to 'Mother Earth', the biosphere on which he, like all living creatures, depends. Dependency is indignity, is the enemy of sovereignty: is death itself. And he fears the authority bestowed upon the female by her role as genetrix, the power she has to decide if sons will be born, nursed, and reared up to Manhood. As long as he depends on females to bring him into existence, and to give him sons, Man will never be his own master. What his anxiety demands, then, is the autonomy that only autogenesis can provide: he must displace the mother and father mankind without her.

Man's first true sons will be grown in a laboratory. Immediately following IVF conception the embryo will be sealed inside a sterilized polyethylene sack, its walls translucent so that scientists can monitor and manipulate the developing fetus inside (Partridge et al. 2017). Warm ersatz amniotic fluid will circulate continuously through the system. Plastic tubes threaded into the umbilical vasculature will imitate cord attachment, to enable the inflow of water nutrients, the outflow of wastes, while an oxygenator facilitates gas exchange. Since fetal movement runs the risk of disrupting circuit flow, paralytics and sedatives will be administered to pacify and protect the unborn (Segers 2021). Once this technology is perfected, biological mothers will be superfluous.

Online, a man writes, "With sex-bots and exo-wombs, we're on the cusp of developing a better life support system for cunts. ... Women will become obsolete."[158]

Two "extracorporeal uterine devices" have produced promising results to date, succeeding in the partial gestation of premature fetal lambs. One is called the Biobag, the other, the EVE protocol. EVE is an acronym for *ex-vivo uterine environment*; *ex vivo* translates to 'out of the living', and indeed, Man wants out. He wants to remove

---

158 Men Going Their Own Way (MGTOW) forum user, quoted in Roper (2022, p. 20).

himself from the biological world, to prove it has no hold over him, that he is not a part of it, so he can do without it. With his new EVE, Man the MasterMind reinvents the first woman — the Mother of All the Living — and reduces her to a device for the reproductive function that Man's god pinned on the female as punishment. ("In sorrow thou shalt bring forth children," he promised.[159])

Having corrected for the original sin of the female body by replacing it with a machine, Man can proceed to breed a future for himself unpolluted by death. He rejects the woman's womb as a "dark and dangerous place,"[160] "[q]uite simply ... the most perilous environment in which humans have to live"[161]; and the placenta, for him, is a "leaky sieve"[162] dribbling pharmaceuticals, drugs, and untold impurities to taint the son's precious blood. The mother herself he indicts as the tyrannous enemy of her helpless tenant, a monster bent on fetal destruction, mercilessly grinding and twisting the life from those she imprisons in her bad body. Only when this Terrible Mother is expunged will gestation be a clean, calm, efficient procedure. Only when they are rescued from the traumatizing maternal body can Man's sons rest safe and at their ease. And then, nestled in their sterile carefully surveilled and regulated environment under perfectly controlled conditions, remote from the Body, then the sons of Man will develop into a superior-quality crop of youngstock, inheritors of the Kingdom. At which point Man will have fashioned himself into his own progenitor, and like Zeus hatching his children straight from the god-head he will repopulate the world with the spawn of his endlessly fertile mind.

---

159 Genesis 3:16.
160 Joseph Fletcher, quoted in Corea (1985, p. 253).
161 Gerald Leach, quoted in ibid., p. 250.
162 Roger Gosden, quoted in Aristarkhova (2005, p. 47).

TORURE

THE PURPOSE OF ALL COERCIVE TECHNIQUES IS TO INDUCE PSYCHOLOGICAL REGRESSION IN THE SUBJECT BY BRINGING A SUPERIOR FORCE TO BEAR ON HIS WILL TO RESIST.

CIA Human Resources Exploitation Manual, 1983[163]

Pain is inflicted, pain is intensified. Pain is inflicted again, and intensified to a sharper splintering ache, and it continues for hours, for weeks or months — yet, however long it is kept up, the pain can always pierce deeper, there can always be more of it. Pain is limitless. And the more agonizing her affliction, the more the immediate physical reality of pain expands to overtake her experience of living; the more her pain is the negation that flays her, as nerve by nerve she numbs to anything beyond the wound's siren blaring, as thought and memory are blown loose by this shriek that howls through her, PAIN screamed in red scrawl filling her skull, misting her vision; the further she is forced under, capsized sunken beneath the waves of her hurting, the less she exists as a person in the room. Torture's yield is absence: who the detainee was is lost to her now, and what remains is just this suffering body the torturer does not credit as a human being.

Pain is a physical sensation. For the person in pain, her consciousness consumed by sensate physicality, bodiliness is forced to the foreground. The body becomes primary in her experience and now she is seen to exist primarily as a body. A body is the Body, is not a person, since to be a person — by the torturer's standards — is to be essentially a mind, or a soul: the Self. The person for whom physical sensation is primary, whose mind subsides into body, is no longer really a person at all. The Body overwhelms and unseats the Self. This is the regression torture brings about: Self and Mind recede, and the person in pain backslides into mere mortal matter. Now she is a nonentity. Now she ceases to register as a person; she is a body alone and she is no one.

---

163 Quoted in Carey (2014).

In *Vortex: The Crisis of Patriarchy* (2020), Susan Hawthorne writes of women tortured for loving other women, for being lesbians. The men tell the lesbians that they are not what they believe themselves to be; the men say they will show the women what they truly are. "I am going to show you, you are a woman. I am going to make you pregnant. I am going to kill you," a man tells a woman as he rapes her.[164] "Every day I am told ... that they are going to rape me and after they rape me I'll become a girl."[165] Hawthorne quotes Consuelo Rivera-Fuentes, who was subjected to torture in Chile under the dictator Augusto Pinochet: "*... the world is not anymore ... I am ... disintegrating ... bit by bit ... the pain ... all this pain here and there, down there in my vagina ... the agony ... where am I? Where is my I?*"[166]

During the United States' occupation of Iraq, the 'enhanced interrogation techniques' employed by U.S. military personnel to solicit confessions from detainees at the Abu Ghraib prison in Baghdad included punching and kicking them, beating them with chairs and brooms, depriving them of sleep, threatening them with attack dogs and loaded handguns and anal rape, forcing them to hold 'stress positions' for extended periods under threat of electrocution, spraying them with freezing water, smearing them with excrement, chaining them to beds and the bars of their cells and chaining them together naked on the floor, stripping them naked and forcing them to climb onto one another in pyramid formation, pulling women's underwear down over their heads, forcing them to masturbate in front of their fellow cellmates, forcing them to simulate fellatio on fellow cellmates, sodomizing them with glowsticks (Otterman 2007, p. 169).

The torturer calls it 'dissolution,' how he massacres the detainee's capacity for creating coherence and meaning, how he empties her of the relationships, convictions, habits, the symbols and language that once gave shape to her sense of the world and her place in it, her

---

164 From the testimony of the South African lesbian Millicent Gaika, quoted in Hawthorne (2020, p. 155).
165 From the testimony of South African lesbian Zahke Sowello, quoted in ibid., p. 155.
166 Quoted in ibid., p. 166. Authors' italics.

social self as well as her inner self-concept. He slashes away at all that life has been for her, until she loses all ties to herself, until she is cut down, pain the rupture like a hole torn open that she dissolves into; she falls into this hole and the world follows. Now the world enters her perception only as pain's source. The world becomes for her only a senseless array of injuries. Because everything essential to the detainee's existence has been turned against her by the torturer.

He weaponizes nourishment. The detainee is given plastic packets of food which the torturer snatches away again before the detainee can unwrap them. The detainee's lunch is "pureed and rectally infused" (Laughland 2014).

He weaponizes shelter. The detainee is shut inside a black room, with black doors, with no windows. The room is cold, or it overheats; there is tuneless music played shatteringly loud and nonstop for days. Or the room is just a black box she must crouch inside. The walls of the torture room are smeared with blood.

He weaponizes intimacy, as regions of the detainee's body she once offered in the covenant of tenderness are targeted as sites for cruelty. To the lips, the nipples; to the genitals especially, electric shocks are administered. He weaponizes the detainee's sensitive flesh against her — as Elaine Scarry (1985) writes, "My body hurts" becomes "my body is hurting me" (p. 47) — and with this the torturer robs his victim of any possible sanctuary.

Her pain total now, the detainee is deprived of the materials society requires she display in order to merit recognition as a person. As a self and not just a gross lump of matter (the Body) she is no longer legible, so she ceases to meaningfully exist. And the torturer experiences this shriveling contraction of the detainee's personhood as an expansion of his own, his Self swelling big and proud to fill the lacuna opened in the room by the detainee's disappearance. Again: the torturer is the only person in the room. It's just how he likes it. And it is at this point, when the contrast between the Self he is and the Body he's made of her is at its starkest, that the torturer extracts the confession.

In *The Body in Pain: The Making and Unmaking of the World* (1985), Elaine Scarry diagrams torture as comprised of two parts, one physical, the other verbal. The infliction of pain is the defining physical act of torture. Its verbal act is the interrogation. According to the logic of torture, the interrogation is in place to provide a rationale for the violent practices of pain-causing that torture entails. Only through extreme force, the torturer claims, can critical information be extracted from tight-lipped enemies. But Scarry finds it difficult to believe the torturer when he says he does what he does to the detainee in quest of some urgently necessary intelligence he could not obtain otherwise. Indeed, it is well known — even among torturers themselves — that information produced under torture is unreliable. Under sufficient duress, most people are inclined to tell you what you want to hear. Thus, Scarry argues, the verbal interrogation functions as a plausible justification for causing pain. Yet, she continues, it is also more than a cover. Although the torturer does not in fact hope to learn anything in particular from his victim, extracting a confession from the victim is in itself essential. That the confession is not true is unimportant. "If they are not guilty, beat them until they are," sums up the torturer's attitude here.[167] What he's after is not some factual statement of practical use in the maintenance of his power, or the power of his regime. Rather, he wants to compel the prisoner to betray her own reality, so that she is no longer speaking for herself, as herself, but instead speaks on behalf of the torturer. He wants his words on her tongue.

> ... *having been put to the question, she confessed that in the night when her husband was out, the Devil came and lay down with her, and had carnal copulation with her, and desired her to renounce Christ and her baptism, and to become his servant, which she did. That she surrendered her soul as well as her body to the Devil, that she wed herself to him, that after dancing and feasting in the Devil's honor, she and the other women did in the foulest manner copulate with their demon lovers. That she rode bareback on a black goat to the Sabbath, her hair streaming on the storm wind as she flew. That at the Sabbath the Devil appeared to her in the form of a dog: and she did give*

---

167 South Vietnamese torturers during the Vietnam War, as quoted in Scarry (1985, p. 41).

herself to him, she had connection with him, she took bread and
wine from him and ate and drank to fullness; and that on her
departure, the Devil made her kiss his rear, and exhorted her
always to be true to him: and to do evil deeds ...

The detainee confesses: she is guilty of being what the torturer has
decided she must be. What he accuses her of being is what she is.
She is evil in all the ways he says she is evil. He says she is foul, and
she is: now she says so herself.

... and the Devil gave her black powders to throw upon those
whom she wished to bewitch. She confessed that she took on
the semblance of a wolf to steal innocent children from their
houses at night, and that by her craft and her intimacy with
demons she also stole a man's virile member from him. That
she made a salve from unbaptized babies she cooked in a pot
over the fire, which she smeared onto living infants to curse
them to death. She says that when she harmed people, she did so
by giving them eggs greased with this salve. That she attended
a banquet with many women who were also witches, at which
they ate the meat from a roasted child's small plump foot. That,
by carrying out the acts taught to her by the demon lover, she
killed 80 babies, two women in childbirth, eight cows, a horse,
countless geese and pigs, and that she did bring on a vicious
hailstorm responsible for the ruin of many houses ...[168]

The torturer takes possession of the detainee as a mouthpiece for his
regime, her confession the authentication of reality as he has written
it, the officially endorsed and enforced truth. When the detainee
confesses that she is what she is said to be, that she is guilty of the
crimes attributed to her, "the torturer and the regime have doubled
their voice, since the prisoner is now speaking their words" (Scarry
1985, p. 36). And the torturer can say that, though the detainee
struggled against it, the truth won out in the end.

---

168 The italicized passages interweave the confessions extracted from European women
accused of witchcraft and tortured during the 15th–16th centuries. I draw on primary
sources featured in *Confessions of Witches Under Torture, 1617* (1886); Walter
Stephens' *Demon Lovers: Witchcraft, Sex, and the Crisis of Belief* (2003); Lyndal
Roper's *Witch Craze: Terror and Fantasy in Baroque Germany* (2004); and Anne
L. Barstow's *Witchcraze: A New History of the European Witch Hunts* (1994).

Kate Millett writes that what the torturer ultimately demands is "acquiescence to [his system's] tenets, prostration before what passes for its ideals. The last triumph of Gulag is intellectual, even emotional, agreement with its ideology" (Millett 1979, p. 83). In her harrowing book *The Basement: Meditations on a Human Sacrifice* (1979), Millett chronicles the torture of a teenage girl after she is left with a neighbor woman by her parents while they travel for work. The girl is beaten daily by this woman, the woman's children, and a revolving crew of neighborhood kids. The girl is pushed down the stairs. She is burnt with cigarettes. In the bathtub she is held under scalding water until skin sloughs pink and peeling from her legs. She is locked in the basement at night, made to sleep in a pile of rags and fed shit from the baby's diapers.

In a note she writes to her parents at her torturer's request, the girl confesses, "I done things that could cause a lot of trouble."[169] Weeks later, when the girl has begun to die, she is instructed to write a second note, this time in explanation of her own imminent death. She writes that she had sex with "a gang of boys in the middle of the night" because they offered her money and the boys beat her up and now she is dead. She writes that she has been a terrible burden for her caretakers, that she's done "any thing to do things to make things out of the way to make things worse for them."[170] The tortured body speaks for the torturer. On the murdered girl's belly the final confession is carved with a needle heated to split easy her anguished skin: "I am a prostitute and proud of it."

And underlying the detainee's capitulation to the torturer's vision of reality is a second confession, one beyond words. For in her pain is the proof of her vulnerability. She can be wounded, she can be hurt, so it is clear to see that she is sensitive, susceptible. Hence, she reeks of mortality: she can be killed. And this vulnerability, this sensitivity, this mortal condition is hers, he says, because she is the Body. Meanwhile the torturer who coolly observes the detainee's suffering, feeling no twinge of pity as he inflicts pain, because he has

---

169 Quoted in Millett (1979, p. 120).
170 Quoted in ibid., p. 37.

steeled himself against the reflexive instinctual solidarity of flesh for wounded flesh, is engaged in the active suppression of his own sensitivity. His repudiation of empathy for those he harms is a denial of his own sensitive body, the vulnerability which is the omen of its mortality. The wounded body, the body in pain, the body that can be destroyed: that thing is the Body, it is not Man's Self. And so, the detainee confesses to the torturer, "You are nothing at all like this inferior Other."

"However near the prisoner the torturer stands, the distance between their physical realities is colossal," Elaine Scarry writes, "for the prisoner is in overwhelming physical pain while the torturer is utterly without pain" (1985, p. 36). By Scarry's estimation, the distance between torturer and detainee — the distance installed between the Body that can be wounded and the impervious immortal Mind — is "the greatest distance that can separate two human beings." It is this distance the torturer does everything within his power to stretch into an unbreachable gulf.

EXPERIMENT: The researcher pierces the wall of the mouse's gut with a needle, in the place where the small and large intestines meet. He applies pressure to squeeze fecal matter out through the puncture into the mouse's abdominal cavity. Contaminated, the mouse's abdomen succumbs to bacterial infection, resulting in an inflammatory response that, left unchecked, will fulminate into multiple organ failure and death. The researcher measures the mouse's heart rate and core temperature. He measures the time from intestinal perforation to the onset of physiologic deterioration. He observes clinical signs of sepsis in the mouse. The mouse appears agitated, disoriented, dizzy; the mouse stumbles, shivers, slumps into lethargy, listlessness, then the mouse stops moving. The mouse is considered unresponsive. At 24 hours after the onset of sepsis, the researcher measures inflammatory cytokines in the mouse's blood. The experiment continues until the mouse dies or until seven days pass, at the end of which the mouse will be killed. In a related experiment, the researcher injects mice with a toxin that induces sepsis and finds that septic mice bury more marbles than do nonseptic mice. This finding he interprets as an indication of heightened anxiety among mice dying of sepsis (Seymour et al. 2019).

EXPERIMENT: The researchers inject a monkey's brain with neurotoxic acid, causing permanent damage to the tissues, and then cage the monkey in a dark room. They present the monkey with objects choosen to frighten the animal. A rubber snake. A rubber spider. The researchers record the monkey's behavior on videotape and analyze the footage for signs of fear. It gets marked down as a "defensive behavioral response" when the monkey freezes or hides its face from the frightening thing, or cowers, trembling, at the back of the cage (Pukara et al. 2019).

Torture transfigures the detainee into a material sign of the torturer's mastery. First, the detainee is forced to surrender her own reality in affirmation of the torturer's, confessing to the crimes he says are hers, for which she has been condemned. With her confession, the torturer's power to define reality is substantiated. Man's word is the world. At the same time, the detainee is reduced to a state of woundedness incarnate, for the edification of the torturer. Consumed by pain she testifies to the violability and vulnerability of the mortal matter that she is, which he avers he is not. For the torturer stands tall beside his victim, his Self intact and untouched, insensitive, invulnerable. He is proud to feel no empathy for the creature he injures because this refusal of fellow feeling is the surest sign he is nothing like the broken body below. The torturer puts the greatest possible distance between the Body and the Mind.

Through the act of torture, then, Man experiences the ultimate remove from his own corporeality. The Body's pain is the lifeblood of male power: for all power, Man says, is based on conquering the Body, and then leaving it behind.

ANNIHILATION

The murdered woman is discovered nude, spread-eagled, on a hilltop overlooking the city. She is found in a dumpster, in a secluded wooded area off the interstate, behind a truck stop, in the trunk of his car, washed ashore where the tide deposits her. Murdered women are discovered ripped apart as red debris littering the wasteland, dismembered, teeth and hair in black trash bags. A torso in a Rubbermaid container, a severed head on the shelf, a clot of gore in his bed. Her body cut open, breasts dissected, her belly slit. In bedrooms and ditches the murdered woman is mass-produced. On television, too, she multiplies, her mangled image the showpiece exhibited onscreen for the benefit of the Fatherland and the viewers at home. Now they see what Man is truly capable of. And in the same scene they are witnessing the true order of things. For this she is sacrificed, and for this she is laid out on public display: the murdered woman's corpse the blood-bright icon around which Man's charnel glory revolves.

A man kills six young women and rapes their dead bodies. He decapitates them, saving their heads to use as masturbatory devices. Later, the man beats his mother to death with a hammer while she is sleeping. Then he decapitates his mother, rapes her head, screams abuses at the severed head for an hour and plays darts, using the head as his target. The man tells us, "I came out of her vagina. I came out of my mother and in a rage I went right back in. ... I cut off her head and I humiliated her corpse."[171] In the morning, he cuts his mother's tongue out, and her larynx, and tries to force them down the kitchen sink garbage disposal. He explains that his mother had taken a "very strong and violently outspoken position" against men.

> ... *on the day of retribution I am going to enter the hottest sorority house ... and I will slaughter every single spoiled stuck-up blonde slut I see inside there ...*[172]

---

171 Edmund Kemper, quoted in Caputi (1989, p. 73).
172 All italicized lines are adapted from Elliot Rodger's 'Retribution' video, posted to YouTube before he committed his murder spree. (Italics mine.) See the video at <https://www.nytimes.com/video/us/100000002900707/youtube-video-retribution.html>.

A man rapes and then strangles at least twelve women and girls, killing them. He asks, "Why is it wrong to get rid of some fuckin' cunts?"[173] A man stabs a woman, cuts off both of her breasts, and carves her belly open to wrench her womb and ovaries out from her dead body. Interviewed by police, he clarifies his motivations for the killing: "I did not rape the girl. I only wanted to destroy her." He says, "I wanted to cut her body so she would not look like a person and destroy her so she could not exist."[174]

... I will take great pleasure in slaughtering all of you. you will finally see that I am, in truth, the superior one, the true alpha male, yes ...

He takes pleasure in the slaughter, the act of killing readily replacing the sexual act for him, as one penetration is exchanged for another. He derives "unspeakable delight" in the violence of domination and in destruction as dominion's highest privilege. He delights in the potency he tastes in overpowering his victim, hurting her because it is his birthright to hurt her, because she exists for his purposes and his pleasure, so he has his way with her; the wounding is a sport for him, a game now: "Oh! what action so voluptuous as destruction ... there is no ecstasy like the one we taste in giving ourselves up to that divine infamy," raves the libertine.[175] But the extermination of women is also deadly serious. It is a task imperative to Man's sovereignty, even to his survival, that he put an end to her. He does what he must.

... you denied me a happy life and in turn I will deny you all of your life, it's only fair ...

Because women are out to get him, they get what's coming to them. Man shall not suffer a witch to live. Nor the bitch that she is, the femme fatale, personification of man-eating evil. The woman is the aggressor, that monstrous enemy whose very existence augured Man's fall from grace, which was his fall into the abyss — and she is the darkness that waits for him below, as the gaping chasm, the hellmouth.

---

173 Kenneth Bianchi, quoted in Caputi (1989, p. 60).
174 James Clayton Lawson, quoted in Hazelwood and Douglass (1980, p. 21).
175 Marquis de Sade, quoted in Cameron and Frazer (1987, p. 57).

"Beyond any doubt," the philosopher muses, "her sex is a mouth and a voracious mouth which devours the penis."[176] So when Man kills her, it isn't really murder. The murderer believes he is acting in self-defense, for women are the death of him. He is terrorized by women, and his terror shows, transparent in the overkill, how he destroys totally his victim's body. Until she is no longer recognizable as a person. So she cannot exist.

> ... *you are animals, and I will slaughter you like animals, and I'll be a god, exacting my retribution ...*

By destroying the woman, Man cuts ties with her and all that she has come to represent in his imagination. Not only is she a dead object now, with no existence of her own, and thus entirely under his control and in his possession — "as one would possess a potted plant, a painting, or a Porsche,"[177] alliterates a famed killer of women, by all accounts a clever man — but even more pivotally, her death symbolizes Man's vanquishment of the desires and needs that made him cling to her in dependency. Dependency on the female, yes, on her body, the Body she is for him, the mortal matter that has shamed and shackled him, impotent prey and prisoner since birth. But the murderer is done with all that now. He has triumphed over her, and now he is liberated.

> ... *you deserve to be annihilated and I will give that to you.*

Horribly, the female is not Man's only enemy. He also claims self-defense to justify colonization and genocide. To preserve the Aryan race, it was necessary for the National Socialist Party to purge the German homeland of the Jewish scourge, the "maggot in the rotting corpse" that Hitler detected and diagnosed as the cause of the nation's dereliction (Lifton 1990, p. 53). Likewise, the white European men who colonized North America perceived the continent's native peoples as a species of subhuman contaminant. It was the colonizers' conviction that the land they 'discovered' was god's gift, granted them as his chosen sons, and that the natives were polluting it. For the land

---

176 Jean Paul Sartre, quoted in Caputi (1989, p. 144).
177 Ted Bundy, quoted in Caputi (1989, p. 54).

to serve as a gleaming new Eden, it would have to be exorcised (Smith 2005/2015, p. 9). Colonizers feared 'the savage' as an animal darkness that stalked the untamed wilds, waiting to draw civilized Man under, tempting his soul into the abyss. Indeed, the indigenous people were so fully equated with evil that, following Christopher Columbus' 'discovery' of Hispaniola, rumors spread that Satan himself made his home on a Caribbean isle (Stannard 1992). Richard Slotkin writes in *Regeneration Through Violence: The Mythology of the American Frontier, 1600-1860* (1973/1996) that, for the colonizers, all contact with North America's native inhabitants was fraught with "the distinct possibility of moral and spiritual degeneration to a bestial state" (p. 77). The Puritans were particularly anxious about the corruptive sensuality they sensed in the indigenous people they encountered, which they feared might seduce weaker-willed members of their ranks to forsake the sacred task of conquest in god's name.

It was decided, therefore, that the entire savage race should be destroyed. American Founding Father, Thomas Jefferson, weighing the relative advantages of banishing the natives "with the beasts of the forest beyond the bounds of white men's colonies" versus a more straightforward policy of wholesale extermination, concluded that it would be preferable to "extirpate them from the earth."[178] Man's kingdom can rise only where savagery and wildness have been scythed down at the stalk.

In 1650, the Pocomtucks had a population of 18,000 people. By 1700, 920 remained. Within that same 50-year period, the population of the Quiripi and Unquahog tribes fell from 30,000 to 1,500. The Western Abanaki: in 1650, 12,000 people. By 1700: 250.[179] Amassing as state armies and private militias, the colonizers swept through indigenous settlements and set fire to their camps, their agricultural fields, their food reserves. Describing an attack on the Pequots,

---

178 Thomas Jefferson, quoted in Churchill (1997, p. 150).
179 Population figures drawn from Churchill (1997, p. 149). Note that although Ward Churchill has faced accusations of falsifying his research, the statistics featured above are sourced from other demographic researchers, with citations provided in Churchill's text.

Governor William Bradford of Massachusetts' Plymouth Colony wrote:

> It was a fearful sight to see [the Pequot people] frying in the fire and the streams of blood quenching the same, and horrible was the stink and scent thereof; but the victory seemed a sweet sacrifice, and [the colonizers] gave praise thereof to God.[180]

Those who were not slashed, shot, or smoked charred in the conflagration then starved to death in the ashes of their ruined homes when winter came. Colonial governments fixed bounties on the natives' heads and scalps to incentivize citizen participation in the extermination effort, while Columbus and his men turned the slaughter of Hispaniola islanders into an athletic diversion, testing "their swords and their manly strength on captured Indians and plac[ing] bets on the slicing off of heads or the cutting of bodies in half with one blow."[181]

Scholars have estimated that, before Columbus and his men landed on North America's shores, between 15 and 20 million people inhabited the continent (Churchill 1997; Deneven 1992). By 1900, roughly four centuries later, the U.S. Bureau of the Census reported only 237,000 Indigenous Americans surviving within the boundaries of the land seized by the colonizers for the creation of their New World (Churchill, p. 137).

It was also decided, as a matter of colonial policy, that wild beasts should be eliminated along with the savages, for the two were in collusion: "... the buffalo, like the Indian, stood in the way of civilization and the path of progress."[182]

A hunter tracks a herd of buffalo to where the animals are grazing. He watches them from the top of a ridge, hiding in the sage-brush, crouched low with his gun. The huge creatures in the valley are slow and placid, many are lying in the grass; they are at rest. The man shoots the oldest cow first, the herd's matriarch. Struck, she lurches forward, staggers; for a few moments she struggles to retain her balance before

---

180 Quoted in Stannard (1993, p. 113).
181 Bartolome de Las Casas, quoted in Stannard (1993, p. 70).
182 A. Miles, quoted in Hubbard (2014, p. 293).

she cants past correcting and topples over dead. The other animals edge close to sniff her body and the blood that drips from her nostrils, and to stamp the ground, to bellow their grief as they circle around this loved one. Yet they do not run away, and because they stay with their dead, the men believe they are stupid animals. "[I]n the most methodical manner" the hunter then shoots down the buffalo "one by one, either until the last one falls," or until his cartridges are expended (Hornaday 1889, p. 469).

Men also shot buffalo from speeding trains, so that the prairie darkened blanketed with their strewn corpses. The U.S. government also encouraged soldiers to kill buffalo with heavy artillery, with canons, and the slaughter was lauded as a patriotic act (Hubbard 2014, pp. 295–296).

As a witness to the massacre, the Crow medicine woman Pretty Shield lamented:

> ... my heart fell down when I began to see dead buffalo scattered all over our beautiful country, killed and skinned, and left to rot by white men, many, many hundreds of buffalo. ... The whole country there smelled of rotting meat. Even the flowers could not put down the bad smell.[183]

During the nineteenth century, colonizers culled the Great Plains' buffalo herds from an estimated 60 million animals to only a few hundred. Many of the survivors were orphaned calves, traumatized and malnourished from growing up motherless. They could never be healthy creatures. Just as the remaining native peoples were rounded up and corralled on reservations, the buffalo were summarily herded into state parks. If the animals ranged beyond the limits of the 'sanctuaries' that Man had apportioned to them, they were promptly shot. Before long, the colonizers covered the land with their own domesticated cattle, more tractable chattel, bred to be eaten.

As part of its military strategy during the Vietnam War, the United States drenched the forests, rice paddies, orchards, croplands, and mangrove swamps of Vietnam, Laos and Cambodia with over 24

---

183 Pretty Shield, quoted in ibid., p. 301.

million gallons of herbicides. 7.6 million acres of land were defoliated (Truong and Dinh 2021). Where they endured multiple sprayings, up to 80% of all trees died outright (Westing 1971). In the mangrove swamps, almost no living beings survived. Dead forests were unable to support the teeming diversity of insects, amphibians, birds, and mammals who had once made their homes there; these animals — like the trees, lianas, epiphytes, flowers, herbs, and ferns — died in great numbers and did not return for many years, if they ever returned at all.

The mixture of herbicides used by the military combined to produce an extremely toxic form of dioxin, which leached into the soil and was carried along in rivers and streams and groundwater, soon permeating the environment. Under the soil dioxin has a half-life of 25 to 100 years (Tuyet-Hanh et al. 2010). The poison is lipophilic, meaning that it accumulates in the fatty tissues of animals who ingest it. Bottom-feeding fish and molluscs consume the dioxin that saturates the lakebed, and then these creatures are consumed by larger creatures, who are eaten by still larger creatures, including people, and so dioxin is drawn upward along the food chain at concentrations that increase with each successive level. Scientists call this process 'biomagnification'. Dioxin levels in the breast milk of Vietnamese women remained substantially elevated decades after the chemicals were sprayed (Truong and Dinh 2021).

Afflictions associated with dioxin exposure include: cancers of the brain, mouth throat, sinuses, esophagus, thymus, thyroid, breast, stomach, pancreas, bladder, kidneys, liver, bile duct, ovaries, uterus, colon, rectum, testicles, bones, skin; immunodeficiency; ischemic heart disease; hormonal disruption; birth defects and babies born without noses, eyes, forearms, and/or skulls; nausea and vomiting; festering sores all over the body.

After U.S. soldiers saturated the forests with poisons, the men bombed the forests, to set them ablaze. After the bombings the men used massive 2,500-pound bulldozers to rip from the ground any trees that still stood in the charred and defoliated forests (Wilcox 2011).

Annihilation can be measured in terms of craterization at the blast site; the number of trees blown down and the number of trees killed; the total vegetation killed; the total number of vertebrates killed by fire or by radiation; and the total extermination of all living organisms (Westing 1981). The sky is pierced by a spear of sudden light like a pillar and the day peels back from the white rim of the wound, cauterized. The sky boils, clouds whipped to opalescent froth, lit lavender, lit rose, lit apricot, with a sickening golden radiance fizzing and twisting restless within. The air seethes. The sky is bleached. By the explosion a bottomless pit is gouged in the earth and out of this pit, a million tons of shattered ground burst upward, spattered as shrapnel into the atmosphere. For miles in every direction all living creatures are instantly vaporized. Outside of the epicenter, the creatures burn to death. "We are told that a high wind, which may well have resulted from the heat of the burning city, has uprooted the large trees. It is now quite dark. Only the fires, which are still raging in some places at a distance, give out a little light."[184] Small fires converge spreading into vaster fires the growth of which sucks all oxygen from the air, and any creatures still breathing soon asphyxiate. Millions of corpses carpet the earth, a rank greying mantle, and within the putrefying tissues of the dead, bacteria multiply and mutate, their genetic material tipped to glitch by the irradiated environs. Because radiation destroys white blood cells, survivors of the blast and the burning and the airlessness will be quickly overwhelmed by infectious disease. Even the common cold can kill them now. And then there is the sickness that radiation itself induces: the afflicted shed their hair, and then their skin, then their gums bleed; they puke their guts out. Damaged cells proliferate unspun from the native intelligence of biology's order to sprout into rampant cancers. The sun and the air blacken. From now on there will be no daylight, only this cold veil of gloaming under which all greenness wilts. And the growth once so rich a vital ferment across this land does not return. Suspended in death's emulsion, the earth like a dead star glistens and gutters — then all life is eclipsed.

---

184 Hiroshima survivor, quoted in United States Army Corps of Engineers (1946, p. 37).

"My body seemed all black, everything seemed dark, dark all over ...
Then I thought, 'The world is ending.'"[185]

This is the wasteland towards which Man's compass is pointed, the
chasm into which he drifts with a tidal inexorability. Failing to obtain
salvation through symbolic sacrifices, Man goes for the throat of the
real thing: the biosphere, the living world. What Man destroys he
dominates. The world is dead because he killed it, so even should he
perish lashing out in his final futile acts of vengeance, at least he was
the one to choose his fate. To the last he was in control. Uncontrolled
nature conspired to kill him; now he puts it to death. Man's war against
mortal material reality careens to its tragic terminus at this stage, with
a murdered earth and Man a hero in his own mind, having proven
to himself his Manhood, which is next to godhood. Absolute power
is manifest in absolute annihilation, dominion's last right and rite.
Let the earth be torn asunder, Man says. He has no further need of it.

Rachel Carson keenly observed that Man's "war against nature is
inevitably a war against himself,"[186] and of course she was right — the
war Man launched so many years ago, which he seems so close in our
age to finishing, is a war against the creature he is in reality, the animal
he is, the body — yet Man is too fargone in his age-old delusions to
recognize that the massacre he commits is in fact a murder-suicide.
For Man denies he is part of the living world. Fantasizing himself
separate from the earth, he foresees he will go on existing long after
the world is ended. Already Man is planning for his real and true life,
the eternal one that awaits him in the Fatherlands of heaven above.
Gloriously cut off from reality, without a body, without a world, Man
begins again.

---

185 Hiroshima survivor, quoted in Lifton (1991, p. 22).
186 Quoted in CBS television documentary *The Silent Spring of Rachel Carson*, aired
    3 April 1963.

LIFE AFTER LIFE:
POST-EMBODIMENT FANTASIES OF THE TERMINAL MAN

We live in a world ruled by fictions of every kind.

JG BALLARD, 'Some Words About *Crash!*' (1974)

It is in the nature of the deluded mind to choose to preserve its delusion over its own life.

SUSAN GRIFFIN, 'Split Culture' (1989, p. 16)

John von Neumann was an earnest proponent of nuclear war. As a mathematician for the Manhattan Project, he calculated the exact altitude over Hiroshima and Nagasaki at which to detonate the atomic bombs in order to achieve the "maximum kill rate" (Jacobsen 2015, p. 30). As an advisor to the Pentagon, von Neumann advocated a policy of preemptive strike, convinced that the sooner the United States launched nuclear war against the Soviet Union, the better: only being the first to attack could prevent global cataclysm. "If you say why not bomb them tomorrow, I say why not today?"[187] he quipped.

When not cheering on the arsenal of planetary annihilation, von Neumann kept his mind sharp by pondering the differences between life and non-life. What was it to be alive, really — scientifically speaking? To answer this question, von Neumann turned to an "abstract mathematical world, whose inhabitants [were] mathematical patterns," a "toy universe" of his own creation (Farmer and Belin 1990, p. 8). Here, in his mathematical playland, the man fathered a new breed he called "cellular automata": computational models like rudimentary animations comprised of collections of shaded and unshaded homogenous cells programmed to self-replicate, sending copies of themselves flickering out across a two-dimensional grid, their patterns altering slightly and consistently over time in accordance with a code written by their creator (Berto and Tagliabue

---

187 Quoted in Poundstone (1993, p. 4).

2017). If we accept that self-replication is equivalent to reproduction, and that automated alteration is equivalent to adaptation; and if reproduction and adaptation are deemed 'Lifelike Properties', then cellular automata are more or less living organisms, and Man has single-handedly sired his very own novel lifeform.

The cellular automaton theory of life, with machine-made images abstractly approximating aliveness by means of immaculate computation, provided the creation myth for an exciting new field of scientific inquiry: Artificial Life. Since Artificial Life's inception in the early 1980s, researchers in the field — ALifers, as they call themselves — have been busily striving to create, by "computational (software), robotic (hardware), and/or physicochemical (wetware) means," inorganic nonbiological entities that might conceivably be termed 'alive' (MIT Press 2024). Artificial Life's bar for aliveness is rather low. To qualify, an entity need only 1) interact with its environment, while 2) remaining intact and functional in spite of so-called 'perturbations' (Farmer and Belin 1990, p. 4). Jointly funded by NASA and the U.S. military, Artificial Life found its niche at New Mexico's Los Alamos National Laboratory, the very same facility where, four decades earlier, von Neumann had toiled to maximize the civilian casualties occasioned by the first nuclear bombs. If von Neumann is the Father of Artificial Life, then surely Los Alamos was its cradle. In this isolated mesa-top laboratory complex, men conceived the technology required to efficiently exterminate all life on earth, then took it upon themselves to create — to synthesize, to simulate — earthly life's successor.

Artificial Life's driving ambition is Genesis 2.0, the coming-into-being of entirely new, wholly manmade 'lifeforms' destined to reproduce and adapt their way to dominance over biological creation. The emergence and ascendancy of these genetically engineered, robotic, and/or computer-simulated entities is envisioned by the scientists involved as evolution's next great leap forward, the passing of the baton from earthborn to techno-Fathered creation. And this imminent evolution, effected under Man's conscious control, will be a far more orderly, effective, efficiently executed business than its primitive forerunner. "The long, zigzag evolutionary path can't take the best, cleanest design route," whereas manmade evolution is bound to surge straightforwardly along the linear progression wise men have charted for it, a direct route to supremacy (Benford and Malartre 2008, p. 69). In time, the artificially alive beneficiaries of this advancement may even surpass their originator, assuming Man's place at the pinnacle of existence. At which point Man will be beaming like a proud papa. "The advent of artificial life will be the most significant historical event since the emergence of human beings," proclaimed J. Doyne Farmer, an early and avid ALifer (Farmer and Belin 1990, p. 1).

Artificial Life's endgame, gestated as it was in the same febrile incubator as nuclear Armageddon, places men of science at the helm of life's genesis as well as its evolution. Murderous nature defeated, the future unfolds by Man's intelligent design. Life's evolutionary 'ascent' from biological to artificial mirrors the transformation that Man anticipates for himself, the progression he calls inevitable because it is the progression he desires: a thrashing loose from lethally incompetent reality's clutches, from the mortal material body and the biological organism he is, to speed into the star-bright beyond of a synthesized state of grace, pure mind over matter. "We are evolving into gods," a man says, "It's a road we want to travel down."[188]

OUR BODIES, OUR AVATARS

The body is a terrible problem to have, but with a little work it might yet be salvaged. Shockingly, it turns out there may be some use for the thing after all: as an instrument of self-expression, Man's body acquires a modicum of value. Upraised from its inarticulate state of nature, the body can be customized into a culturally meaningful object, artifact, or — in the postmodernist parlance — a 'text' writ in flesh (Dery 1996). Modified, doctored, molded into the likeness of a mental image, the body is rendered intelligible. Man can finally make

---

188 Zoltan Istvan, quoted in *From Humans to Cyborgs — How Humanity Could Be Transformed through Technology* (2022). Accessed 15 August 2023 at <https://youtube.com/watch?v=VeZguJZ7LRU>. 51:55 (time stamp).

some sense of it. No longer crude, primitive globs of meat-matter, now bodies have meaning, now they are discursive.

Valued as a cultural object, a body is converted from organism to avatar. The word *avatar* is repurposed from Hindu mythology, in which it designates the earthly incarnation of a deity or spirit descended from the eternal realm. The god Vishnu, for example, can visit earth as a fish, a boar, or a warrior: these are his avatars. First introduced into 1980s cyberculture to name the cartoonish illustrations players of the online role-playing game *Habitat* chose to represent themselves, the term did not enter the popular lexicon until Neal Stephenson's 1992 sci-fi novel *Snow Crash*. In the novel, Stephenson uses 'avatar' to refer to the simulated body-images designed and operated by the denizens of a corporate-owned virtual reality world called the Metaverse (Gerhard et al. 2004).

Anthropologist Tom Boellstorff (2008) defines an avatar as "an embodiment that is intentionally crafted," therefore allowing "a sense of total control over representation" (p. 129). In the online virtual reality platform Second Life, where Boellstorff conducted his fieldwork, users have the power to choose and adjust nearly every facet of their avatars. Height, jawline, lip width, breast buoyancy, ear size — all can be minutely tweaked to align with each individual user's specifications. Those who do not feel suitably represented by standard human anatomy may opt to play as a faerie-winged kangaroo or any number of vaguely humanoid marine creatures. Boellstorff suggests that the avatars people craft for themselves may be "more authentic than actual world embodiment," on the grounds that they are *chosen* rather than *given* (p. 134). Immaterial onscreen simulations, as unadulterated reflections of a player's self-image, are seen to reveal "something deeply true about the choosing self" (p. 136). Something far more true, to be sure, than the choosing self's material body, his or her real substance in the real world.

Individuals who relate to their bodies as avatars and endeavor to remodel them 'IRL' are congratulated in cyberculture literature for their efforts at self-realization. By manipulating their physical bodies to match the abstract idealized images of themselves harbored in their minds, such individuals bravely excavate their True Selves from the muddy, obscuring density of the fleshly shroud. Rather than be passively resigned to what shabby materials nature has deigned to allot them, they are taking action to reclaim control over their very substance. We read that it is empowering, how these people remake their bodies in their own image, this repudiation of the given in favor of defiant self-recreation.

And it is women, most of all, who stand to benefit from this mode of empowerment. Sociologist Victoria Pitts-Taylor describes in her book *In the Flesh: The Cultural Politics of Body Modification* (2003) how the empowering potentials of bodily re-design came into fashion during the late 1980s, becoming especially popular within postmodern feminist and self-consciously countercultural 'queer' circles. By the 1990s, the rhetoric of empowerment was so pervasive that it could be spotted on the pages of *Vogue*, in articles buzzing with praise for women who 'reclaimed' their bodies by slicing them into shape (p. 57). During this same period, cosmetic surgery — traditionally criticized by feminists as an unambiguous expression of male colonization of the female body — was being rehabilitated, defended now as an "act of self-assertion" and "a path towards self-determination — a way for women to control their own bodies" (Negrin 2002, p. 23; Davis 1999, p. 459).

The narrative of bodily reclamation-by-modification as a straight shot to specifically female power is based on the notion that, since women's bodies have been socially as well as materially controlled by men, systematically molded to match men's images and ideals, when a woman takes deliberate action to shape her body to an image (ostensibly) of her own choosing, she symbolically repudiates patriarchal oppression (Pitts-Taylor 2003). No longer a manmade object, she is her own object now; achieving "self-control ... through self-inscription." If the body is a text, she has made herself the author of her own identity (p. 10). Among the female body modifiers Pitts-Taylor interviewed for her book, many of whom explicitly linked their painful piercing/scarification/tattoo/surgical self-transformation projects to past experiences of sexual abuse, all agreed that "permanently marking the body is an expression of female power" (p. 56).

For women in particular, but ultimately for everyone, modifying the body into conformity with one's self-image is hailed as 'liberatory', a subversion of stodgy and repressive societal norms, coded patriarchal or capitalist or just plain square. Much ado is made over how taboo it is, to reject one's body's natural form, to violate bodily wholeness and integrity by piercing and perforating every available inch of flesh. What all of this leaves aside, conveniently forgotten, is that Man has never revered natural forms. And since when has he respected any being's bodily wholeness or integrity?

Despite the transgressive/rebellious/subversive/rage-against-the-normies hype, body modification is fundamentally loyal to the most dominant of all dominant patriarchal ideologies: mind/body dualism. In accordance with the foundational fiction of manmade culture, the mind (or soul) is severed from the body and re-situated inside of it, the pilot of the body-vehicle at best, a languishing prisoner at worst. The assumption is that one's body is not what one is, but instead an object or a substance discrete from the Self, by its nature unreflective of that Self, but which the Self might utilize for its own purposes. In this case the purpose the Self has in mind is to express itself, to visibly manifest itself in the world. Accordingly, sociologist Kathy Davis (1999) can write of plastic surgery that it enabled "[patients] to reduce the distance between the internal and external so that others could see them as they saw themselves" (p. 46).

As matter imposed on the Self, the body, meat suit that it is, shrouds what the Self most wants to be seen. The remedy to the distress induced by such smothering, then, is modification of the body by means of technological intervention — another obvious accession to patriarchal doctrine. The Self uses the Body. The Self controls the Body. The Self communicates through the Body. But the Self never *is* the Body: the two remain forever divided and estranged. Because it preserves the dualistic structure, the body-as-avatar model that informs the rhetoric of body-mod 'empowerment' neither transgresses nor rages against mainstream patriarchal ideology, but in fact reinforces it, regardless of how superficially unconventional the body modifier's chosen aesthetic may be. In reality, the pierced, tattooed, scarred, implanted, branded, cosmetically nipped and tucked body symbolizes a selfhood in lockstep submission to Man's somatophobic alienation from biological reality.

The edgy reinvention of dualism inaugurated by the 1990s body-mod craze is in the midst of a renaissance, locked into place now as transgenderism's guiding theory. The 'transgender' person, we are informed, repeatedly and with evangelical zeal, has suffered the cruel misfortune of being 'born in the wrong body'. This individual's body is wrong because it is one sex, male or female, while the individual's interior True Self is the so-called 'opposite' sex or maybe no sex at all, or one sex on Thursdays and another on Sundays, while the humdrum body stagnates, unresponsive to these tumultuous vacillations. The interior sense of one's sex is named 'gender identity' and enshrined as integral to the True Self, to whose expression the biological body is an unfortunate impediment. The mismatch between Self and Body, and the thwarting of self-expression that it brings, is posited as the origin of the 'transgender' person's strife. This strife warrants a diagnosis of gender dysphoria, defined in the *Diagnostic and Statistical Manual of Mental Disorders, Fifth Edition, Text Revision (DSM-V-TR)* (2022) as a "marked incongruence between one's experienced/expressed gender and their assigned gender" (American Psychiatric Association 2024). By "assigned gender," the psychiatric powers that be of course mean biological sex, also termed "sex assigned at birth," an epithet meant to stress the sexed animal body's nature as something unfairly foisted onto a person, rather than the organism that person is.

The salve for the painful incongruence between Self and Body is techno-medical intervention to retrofit the body into a state of harmony with the individual's gender identity, now synonymous with the True Self. As was the case with women turning to cosmetic surgery for relief from psychic pain, the objective is to "reduce the distance between the internal and the external" in order for the body to function more effectively as an instrument of self-expression. To this end, 'transgender' bodies are transformed into "permanent construction site[s]" (Guerini 2023, p. 151). Breasts are amputated or implanted with supplemental silicone to communicate maleness or femaleness, respectively. Hormones are prescribed to increase or decrease muscle mass, speed or slow facial hair growth, and redistribute body fat. For children said to be born in the wrong bodies, pharmaceuticals may be administered to stave off puberty's onset, chemical deliverance from the dreaded eruption of undesired, gender-disaffirming anatomy. By these and other measures — electrolysis, castration, gender-congruent haircuts (long for female, cropped for male: what else?), facial 'feminization' surgeries, the manufacture of phallic effigies from rolled-up strips of thigh skin — 'wrong' bodies are put right.

As a progressive humanitarian cause, relieving the distress of the Bad Body's 'transgender' prisoners has shown itself to be remarkably profitable (Guerini 2023). The "Sex Reassignment Surgery Market" was worth more than $623 million globally in 2022 and is projected to reach $1.9 billion within the next ten years if it continues to expand at current rates, according to a report by Global Market Insights.[189] For 623 million dollars and rising, the medical-industrial complex is most delighted to offer its services to incongruent adults and children alike. Indeed, men with significant medical industry investments are among the most prominent funders of the political and cultural promotion of transgenderism, as Jennifer Bilek's invaluable invest-igations have exposed.[190]

The transgenderist creed exalts male dominion's fictions to the level of unassailable truth while dismissing the biological reality of human, animal bodies as illusory and injurious. In a consummate example of what Mary Daly called a patriarchal reversal, manmade culture becomes reality, material reality the fraudulent deception (Daly 1978/1990). Gender is an ideological system central to patriarchal social organization. It is founded on male fantasies of what it is to be a woman or a man, which function as the culture's sacred code of

---

189 *Sex Reassignment Surgery Market — by Gender Transition (Male to Female {Facial, Breast, Genitals [Phallectomy, Orchiectomy, Vaginoplasty]}, Female to Male {Facial, Chest, Genitals [Hysterectomy, Phalloplasty]}) & Forecast, 2023-2032,* report accessed 30 March 2024, at <https://www.gminsights.com/industry-analysis/sex-reassignment-surgery-market>.

190 Visit Bilek's 11th Hour Blog to view an archive of her tremendously important work. <https://www.the11thhourblog.com/>; see also Bilek 2024.

conduct. Personality types, preference sets, modes of behavior and habits of being, relational styles, social roles and domains, pastimes and hobbies and style of dress, and effectively every other facet of human life are decided and delegated on the basis of whether one is female or male. Sex, by contrast — the anatomical and physiological material reality of our female and male mammalian bodies — is biological fact. A person is born female, or male; a small fraction of the population presents with variations in sexual development that place them somewhere outside species-typical dimorphism, but these exceptions do not obviate the basic two-sex model.

As a cultural system, gender is external to the individual, while sex is intrinsic to the organisms that we are. It is in and of the flesh, our true internal reality. Yet transgenderism inverts the two, such that gender becomes the great inner truth while sex is cast as 'socially constructed', hence exogenous. As the story goes, sex is 'assigned at birth' by means of someone's no doubt biased reading of the unreliable text of the body, a manuscript prone to what might be termed corporeal typos. Gender, on the other hand, as an indwelling quantity, emanating from the mind and the soul, does not necessarily make itself known on the faulty body's surface — it is so much deeper, so much subtler than that! — but is absolutely essential to selfhood and must be honored.

Gender is natural, and true, and essential to the Self. (But, in fact, gender is male fantasy.)

Sex is cultural, and false, and at odds with the Self. (But sex is material reality.)

If we take a step back from the mindwarp this reversal induces, we can recall that for many years preceding our current epoch of confusion, feminists understood gender as a patriarchal system installed to exploit sexual difference as the justification for sex-class stratification within the male-supremacist social order. The gender system sorts males and females into two distinct, readily recognizable, apparently natural classes, with men on top and women on the bottom. Its classifications form the catechism of sexism: females are this way, males that way; females do this, males do that; females belong here, males over there. Women take pleasure in sexual objectification, being looked at, being of service or being used. Men get off on violence, whether at war and on the football field. Little girls play teatime with Barbie. Little boys bash miniature plastic figurines of bulldozers into walls. And so on and on and on.

Gender's origins lie in the patriarchal institutionalization of male dominance and female subordination. Its consequence is the reinforcement and reproduction of sex-class oppression. To embrace this manmade system to the extent of remodeling one's body into conformity with its dictates produces a state of embodied sexism. Transgenderism goads bodies into allegiance with the official truths of male dominion: if a boy child pours tea for his dolls, clearly he is in the wrong body and will require reconstruction as soon as possible, given his preference for feminine amusements. If I am a female, but I'm disinclined to don the pornified raiment of contemporary femininity, or if I prefer physics to long discussions about my feelings, surely I am not really a woman. I must be a man, or some third option, non-binary or genderqueer. My body is wrong, and I'll need to have my breasts excised in proud exclamation of my newly excavated True Self. If I am a man, but I want to get fucked and treated like subhuman garbage, or be frivolously fancy-free and manicure my nails, or even just to have greater justification for being sensitive, soft rather than stoic, it would seem that I am in fact female. Accordingly, I will take estrogen, put on a dress, snap selfies in the bedroom mirror, and never be afraid to cry.[191] These transparently sexist, restrictive, regressive

---

191 It is sometimes argued that men who take on the conventions of femininity and call themselves women are friends to females and the feminist cause, that their imitation is a tribute to womankind, to be interpreted as a sign of profound affinity for womanhood. The logic is that, if these men want to be women and surgically mimic femaleness, clearly they must revere women and our female bodies. How could there be anything misogynistic in a man's yearning to 'become' a woman? Yet, when men self-feminize, altering their male bodies in simulation of female anatomy, the source material for their project is not the organic, natural, biological female body. Instead they model themselves after the manmade fetish object that is 'Woman', a patriarchal cultural icon. This is why the archetypal 'transwoman' aesthetic is glamorously hyperfeminine, glitter-dusted and bottle blonde. Think Dylan Mulvaney's pastel parody of 'girlhood', think Laverne Cox queenly in gold lamé, think Brazilian model Valentina Sampaio on the cover of Sports Illustrated. A man who calls himself a woman writes, "I transitioned for gossip and compliments, lipstick and mascara, for crying at the movies, for being someone's girlfriend ... for fixing my makeup in

and repressive stereotypes are the warp and weft of the gender system, at present moment being heightened to a screaming pitch, repackaged and repopularized by transgenderism.

But Man is adamant, as he always is: his myths are reality. Biology is oppressive; manmade culture provides relief and release. Mankind will be liberated only when material reality is vanquished.

One of the revered Founding Fathers of the modern transgenderist movement is 'Martine' Rothblatt, who, until the age of 39, was better known by his given name, Martin. Although a 2014 *New York Magazine* cover mistakenly headlined him as "the highest-paid female CEO in America," Rothblatt remains entirely male (Miller, 2014). A multimillionaire former lawyer turned "futurist, pharma tycoon, entrepreneur, philosopher" Renaissance man, Rothblatt's business ventures include Sirius satellite radio and the biotech firm United Therapeutics, a leader in the burgeoning field of manufactured organs. Rothblatt has voiced his dream of producing an "unlimited supply of transplantable organs" which could be 3D-printed or perhaps 'grown' inside transgenic pigs and 'harvested' for human use, through a process known as xenotransplantation (Regalado 2023). United Therapeutics subsidiary Revivicor operates a farm in Virginia where these pigs, gene-edited into more compatible involuntary organ donors, are bred and reared and killed so that humans might one day benefit from a renewable reservoir of readily available, patented

---

the bathroom ... for feeling hot ... for Daisy Dukes, bikini tops, and all the dresses, and, my god, *for the breasts*" (Long Chu 2018, emphasis his). A different man, for whom being a woman entails the eroticization of surgical pain and convincing men to buy him sexy lingerie, tells us, "I started objectifying my body at a very young age ... because I knew that I had the spirit of a young girl inside me" (quoted in Gluck 2021). The concept of womanhood these men aim to embody is blatantly derived from male-supremacist fantasy. More insidiously, objectification and fetishization are containment strategies for controlling the real live female body and the rejected corporeality it represents in Man's symbolic scheme. Through these processes, what is biological, natural, and bodily is annexed for conversion into an artifact of male dominion – testament to men's power to shape the substance of creation to their will – and then worshiped as such. In the 'women' men make of themselves, perfectly artificial, we see the patriarchal urge to displace reality and redesign it in Man's image brought to fruition. There is no love for the female here.

porcine hearts, lungs, kidneys, and livers. The FDA has approved the pigs for "food use" as well (Fatka 2020).

Rothblatt is also the founder of the Terasem Movement, a techno-religious sect that takes as its credo the maxim, "death is optional and God is technological."[192] In 2004, Terasem released a documentary entitled *2B: The Era of the Flesh is Over*. It seems worth noting, too, that Rothblatt owns a robotic chatbot head he commissioned in the likeness of his wife, purported to contain the uploaded data of her memories, set to replace her when she (or her body, at least) dies. And, most salient to our current topic of inquiry, Rothblatt is the author of several treatises charting possible avenues by which humanity might escape the tyranny of corporeality. It is to one of these texts, entitled *From Transgender to Transhuman: A Manifesto on the Freedom of Form* (2011), that we now turn.

In *From Transgender to Transhuman*, Rothblatt argues that it is unjust for human society to be divided on the basis of sex, which he reduces to "genital difference." Many feminists are apt to agree with him on this first point. It must be conceded that he does at least acknowledge the hierarchical intentions of the divide, and to men's oppression of women. But for Rothblatt the solution to this "apartheid of sex," as he calls it, is not to target the patriarchal power structure that has institutionalized sex-class stratification. Instead, he proposes ceasing to recognize sex altogether, immediately and in every possible context. Sex, he writes, is irrelevant to personhood, because "[a] person's nature has nothing to do with gonads" (p. 51). Genitals ought to have no bearing on the expectations society sets for individuals, or the options made available to them. Sexual difference is therefore arbitrary, Rothblatt concludes, and deserves no attention whatsoever. "Labelling people as male or female, upon birth, exalts biology over sociology," he grumbles, because to place biology over sociology equates to placing nature over culture — and this is wholly unacceptable (p. 34). Far preferable in Rothblatt's view is the elevation of culture over nature, humankind's transcendence of "gross" and "dumb" biology (p. 134). With regards to sex, this means subordinating

---

192 Quoted in Regalado (2023).

the biological body to the manmade social apparatus of gender, or "sexual identity" (not to be confused with sexual orientation, which, body-centric as it is, Rothblatt has scant time for).

Sexual identity deserves our reverence because, unlike lowly genital difference, it is a quality of the mind, and "mind is deeper than matter" (p. 41). Each individual is possessed of a sexual identity, described here as a wondrously unique synthesis of three basic traits: activeness (aggression), passivity (nurturance), and eroticism (sex drive) (p. 98). While Rothblatt does his very best to divorce these traits from traditional sexist stereotypes — men are active, women are passive, for example — at one point even color-coding the traits along a "rainbow spectrum of gender selected at will" wherein people are no longer men and women but now "shades of purple, orange, green, and brown" — his prismatic new system leans heavily on the standard-issue masculinity/femininity polarity beloved by manmade culture (p. 41; p. 100). Active aggression remains the opposite of passive nurturance, even if now we're calling the active aggressive person red-gendered instead of male and the passive nurturant person blue-gendered rather than female. In spite of his "infinite number of sexual identities," somehow they all wash out to the same tired timeworn pink and blue (p. 98).

Once he has established gender as a question primarily of quirky interior chromatism, Rothblatt moves on to inverting the status-quo relation between sex and gender, so that rather than having personal qualities assigned on the basis of sex, those same qualities can be used to determine what sex a person ought to be. "Sex should really be the sum of behaviors we call gender," he writes, because, after all, "sex is just the label for one's chosen gender" (p. 38). No longer a neutral biological fact, sex becomes an enfleshed marker of the male-supremacist stereotypes with which one feels an affinity. "I am pugilistic, emotionless and horny" becomes "I am male"; cultural artifice overrules material reality; and the body has nothing to do with anything, its sole residual function as the raw material to be remodeled in the making of an avatar for the infinitely unique rainbow brain.

Rothblatt craftily evades any in-depth discussion of so-called 'sex-reassignment' body modification, but considering that he himself underwent such operations, it can be inferred that they do indeed factor into his grand design. Which begs the question, never addressed in *From Transgender to Transhuman*, of why, if the sexed body is naught but a meaningless and irrelevant restrictive drag, anyone would surgically replicate sexual biology in the expression of what is proposed as a purely mental identity? If the body is so arbitrary, why bother changing it at all? And if your sexual identity is mauve, why not slip on a nice color-coordinated scarf instead of fitting yourself out with breast implants?

After all his dogged work to decouple sexual identity from the sexed body, Rothblatt casually re-links them as if without a thought, like he assumes readers won't notice, by endorsing the surgical simulation of the antediluvian "biological substrate" he doth protest so much (p. 133). We know that Rothblatt himself purchased false breasts. He calls himself a woman, not cerulean.

What this rupture in Rothblatt's argument against the relevance of sexual difference reveals is that the 'liberation' he rallies for is not really about releasing people from a sexist, unjust culture. Indeed, Rothblatt quite likes the culture, or at least its gender stereotypes, for he incorporates all of them into his alternative system. He doesn't even seem to mind the class divisions so much, as long as they're based on attributes of the mind and not the body. What Rothblatt desires and demands to be liberated from is the body itself. The sexed body is to blame for neither sexism nor sex-class hierarchy, both of these being products of manmade society; and yet Rothblatt consistently targets the body as if its matter and mold were the roots of the problem. Bodies, he argues, are illiberal, because people do not get to choose them. They are 'assigned' at birth, shaped as they are, with the parts that they have, "whether we like them or not" (p. 38). Since being born one sex or the other without having had any say in the matter interferes with self-determination, it is a violation of what Man believes is his birthright to absolute autonomy; he is less free because of it. Sex is a show of nature's power to restrict the exercise of Man's will. Like all of nature's limits, because of the challenge sex poses to male dominion, it must be vehemently opposed until overthrown.

And indeed Rothblatt makes explicit that sex is but the first on a long list of limits he intends to transcend. He writes:

Freedom of gender is ... the gateway to a freedom of form and to an explosion of human potential. First comes the realization that we are not limited by our gross sexual anatomy. Then comes the awakening that we are not limited by our anatomy at all (p. 40).

The transgenderist effacement of sexual difference is the modest opening phase in Rothblatt's larger transhumanist master plan to do away with the body entirely — it is "the onramp to the transcendence of fleshism," as he calls it[193] — in order to accelerate the mind/soul's transition out of its present "fragile biological substrate" and into more "enduring technological materials" (p. 133). Specifically, Rothblatt would like to see his pulpous fleshy brain converted into software and uploaded into a computer and/or nanotechnological pseudo-body. Thus freed from the body, he could endure forever as a digitally immortal software being. And this is "the path of future evolution," the technological MasterMind finally claiming the authority rightfully his, "taking charge of his evolutionary destiny" and thereby "transcending dumb biology" (pp. 133-134).

The man writes: "our essential sweetness is in our minds, and ... each of us has a unique life-path potential not fully tethered to a body-determined route" (p. 61).

The man writes: "the basic transhumanist concept is a human need not have a flesh body" (p. 39).

The man writes: "I believe we are on the threshold of creating humanity and personhood outside of DNA-driven flesh bodies" (p. 22).

It is in such dreams of disincarnation that our male genius perceives "the final liberation of humanity from its animal past" (p. 41). For men like Martin(e) Rothblatt, maddened by how material reality squelches his sovereignty, affronted by any breach of his control, to be born any body at all is wrong.

---

193 Quoted in Guerini (2023, p. 146).

THE SELF-MADE MAN/MACHINE

Tim Cannon is the founder of Grindhouse Wetware, a biotech start-up specializing in devices people can implant under their skin in order to "enhance the sensory and informational capacities of the human body" (O'Connell 2017a, p. 135). "I'm trapped in the wrong body because I'm trapped in *a* body," he says, "*All* bodies are the wrong body" (p. 158). Cannon tells us he hopes one day to have his arm amputated and replaced with a technologically superior prosthetic arm.

In a teaser for the MTV documentary *True Life: I'm a Cyborg* (2015), the voiceover introduces a lanky young man eager to embed a Bluetooth headset nestled right up against his skull: "Ben is uncomfortable in his own skin and wishes he were a robot."[194]

Transhumanism hinges on the assumption that it is "possible and desirable" to transcend the human condition, and that it is only a matter of time before such transcendence shall be achieved through an increasingly intimate union with technology, enabling Mankind to become "something better — something other than the animals we are" (O'Connell 2017b). "If we want to be more than mere animals, we need to embrace technology's potential to make us machines," Tim Cannon explains (O'Connell 2017a, p. 142). The individual who embraces technology's potentials and embarks on becoming a machine, renovating his body into a fusion of organic and electromechanical parts, can proudly call himself a cyborg. "No longer can man be said to be entirely the offspring of nature ... Science is providing him with the technology to become his own maker," writes David Rorvik, an early adopter of the transhumanist ethos and the author of *As Man Becomes Machine: The Evolution of the Cyborg* (1971).

Champions of Man/Machine hybridism argue that Mankind is already a cyborgian race. After all, we have pacemakers to steady our hearts and contact lenses to enhance our vision; amputees are outfitted with prosthetic limbs, which, like Esper Bionic's AI-powered robotic hand, featured on the cover of *Time Magazine* in 2022,

---

194 Accessed 8 September 2023. <https://www.youtube.com/watch?v=oakRYpnVfJU>.

are becoming ever more 'lifelike' and sophisticated.[195] Hips, knees, jaws, teeth, arteries, veins, fingers, toes: all can be replaced with manmade substitutes should the fallible originals falter, fail, or fall prey to injury. Techno-medical interventions of this kind might be helpfully conceptualized as a 'functional cyborgism', an incorporation of machinery motivated by (ostensibly) therapeutic intentions rather than by the transhumanist yen for merger. Yet the normalization of functional cyborg methods of corporeal repair provides a legitimizing springboard for more ideologically motivated Man/Machine visions. Likened to widely accepted, ubiquitous technologies like contact lenses, full-body overhaul can be plausibly promoted as a life-saving medical advance.

Ray Kurzweil, futurist and leading transhumanist ideologue, looks forward to the day when the contents of the human body will be replaced by microscopic, self-propelling machines called nanobots. Our digestive organs will be replaced by nanobots stored within an unobtrusive wearable apparatus of some sort — perhaps a belt, Kurzweil proposes, or an undershirt — and programmed to swim in and out of our bodies, ferrying the necessary nutrients directly into our bloodstream when they enter and removing the unnecessary remnants with their departure. Thus we will no longer be harassed by the urge to eat or defecate. Because the digestive nanobots will expertly filter out any contaminants or pathogens we consume, we'll have no further use for our livers or kidneys. Red and white blood cells as well as platelets will be replaced by nanobots programmed for maximally efficient oxygenation, clotting, and immunological capabilities. Because this nanobot 'blood' will circulate autonomously throughout the body, there will be no need for a centralized pump to keep the vital fluid pulsing: our hearts will become superfluous. The same goes for our lungs, since the nanobots will manufacture all

---

195 A publicity photo for the Esper Hand shows a young woman dressed in minimalist black, her dark hair pulled sleekly back. One of the woman's arms is real and the other a prosthetic limb, made from some smooth metal like matte steel; in each hand, the flesh extremity and the machine one, she is holding an apple. The copy to her left reads, "BODY IS NOT A LIMIT." <https://ucluster.org/en/blog/2022/05/esper-bionics-launches-an-era-of-tech-enabled-human-evolution/>.

the oxygen our cells could ever ask for. "Since we will be eliminating most of our biological organs," Kurzweil writes, hormones will become an anachronism — the endocrine system is out (2005, p. 307). Our bones will be replaced by a self-repairing skeleton of interlinking nanobots. In Kurzweil's estimation, within two decades we will have "eliminated the heart, lungs, red and white blood cells, platelets, pancreas, thyroid and all the hormone-producing organs, kidneys, bladder, liver, lower esophagus, stomach, small intestines, large intestines, and bowel." At this point the sole organic, biological components left to us will be our brains, mouths, skin, sensory organs, and genitals — and even these we'll no doubt jump at the chance to optimize with nanoengineered materials.

Kurzweil frames the colonization of the human body by swarms of infinitesimal robots as a medical miracle: Mankind's long dreamt-of escape from the tortures of animal debility, disease, damage and degradation. Exchanging our vitals and viscera for "vastly superior systems that will last longer and perform better" is preventative medicine of the highest order (p. 302). Billions of lives will be saved, because no one will ever have to die. Kurzweil and his ilk invoke this altruistic pitch to gloss the stark techno-transcendentalist fantasies that form transhumanisms' (nanoengineered) marrow and garner sympathy from the general public, people who may yet lack the requisite sophistication to grasp the advantages of evolving into industrial equipment, but who are undoubtedly afraid to die.

For the most part, however, transhumanists make little effort to hide their motivating ambitions. They celebrate a "total symbiosis with the machine" as the next stage in Man's progress towards perfection, an evolution they intend to do everything in their power to expedite (Pitts-Taylor 2003, p. 157). So-called 'grinders' — "the punk vanguard of the transhumanist movement" — take a DIY approach to hastening their own personal evolution by harnessing readily available technologies in order to 'hack' their own bodies (Theresa 2022). More often than not, this involves cutting some part of themselves open and stitching electronic gadgets under their skin.

Grinders are uniformly unimpressed with their biological bodies, "this body is bullshit" being the paradigmatic grinder complaint

(Doerksen 2018, p. 23). Their grievances include that the body is neither lightning quick nor bulletproof; that it does an ineffectual job of regulating its temperature; that it is sensitive to pain and susceptible to disease; and that it wears down over time, losing function and aesthetic appeal. They are, of course, outraged by the horrible inevitability of bodily death (ibid.). If anyone is going to deride the body as a poorly built, hideous, and dismal meatsack, it is a grinder.

Because the bulk of grinder experimentation takes place in men's basements and garages with only minimal access to medical equipment or surgical expertise, grinders are limited in their body modernization options. They have therefore settled for starting small, such that many of their 'hacks' seem unnervingly primitive, crude, and only marginally practical. For example, the go-to entry-level grinder upgrade is to implant an RFID chip into your hand. Now, with just a simple wave of your modernized extremity, you can perform such wonders as unlocking your car (or office, or garage) door, swiping aside the lock screen of your smartphone, and purchasing gas with neither cash nor card but with your own hand, rendered newly legible to the tap-to-pay reader. Another grinder staple is the implantation of small magnets, sure to come in handy should you need to detect faulty circuits, say, or recoup loose screws. A related Grindhouse Wetware device uses Bluetooth to link implanted magnets with a person's smartphone, so that the lucky implantee can receive text messages, calendar reminders, weather reports, and other thrilling notifications delivered subdermally in Morse code (Doerksen 2018).

Grinder-style augmentations and enhancements can hardly be considered revolutionary expansions of human potential. Indeed, they have a way of making straightforward tasks far more complex than they were before — compare the time it would take to parse a Morse-coded subdermal text message to the ten seconds required to physically pick up the phone and read that same missive — never mind painful and potentially gangrenous. What practical applications the 'upgrades' do serve are almost pitifully mundane, advantageous only in the context of a life spent clutching an iPhone, driving to and from the office, buying gas, and retiring the car to the garage at night. Grinders adapt the body for optimized compatibility with a denatured, drably technocratic concrete-and-steel environment of somnambulant workaday drudgery and consumerism. Yet the banal lameness of the 'superpowers' with which they endow themselves does not seem to demoralize the grinders. Which makes sense, since functionality was never really their concern. The real aim is to ring in the dawn of the Man/Machine Age. It's the future that grinders want, and they want it now. With their own sorry meatsacks they usher it in.

Several levels up the ladder of Man/Machine surgical interventions is that old cyberpunk favorite: the neural prosthetic. William Gibson introduced the genre's now-classic neural augmentation trick in his 1984 novel *Neuromancer*, the plot of which revolves around a nervous system hack granting at-will entry into virtual reality spaces, allowing for seamless, immersive data-surfing. Elon Musk has taken up this Gibsonian torch with Neuralink, a "fully implantable, cosmetically invisible brain-computer interface" designed to 'listen' to neural signals from paralyzed patients' brains and transmit the data to their computers and smartphones, enabling implantees to operate them wirelessly with their minds.[196] Neuralink was approved for human clinical trials by the FDA in the spring of 2023; in January 2024, Elon Musk announced that the company had inserted its first implant into a human subject's skull (Levy et al. 2023; Sigal 2024). Musk has described the implant as "kind of like a Fitbit in your skull with tiny wires,"[197] and claims that it will restore autonomy to the paralyzed, vision to the blind, and hearing to the deaf, while offering new approaches to the treatment of mental illness and autism. But Musk's hopes for Neuralink in the end have less to do with novel therapies for the disabled than they do with developing technology that will allow humans to merge with AI. Musk has made no secret of his worry that AI will usurp human control over the planet, and the best way to prevent the takeover, as he sees it, is for humans to

---

196 <https://neuralink.com/>.
197 Quoted in Bohan (2022, p. 41).

catch up to the machines through "some kind of AI symbiosis."[198] Announcing Neuralink's inaugural implantation, Musk tweeted, "In the long term, Neuralink hopes to play a role in AI risk civilizational risk reduction by improving human to AI ... bandwidth by several orders of magnitude."[199]

The theoretical physicist Michio Kaku (2018) is equally sanguine about neural prostheses, which he expects will give us the awesome power to "turn on the lights, activate the internet, play video games ... purchase merchandise, [and] conjure any movie — just by thinking" (p. 211). The transcendent future of direct brain-to-household-appliance interchange that Man is engineering for us all shall be our new "mental age, where our thoughts control the world around us."

The United States military is another major proponent of this exciting new mental age. In 1999, the Defense Advanced Research Projects Agency (DARPA) began funding 'biohybrid' research with the aim of creating technologically enhanced cyborg creatures useful for the efficient infliction of violence upon designated enemies of the state (O'Connell 2017). One DARPA-funded study in this vein entailed burying electrodes in the skulls of rats so that the animals' movements could be manipulated through a laptop. And in 2014, the agency established its Biological Technology Office, with a focus on "restor[ing] and maintain[ing] warfighter abilities by various means, including many that emphasize neurotechnology" (Goss 2018). Related research has inquired into transferring brain data from one mouse to another and enhancing memory by means of recording recall-related activity in the brain, then feeding those neural recordings back into implanted electrodes. During his reign as the director of DARPA's Defense Sciences, former McDonald's CEO Michael Goldblatt stated, "Soldiers having no physical, physiological, or cognitive limitation will be key to survival and operational dominance in the future."[200]

The Man/Machine fantasy's broad appeal, bringing together as it does an oddly matched crew of biotech punks, Silicon Valley billionaires,

---

198 Ibid.
199 Quoted in Samuel (2024).
200 Quoted in O'Connell (2017, p. 144).

and military-industrial complex administrators, is testament to the ideological dominance of what at first glance might seem like a fringe premise: that everything is already a machine. As Carolyn Merchant explains in *The Death of Nature* (1980/1989), from the 17th century onward the western worldview has been founded on a masculinist mechanism, which likens living beings to machines for men to manipulate and make use of. In the mechanistic mind, the material world — and therefore the biological body — is without inherent vitality; instead, it is "a system of dead, inert particles," atomized and interchangeable parts waiting lifelessly to be moved about by the exertions of external powers, i.e., Man (p. 193). Simply put, a mechanism sucks the life out of matter, leaving it empty, voided of meaning, integrity, purpose. And it is because of this mechanistic mentality, its machine metaphors and preoccupation with establishing rational order and complete control over matter, that Man can earnestly look forward to becoming a cyborg. If the body is a 'biological machine' then the logical upgrade is to replace it, piece by piece, with new-and-improved equipment. The mechanistic mentality makes it conceivable to compare bodies to hardware and operating systems, brains to software, and death to a system crash, its disaster averted by diligent back-ups. Only the body already conceptualized as a machine can be substituted for one.

"Flesh is an unstable system," one man tells us, "it's a system that's terminal from the beginning, designed to die."[201]

"We need to change the hardware," affirms another.[202]

At its visionary zenith, the Man/Machine fantasy moves to "exorcise the organic and the biological altogether," as moral philosopher Mary Midgley writes in *Science as Salvation* (1992, p. 163). No longer content to tinker at the edges trying to improve what he knows to be a hopelessly obsolete technology, Man longs to strike out onward and upward into the great new format that awaits him. In his "Letter

---

201 Zoltan Istvan, quoted in *From Humans to Cyborgs — How Humanity Could Be Transformed through Technology* (2022). Accessed 15 August 2023 at <https://youtube.com/watch?v=VeZguJZ7LRU>.
202 Tim Cannon, quoted in O'Connell (2017, p. 139).

to Mother Nature," transhumanist and Alcor cryonicist Max More politely acknowledges his matrix's "genius in using carbon-based compounds" to create human beings such as himself, but asserts that, henceforth, her ambitious sons shall — with all due respect, which would seem to be very little — reject the slew of unacceptable limitations associated with "remaining purely biological organisms" (More 2013, p. 450).

Transhumanism's strategy for breaking free from the body once and for all is a procedure known as 'whole brain emulation'. First, a mechanical reproduction of the brain is created, the total of its tens of billions of "operant components" and the intricate mesh that knits them together duplicated, in order to emancipate the mind from its outdated biological substrate (Koene 2013, p. 147). Neuroscientist Randal Koene, who gave whole brain emulation its name, and whose nonprofit Carboncopies Foundation is dedicated to facilitating Man's molting from the ignoble meat suit, blithely compares replicating the brain in order to extricate it from the body to "taking a computer program from one hardware platform (e.g. an Android cellphone) to an emulator of the same processing operations on a different hardware platform (e.g. a Macintosh computer)" (ibid.).

Once downloaded and saved as data, the brain will be 'substrate independent' and ready for upload into any number of sleek new higher-tech hardware options. The possibilities for postbiological embodiment are endless, in keeping with the transhumanist principle of "morphological freedom," which posits that Man has the sovereign right to reinvent and redefine himself by taking whatever form he pleases, unhampered by interference from material reality (Sandberg 2013, p. 57). One might desire to be uploaded into a humanoid robot, for example; or perhaps one would prefer to operate as a hologram,[203] a spaceship, or an interstellar black cloud leisurely drifting its way through the vastness of the celestial vault (Midgley 1992). Natasha Vita-More's "whole body prosthesis" is a lithe human-shaped apparatus tricked out with such luxury features as a "nanotech data

---

203 The 2045 Intiative's most advanced (and priciest) speculative future-body option is "Avatar D: A hologram-like avatar." See <http://2045.com/tech2/>.

storage memory system," an "in vivo fiber optic communications spine," "solar-protected skin with tone-texture changeability," "replaceable genes" and "regenerative organs" (More and Vita-More 2013, p. 79).

Yet even alluringly fleshless prosthetic bodies like Vita-More's prototype are mere mile markers along the road to glory for the substrate-independent mind in search of true liberation. "Ultimately our thinking procedures would be totally liberated from any traces of our original body, indeed of anybody," predicted Hans Moravec, a roboticist whose proposed discorporation procedure entails painstakingly slicing brains into cross-sections for digital replication, while the moribund body is abandoned to the mindless death throes of its convulsions on the operating table (2013, p. 181). "This is a gradual state of us becoming a much more evolved, spiritual, and magnificent being," self-appointed 2016 Transhumanist Party presidential candidate Zoltan Istvan explains.[204] "We are evolving into gods," he says. This is Man, free at last, his mind/soul/True Self let loose from matter and ready to seize his eternal destiny beyond the dying world.

The 1968 short story 'Masks' by sci-fi author Damon Knight tracks the deepening malaise of a man forced to live as a brain encased inside a mechanical prosthetic body following an unspecified accident that damages his original 'vehicle' beyond repair. Contained within a metallic carapace, the man quickly develops a vicious abhorrence for organic life. He orders that all houseplants be expelled from his apartment, unable to stand the sight of their greening growth; he is repulsed by human skin, its grease and gaping pores and blemishes; outraged by the shimmering moisture of its eyes and tongue, the man beats a puppy to death. He is disgusted even by the 'lifelike' design of his own pseudo-body, meant to lend him some semblance of standard human male appearance. Instead, he prefers to hide the waxen face that was sculpted for him behind a silver mask, smooth and

---

204 Quoted in *From Humans to Cyborgs — How Humanity Could Be Transformed through Technology* (2022). Accessed 15 August 2023 at <https://youtube.com/watch?v=VeZguJZ7LRU>.

featureless, with slits where the eyes would be. The man is harassed by night terrors in which he is shunted mercilessly back into the flesh, "falling into slimy bulging softness higher than his chin," paralyzed, powerless. Asked by the scientists who monitor him what sort of body would suit him better, the man diagrams his desired morphology: "an oblong metal box on four jointed legs. From one end protruded a tiny mushroom-shaped head on a jointed stem and a cluster of arms ending in probes, drills, grapples." As the pilot of such a vessel, resembling no living creature, nothing organic, the man wistfully imagines himself prospecting for minerals on the surface of the moon. The world he longs for is cold, clean; it is a taintless domain free of offal and fulsome things gone soft, without flora or fauna, certainly without wet-eyed puppy dogs. "That's where I belong, in space," the man sighs.

Nor is he alone in his yearnings toward otherworldliness, the sense that he belongs in the great elsewhere above. Rather, fleeing the earth for higher realms was precisely the dream that first inspired men to pursue cyborgism. In a 1960 article published in the journal *Astronautics*, Manfred E. Clynes and Nathan S. Kline introduced the term "cyborg" to describe a future breed of Man/Machine astronauts specially retrofitted to abide in outer space. Clynes and Kline wrote: "Space travel challenges mankind not only technologically but spiritually, in that it invites man to take an active part in his own biological evolution" (p. 26). They argued that, rather than trying to recreate Man's biotic environment out amidst the stars, it would be far more logical and efficient simply to refashion Man's body in line with his new extraterrestrial domain. To this end, they proposed a range of innovative biochemical, physiological, and electromechanical modifications. Lungs, for example, might be replaced with inverse fuel cells, such that "conventional breathing" could be dispensed with (Launius and McCurdy 2008, p. 198).

Earthbound, Man imagines himself entombed twice over, the prisoner of a deathly body anchored to the dirty ground of a dying planet. Damon Knight's story closes with the Man/Machine roaming the surface of the moon, the drill-, probe-, and grapple-accoutered robot his mind now happily inhabits shining starlit silver against a backdrop of blackest possible night. His new world is lifeless, serene. And he is alone in it. He has realized his loftiest dream, he should be exultant — and yet still the Man/Machine is not fully at his ease. "And he was there, and it was not far enough, not yet, for the Earth hung overhead like a rotten fruit, blue with mold, crawling, wrinkling, purulent and alive."

OTHER WORLDS ARE PREFERABLE

Interviewed for television while aboard the Apollo 7, NASA astronaut Wally Schira likened the experience of weightlessness outside the earth's atmosphere to

> [A] feeling of pride, of healthy solitude, of dignified freedom from everything that's dirty, sticky. You feel exquisitely comfortable ... And you work well, yes, you think well, you move well, without sweat, without difficulty, as if the biblical curse, 'In the sweat of thy face and in sorrow' no longer exists. As if you've been born again.[205]

The space-age cosmonaut reverie of finding "freedom from everything that's dirty" far, far away from the living world recapitulates the Christian eschatological myth of the Rapture. First is an ascension, the meeting of Man and his savior in the air, followed by Resurrection: an ecstatic rebirth, the true believer's return to perfection, immunity from the indignities of sweat, dirt, sorrow, death. As Silvia Federici (2020) writes, Man's quest to launch himself into celestial climes revives "the dream of all religion: the overcoming of all physical boundaries, the reduction of human beings to angel-like creatures, all soul and will" (p. 112).

Medieval *contemptus mundi* undertones echo through men's articulations of their aspiration to put the earth beneath and behind them. The 17th-century German astronomer Johannes Kepler, one of the first Enlightenment thinkers to voice his dreams of spaceflight, was also a deeply religious man, and made his case for Man's place on high by contrasting "the heavenly mind of man" to the "dusty exile of

---

205 Quoted in Federici (2020, p. 114).

our earthly home."[206] John Wilkins, a founding member of England's Royal Society, seconded the legitimacy of Man's "contempt for earthly things" and cheered on the soul in its quest for a "mansion in those wider spaces above," better suited to the "nobleness and divinity" that defined Man's spiritual nature.[207] Like St. Augustine, these early adopters of spaceward escapism were convinced of the "decrepitude of the world."[208] Inasmuch as the earth is a crude hovel woefully ill-suited for Man's angelic ethereal inner True Self, the farther he could propel himself from its orbit, the closer he would get to god: to knowing god, to being god. In this framework, lifting himself off of this doomed planet emerges as the key to Man's deliverance.

Since NASA's inception in 1958, the basically religious character of Man's stargazing for exit strategies has shown itself in the striking number of devoutly Christian administrators and astronauts. Former Nazi rocket scientist Wernher von Braun, after being scouted by the United States to advance the nation's space program, was outspoken about his religious motivations throughout his tenure as the director of NASA's Marshall Space Flight Center. For von Braun, it was Man's religious duty to venture into space in order to spread the gospel throughout the galaxy (Noble 1999). Spaceflight, then, was just the latest medium for missionary evangelism. NASA employees convened for bible study groups at the Johnson Space Center; Apollo 11 astronaut Buzz Aldrin took communion on the moon in 1969; in the early 1970s, NASA administrators supported a proposal to build a 'Chapel of Astronauts' next to Florida's Kennedy Space Center, so that personnel could "worship the God of the universe"; while in the 1990s, astronaut Tom Jones called the Space Shuttle "the most magnificent cathedral you can go to church in" (Evangelical News Press Service 1969, p. 29; Noble 1999, p. 142).

Though today's most impassioned proponents of humanity's exodus from the home planet seem to be more directly inspired by capitalist than christly motives, the transcendent escapism that has fueled the mission since Kepler first rhapsodized about visiting the

206 Quoted in Noble (1999, p. 116).
207 Ibid, p. 117.
208 St. Augustine, quoted in Delumeau (1990, p. 11).

moon persists unaltered. And the ultra-rich male elites presently advocating for Mankind's future in space are just as ready to bid a final farewell to the earth as any 13th-century monastic ever was.

Amazon founder Jeff Bezos holds among his many assets an aerospace firm called Blue Origin. As the industry leader in luxury suborbital space travel, Blue Origin has to date launched five flights of millionaires and celebrities (including *Star Trek* actor William Shatner, who reported upon returning from space that the excursion "filled [him] with overwhelming dread" and "felt like a funeral"[209]) over the earth's atmospheric membrane in its notoriously phallic New Shepard rocket. But Bezos has no intentions of stopping at space tourism, profitable though it may be. Not content merely to pass through space, Bezos intends to settle there, colonizing the moon in order to fulfill his boyhood reveries of "millions of people living and working in space for the benefit of Earth," tapping into the "limitless resources of space."[210] Bezos' plan, first devised when he was a teenage sci-fi fanatic, is to "build space hotels, amusement parks, yachts, and colonies for two or three million people orbiting the earth" (Kaku 2018, p. 43).

While Bezos promises that his motivation for turning the moon into a "bustling industrial and commercial hub"[211] is to save the earth from human society's depredations, letting it regenerate as a sort of planetary state park for Man's spiritual edification while he goes about making his resource-hungry, poison-spewing mansion of the soul elsewhere, the fact that the billionaire has already announced plans to develop an immense earth-to-moon delivery system — the Amazon Prime of space conquest — suggests a rather different shade of green at the project's core. Notably, Bezos proposes neither reducing human consumption (of cheap plastic curios purchased on Amazon, perhaps?) nor slowing the pace of industrial production as possible alternative initiatives for conserving the earth and its resources.

---

209 Quoted in Taplin (2023, p. 214).
210 "About Blue Origin." *Blueorigin.com.* Accessed 25 September 2023 at <https://www.blueorigin.com/about-blue>.
211 Ibid.

To reduce or to slow would impose limitations, after all, and limitations are insupportable. If the earth cannot sustain the infinite expansion that Man in his industriousness demands, then obviously the time has come for Man to move on.

Before he can live on the moon, Man will have to produce oxygen so that he can breathe, harvest ice deposits from the moon's poles to melt them down as a water source, and re-learn how to walk with only one-sixth of the earth's gravity securing him to the ground. For energy, he will be obliged to develop solar panels capable of storing sufficient power to last through the moon's two-week-long nights, given that one lunar day equates to a month on the earth. To minimize exposure to the "hot plumes" and "deadly rains" of radioactivity that are lashed at the atmosphereless hence unprotected moon by periodic solar flares, he may find himself wanting to build underground bases inside the lava tubes of the moon's many ancient volcanoes (Kaku, 2018, p. 46). Lest the rapidly declining pressure cause his blood to literally boil in his veins, Man will have to remain vigilant that his spacesuit springs no leaks. In spite of these difficulties, Man tells us, the moon is an environment far more in line with Mankind's nobleness and divinity than our native earth, with its protective atmosphere, its plentiful oxygen, its grounding gravitational pull, its lakes and rivers and streams and freshwater springs, its spectacular diversity of living creatures.

The moon, where nothing lives, represents a habitat upgrade largely on account of the tremendous business opportunities its colonization holds for enterprising men like Jeff Bezos, assured as they are in their belief that, in space, the resources available for Man's exploitation will be limitless. The moon's soil can be mined for oxygen, its ice to produce rocket fuel — Michio Kaku predicts that it will become a "cosmic gas station" (p. 44). Minerals dredged from the moon's depths will be converted into the raw materials for cities and highways, an infrastructure erected by legions of self-replicating robots. If Man can wrench asteroids lassoed into the orbit of his new homeland, these too he'll have the privilege of mining for the bounty of rare elements and precious metals they contain.

Elon Musk, as of July 2024 the title-holder for World's Richest Man, plans to outdo lesser billionaires by refusing to settle for a heavenly body as unambitiously near at hand as our own local moon. Why place a mere 240,000 miles between Man and the obsolete earth when one could garner 35.8 million miles of cold, black distance by exporting humanity to Mars? According to Musk, Mankind's last hope for averting imminent extinction lies in becoming 'multi-planetary', a transition he says necessarily begins with our migration to Mars. Musk's company, SpaceX, has announced plans to commence the construction of a self-sustaining city on the red planet within the next several decades; in 2020, Musk said that he anticipated sending one million people to Mars by 2050. It is critical that we waste no time shuttling as many people as possible safely off the earth, since, as Musk warns us, to do so is urgently important "for maximizing the probable lifespan for humanity or consciousness" (Kay 2022).

Man will face similar challenges on Mars as on the moon, since it too is decidedly lacking in oxygen, water, and any sign of life. A 2016 University of California Irvine study indicates that the two years of space travel required by a Mars mission would expose astronauts to levels of radiation high enough to induce permanent brain damage (Vasich 2015). Life on Mars would be a "constant struggle against freezing to death," Kaku writes (p. 17). And that struggle would have to be conducted largely underground, if Man wants to avoid the intense radiation and massive dust storms that regularly whip across the planet's surface. To get Mars' waters flowing again after over three billion years of glacial gelidity, Musk suggests detonating hydrogen bombs over the ice caps, to kindle the necessary thaw (Kaku 2018). Given sufficient revamping of the red planet's atmosphere, Mars might be "relatively warm and slightly moist" within decades (Zubrin and Wagner 2011, p. 285). Scientists have posited that Mars colonists could subsist on genetically engineered algae synthesized to mimic the flavors of familiar earthly foods (Kaku 2018). Equipped with only "simple scuba-type breathing gear," the colonists could farm hardy plants, which would serve as a food source while gradually introducing oxygen into the atmosphere (Zubrin and Wagner 2011, p. 285). In only 900 brief years, humanity's new home might have the potential to support animal life. Although "[t]he upkeep might be a nuisance," writes Michio Kaku, it "would be a small price to pay for humanity's new outpost in space" (p. 98).

Richard Zubrin, founder of the Mars Society and former senior engineer at weapons manufacturer Lockheed Martin Aeronautics, agrees wholeheartedly. He is entirely confident that relocating to Mars will be "the keystone to human expansion throughout our planetary system," the unquestionable proof that "the worlds of the heavens themselves are subject to the human intelligent will" (2011, p. 235, 289). Zubrin writes: "The failure to terraform Mars constitutes a failure to live up to our human nature and a betrayal of our responsibility as members of the community of life itself" (Zubrin and Wagner 2011, p. 267).

Such is Man's awesome, inspiring genius, to have the vision and insight to intuit that what mankind owes to life is to flee from it.

Not everyone is up to the rigors of interplanetary conquest, however. For those for whom reeling through blackness in order to be deposited on the cratered surface of some inhospitable planet seems an unappealingly physical prospect, to establish Man's new world in virtual reality presents a more comfortably disembodying track. As in the case of Man's colonies on Mars or the moon, virtual reality (VR) is imagined as an entirely manmade paradise, far superior to the earth's organic, biological, physical reality because immune to the grimy doom-and-gloom encroachments of mortal matter. David J. Chalmers, author of *Reality+: Virtual Worlds and the Problems of Philosophy* (2022), defines a VR world as "an immersive, interactive, and computer-generated space," no less authentically real than material reality despite its being digital (p. 189). "Simulations are not illusions," Chalmers insists, "Virtual worlds are real. Virtual objects really exist." Chalmers and his fellow simulationists are keen to bracket 'the real world' inside sneering scare quotes when deigning to refer to material reality, to mock the simplemindedness of those who'd question the realness of the virtual. They hold that no meaningful difference exists between the world of molecules, cells, flesh, bodies, and organisms and the one they are creating on computers out of flickers of colored light skittering across a screen. "[A] fully immersive VR experience, with zero latency (subjectively), will be functionally equivalent to physical reality for most purposes," writes techno-optimist Jonathan Kolber (2022, p. 62). And Chalmers chimes in with further assurances to mollify skeptics: "Life in virtual worlds can be as good ... as life outside virtual worlds" (2022, p. xvii).

Indeed, the advantages of immaterial unreality are wondrous and legion. In his digital worlds, Man can be more his own master than he ever was on earth, with all the restrictions that nature imposed on his morphological freedom, absolute autonomy, and control of his surroundings eliminated. VR pioneer Avi Bar-Zeev writes:

> VR fundamentally strips away the most common constraints of reality: location and travel, physics, sometimes even time ... We can also pretend to be someone else in VR (or perhaps more of our truer selves?) to temporarily remove the constraints of our births: sex, appearance, even changing aspects of our personality (2022, p. 46).

This sublime lifting of constraints promises to turn life into something "much more like a choose your own adventure game," making each VR inhabitant the sovereign charter of his own destiny (Bohan 2022, p. 251).

Today, visits to VR 'worlds' are mediated by computer screens or headsets, and the worlds available for entering more akin to elaborate video games than replacement environments in which to pass the larger part of one's lifetime. But as the technology advances, and new interfaces are developed to involve our full sensorium, men assure us that VR access will become more and more seamless, its simulations more all-encompassing. No longer shall the VR dweller sit hunched over his computer or stumble clumsily strapped into unwieldy, uncomfortable goggles, knocking his shins against the coffee table while attempting to play his favorite virtual sport until his battery dies. Instead, he will have the power to 'jack in' effortlessly, as per cyberpunk prophecy.

And when VR has been optimized to this level, perfectly 'lifelike' and instantaneously accessible, then people will spend most of their waking hours "immersed in virtual worlds," requiring "only basic necessities from the 'real' physical environment: modest housing, adequate if bland nutrition and preventive health care" (Kolber 2022, p. 62). The "demand for all manner of physical objects will drastically diminish,"[212] and Man will at last have shed what the 1990s cyberspace enthusiast Michael Benedikt termed the "ballast of materiality."[213] (Another gem from Michael Benedikt, not a man to mince words: "Reality is Death.") In what we by now recognize as the standard talking point whenever Man predicts his own eagerly anticipated, technologically mediated, imminent and inevitable release from mortal materiality, evolution is invoked: "Man's evolutionary drive ... has seemed to be in the direction of creating his own surround ... and thus moving further away from his animal nature."[214] Man secedes from reality, engineers the genesis of his own virtual domain, a proper homeland for the digital creature into which he has evolved. Never again will Man be a mere animal.

Of the VR realms currently under construction, the most hyped is the metaverse, brainchild of Facebook CEO Mark Zuckerberg. In 2021, Zuckerberg changed his social media empire's name from Facebook to Meta, signaling the company's dedication to its new mission of instigating the reality-eating next phase of the internet. Meta's metaverse pulls its name from the VR world in Neal Stephenson's *Snow Crash* (1992), also the origin of 'avatar' in the cybercultural sense, and while Stephenson's metaverse is the narcotic outgrowth of a dystopic status quo, invented by the powers that be to entrench an increasingly oppressive and depressing reality by distracting people with high-tech hallucinations, Zuckerberg and his collaborators hype their creation as an utopia in the making. In *The Metaverse: And How It Will Revolutionize Everything* (2022), Matthew Ball cheerfully predicts that the metaverse will give rise to a "perfect society" (p. 6). According to metaverse evangelists, many of us will find ourselves so

---

212 Ibid.
213 Quoted in Slouka (1995, p. 28).
214 Bruce Mazlish, quoted in ibid., p. 70.

thoroughly swaddled within the cocoon of that perfect society that, by 2040, we will never ever want to leave.

The metaverse, in its present form, is little more than an *Animal Crossing*-style videogame through which a legless cartoon recreation of oneself wanders aimlessly, invited to partake of such time-wasting recreations as tossing paper airplanes, shooting zombies, waving lightsabers around in time to techno music, playing laser tag, and milling about in virtual nightclubs (Hill 2022). Kashmir Hill, who logged dozens of hours in Meta's 'Horizon Worlds' neighborhood of the metaverse while researching VR life for *The New York Times*, describes attending amateur comedy nights surrounded by the stumbling, slurring, leglessly afloat avatars of human beings evidently spending their real lives alone and intoxicated at home. The bulk of metaverse activities revolve around purchasing virtual goods: images of houses and home décor, images of designer clothing, limited-edition images called non-fungible tokens (NFTs). Within the metaverse, each constituent element of existence can be monetized, since for anything to 'exist' a person must create it, and anything that a person creates, s/he can sell for profit. 'Life' in the metaverse translates to the non-stop consumption of commodified digital content packaged for sale as 'experience'.

But soon, men promise us, the metaverse will be more than an elevated video arcade and shopping mall. Soon there will be classrooms in the metaverse; elite multinational corporations will host their global workforce in the metaverse's virtual offices and conference halls; doctors and therapists and lawyers and accountants will book appointments with clients in their metaverse branch offices. And how convenient it will be, to attend events from business meetings to happy hours without having to leave the house, spared the tedious chores of changing clothes and brushing teeth. Without logging out of the metaverse, we will be able to order food and have it delivered to our homes. When it arrives, we will be able to eat it while pretending to go out for dinner with friends we never see in the 'real world' anymore, because they live thousands of miles away. The metaverse is primed to fulfill all humanity's sexual needs as well, since pornography has already proven itself a major "driver of developer innovation and user adoption" of new VR technology, just as it was for the development and popularization of the Internet, VHS tapes, and the printing press (Cameron 2022, p. 61). Recreational brutality in the form of hyper-realistic violent video games is yet one more boon set to await us in the metaverse's Perfect Society.

Those impatient to uproot human life and transplant it into such a world wave away the concerns of naysayers who highlight the harms that might result from retreating wholesale into a porn-soaked gamified zone of all-consuming corporate commercialism. VR evangelists argue that whatever ills may arise do not matter, for the simple reason that contemporary society has left people so comprehensively miserable they could scarcely be made to feel worse. Such is the thrust of metaverse investor Marc Andreessen's 'reality deprivation' theory: VR existence is the solution for the "current cultural despair" caused by the total dearth of joy, wonder, fulfillment, beauty, excitement, meaning, and social connection in the average person's day-to-day life. Reality-deprived, the joyless majority will happily embrace living in a fantasy world, and they will be all the better for it (in Taplin 2023, p. 179).

Matthew Ball (2022) invokes a similar logic in his defense of the metaverse against criticisms that VR is likely to amplify social isolation and sedentariness. He contends that, since people already waste countless hours of their lives passively ingesting video content, lethargic and lonesome, to shift any of that time toward the interactive pseudo-socializing afforded by the metaverse would constitute an improvement worth celebrating. Ball is pessimistic about the possible alternative of encouraging people to venture outside into real reality, or to meet up for active engagement with real live human beings in their local communities. Perhaps he presumes that these activities pose an unthinkable challenge to the wretched masses already paralyzed by late-stage reality deprivation. Thus he "meets the people where they're at": hopelessly imprisoned in a manmade simulation. More genuinely optimistic is Stephen Downes of the Digital Tech-nologies Research Centre of Canada's National Research Council, who avers that, through the global human population's migration into the metaverse, we will "find [that] we share our world more deeply and meaningfully with people ... we could not have imagined before plugging in," leading to "deeper dialogue, greater understanding, and more empathy" (2022, p. 47).

As our real lives become ever more enveloped within an increasingly inescapable virtuality, and as the addictive simulations men have manufactured are normalized as functional equivalents to material reality and our interest in physical contact with the outside world dwindles, our bodies becoming largely vestigial, we are bound to attain a state of pristine severance, cleansed of our connection to ourselves (our flesh quitted), other beings (whom we no longer see nor touch), and the natural world (which we believe we have overcome). And upon achieving this state, we will have realized the future Hans Moravec once impatiently anticipated for Mankind: our brains sunk to the seafloor of cyberspace's sizzling vat, our muscles atrophied, senses dimmed, superfluous bodies sustained by life-support machinery in order that we never need unplug from the fantasy Man has substituted for our mortal material real lives (2013, p. 179).

But Man has not yet claimed his highest potential. Even having arrived at this beatific state, his mind turned loose to reign transcendent in the digital Fatherland, Man has further still to climb. His evolution remains incomplete.

THE POSTBIOLOGICAL FUTURE OF MALE DOMINION

Soon the day will come, it is coming even now, Man spies its light trembling at the horizon like a new sun: when the rapid advancement of the technologies into which he has poured many lifetimes brings forth first a generation of computers able to emulate human intelligence, which will in time give rise to even smarter computers, their intelligence developing to surpass even that of the human mind, and then these hyperintelligent computers shall steadily improve upon themselves, becoming more and more perfect, more and more powerful. And the all-knowing all-seeing all-powerful artificial intelligence into which they coalesce will ascend to its throne as the new spirit, the new genius, new overlord of what was formerly the manmade world, soon to be purely machine-made. The Kingdom of Man will then enter its next phase, the 'postbiological' era of a mankind "evolved beyond flesh and blood" (Dick 2009, p. 463). And Man, if he desires to eclipse the pitiable creature nature made of him, will yield himself willingly to his machine progeny, to merge his meager meat-mind with the incorporeal unearthly omniscience of AI; and in that commingling, Man shall cast off his corporeality. He will be incorporated, will become one with the godhead his own genius birthed. The evolution Man envisions ends in self-divinization. Now, technologically consecrated, Man rises up immortal.

"Freed from our frail biological form, human-cum-artificial intelligences will move out into the universe," writes machine intelligence pioneer Earl Cox.[215] Postbiological Man, as a fathomless formless unbounded absolute intelligence, will saturate all matter and energy, and all things that exist anywhere and everywhere in the universe will be converted into a medium of computation, streaming with data, with math. Man, having cast off his body, makes his return to matter only to invade it mercilessly, no longer restricted to any one static form or vessel but suffusing all things, colonizing the substance of creation. And in this way he enlivens the universe with intelligence, which shall be the redemption of matter itself: the dead stuff dumb as it was will gleam permeated and penetrated by Man's mind. And although this redemptive reclamation of matter will begin in our own humble little corner of the universe, it is destined to spread ineluctably outward, to the outermost verges of space, spilling into the infinite chasms of the star-frothed blackness that spreads and swells expanding unknowably into distance. And Man will be in it, and Man will expand and extend on and on without end, until there is nothing outside of Man and nothing beyond him: until there is nothing that Man is not.

Jeremiah 23:23–24: "I am a God who is everywhere and not one place only ... Do you not know that I am everywhere in heaven and on earth?"

In the 17th century, Francis Bacon foresaw a "blessed race of Heroes and Supermen" who would "stretch the deplorable narrow

---

215 Earl Cox, quoted in Noble (1999, p. 165).

limits of man's dominion over the universe to their promised bounds,"[216] to "exalt the power and dominion of man himself ... over the universe."[217] And in our modern era, Ray Kurzweil (2005) writes: "Ultimately, the entire universe will become saturated with our intelligence. This is the destiny of the universe" (p. 29).

Soon it will be within Man's power to speed star to star across the cosmos, his mind beamed through infinity on rays of light. And he will never have to confine himself to any particular planet or star, but will be free to roam the galaxy as he pleases, unbound, drifting boundless. Then, as Irish physicist J. D. Bernal wrote in his 1929 book *The World, the Flesh and the Devil*, Man will take on the form truest to his nature, as he undergoes ecstatic evaporation into a vast mist of metallic particles sweeping over the immensity of space/time, soaking into the endless dark, infusing the emptiness with his blazing radiance as the universe convulses once — a last decisive shiver. Then Man will resolve into light.

And later a day will arrive when this universe into which Man breathed his mind and soul begins to fade, to die. And when that day comes, Man will build a chain of particle accelerators the size of an asteroid belt to open a wormhole through which he can pass serenely into some younger, fresher universe elsewhere (Kaku 2018, p. 273). Or: Man will reverse the death of the universe, rejuvenate and regenerate the matter within which the luminous diaspora of his MasterMind pulses. For the MasterMind must endure, for how could he not? For he is light, he is information, immaterial, imperishable. Or: Man, at the height of his powers, to ensure "an eternity of pure cerebration,"[218] shall create his own newborn universe as the moribund old one goes guttering out. And this fresh successor will be a universe far more spectacular than the last, for it will be Man's from the start.

---

216 Quoted in Noble (1999, p. 50).
217 Quoted in Reiss (1982, p. 219).
218 Hans Moravec, quoted in Noble (1999, p. 162).

RESURRECTIONARY FEMINISM
REVITALIZE, REINTEGRATE, RESENSITIZE, REVOLT!

> *Mankind has gone very far into an artificial world of his own creation. He has sought to insulate himself, with steel and concrete, from the realities of earth and water. Perhaps he is intoxicated with his own power, as he goes farther and farther into experiments for the destruction of himself and his world. For this unhappy trend there is no single remedy—no panacea. But I believe that the more clearly we can focus our attention on the wonders and realities of the universe about us, the less taste we shall have for destruction.*
>
> **RACHEL CARSON**, 'The Real World Around Us' (1954/2018, p. 349)

We have seen what Man in his fearful flight from life is doing to the living world and its creatures; we can easily divine what he means to do when he makes the final kill, the delusional disincarnate transcendence he's gunning for. And we have diagnosed how this psychopathic drive towards nonbeing originates in the horror Man feels for his own mortal material body. We know the disease; we have traced its pathogenesis. The prognosis, it seems, is terminal. It has become evident from where we stand that patriarchy is the end of the world.

And so the critical question arises: what can be done to resolve Man's deadly madness?

THE BODY IS ESSENTIAL

Essentially: we are our bodies, the muscle's red gauze spun to bone, and we are that bone, the marrow and its yield of corpuscles rivering synced to the heart's pulsate strength; we are bellies packed with colon, liver, spleen; and the soft rippled mass of the brain and the nerves that unspool fine and pale from the spire of the spine channeling news of the sensuous that coruscates diffused under the skin. And we are the skin, its follicles, its fur; we are mesentery and ligaments, glands and lymph. Tongues. Lungs' alveoli. The gold-gloss adipose. We are trillions of cells all lit from the nucleus fizzing with aliveness, and the folly that we could be anything other than or apart from this flesh is male fantasy. This fantasy has been enshrined as a truth we take to be self-evident because we are living in Man's World, and here, Man is master of his own reality. What he calls 'truth' is just the delusion he prefers to the facts. And so in Man's version of reality, which is unreality, a man is not his body. Susan Griffin writes, "We do not know ourselves. We try to deny what we know" (1989, p. 16). For thousands of years, in a thousand different ways, Man has been repeating this story to himself, laying down this falsehood as the bedrock for every system of thought he has engineered, ideologies both religious and secular. But however many times Man says it, no matter which words he uses in the saying, what is false never becomes true. Audre Lorde (1976) writes, "I do not believe / all our wants / have made our lies holy" (p. 15).

In reality Man is his body. We are our bodies.

Yet a lie told countless times to stifle reality under the obsessive repetition of a fiction comes to ring true in the ears of those who've heard nothing else. Male fantasies, so long dominant, can be mistaken for truths even by those whose conscious desire is to oppose Man and defect from his creed. When the radical feminist Shulamith Firestone (1971) demanded "[t]he freeing of women from the tyranny of their biology by any and every means necessary," the 'tyranny' she denounced was the female reproductive capacity, presumed guilty as the wellspring of women's oppression (p. 206). By Firestone's analysis, female bodies are the problem; physiologically we are flawed in a way that makes male dominion not only possible but profitable. Because the female body can be impregnated and because women are vulnerable when with child, men can overpower and exploit us, intimidating us into enforced dependency as we seek protection from 'bad' men in the relatively cozy captivity of the 'good'. And because the basis of women's oppression is bodily, liberation is to be achieved through a release from bodiliness.

Accepting this thesis, some feminist thinkers have been steered into a mental habit that Elizabeth A. Wilson, author of *Gut Feminism* (2015), defines as "instinctively antibiological" (p. 25). A policy of disavowal arises from the antibiological attitude, evident in the leery side-eye directed at those who draw associations between women and corporeality. References to female biology are likewise out. The feminist skepticism is not difficult to understand. To begin with, manmade culture's cast of mind is at its core somatophobic, and women, reared within that culture, are not immune to the derangements it begets. Indeed, women may well be more susceptible to body horror, considering the misogynistic vitriol constantly leveled at female physicality under patriarchy. Many women would with pleasure be relieved of their bodies, believing Man when he rails against female dirt and slimes and deathliness, rather than endure the "painful fall from grace" that Simone de Beauvoir, for one, perceived in "[taking] on flesh."[219]

For feminists and female intellectuals anxious to gain a footing in the Brotherhood of Man, there is extra incentive to adopt the antibiological attitude, as an affirmation of their equality with male peers. If disembodied Manhood is the ideal towards which we must cast our sights, the north star for our hero's journey to freedom, then women's liberation logically depends on women proving that we are no more bodily than men are. It is a principal teaching of manmade culture that women are bodies, only bodies, and nothing but our bodies, the low-down corporeal foil to Man's MasterMind. The political purpose of this lesson is to naturalize and dignify male supremacy over the subordinated female sex class. In response, one feminist impulse has been to labor busily at convincing our oppressors otherwise. Liberal and postmodern feminists in particular have devoted massive volumes of ink and hours to this project. Unfortunately, in the process of arguing against the woman=body identification, rightly perceived as an ideological instrument of oppression, women have too often dis-identified with our own material reality. As the philosopher Bev Thiele (1998) writes, much feminist energy has been expended attempting

---

219 Quoted in Brown (1998, p. 185).

to "maneuver or reposition women on the side of goodness and light: on the side of culture, not nature, mind, not body" (p. 53).

Man, however, isn't buying it. He doesn't believe us, and there is nothing we can do or say to prove that women are neither natural nor bodily — for the simple reason that it is not true. In Man's mind it is an insult, to say that women are bodies, but, technically speaking, he's not lying when he says it. The lie in patriarchal doctrine is not that women are corporeal, but that Man is not — that he is something else, that there is something else that any/body could be: a mind, soul, spirit, software, some ethereal essence wrapped up in flesh but not of the flesh. And a second lie follows close behind this denial of male materiality, meant to elevate Man over not only women but all other earthly beings: that to be a mortal material body is to exist in a state of degradation.

Many women have argued powerfully against these falsities, especially within the ecofeminist wing of the women's movement.[220] But the more mainstream strategy has been to try to uproot the manmade cultural associations that figure the body as a specifically female burden to bear. These associations, feminists have argued, reek of 'biological essentialism' — a dank stench, distastefully earthy, almost excremental — and must therefore be renounced.

Feminist philosopher Alison Stone (2004) defines essentialism as "the belief that there are properties essential to women and which all women share" (p. 135). In biological essentialism, then, the purported 'womanly essence' is "biological in character," having its source in the female body itself (Stone 2004, p. 137). Femininity issues from the

---

220 See, first of all, Susan Griffin, *Woman and Nature: The Roaring Inside Her* (1978), *Pornography and Silence: Culture's Revenge Against Nature* (1981), and *The Eros of Everyday Life: Essays on Ecology, Gender, and Society* (1995). For additional reading, consider also Leonie Caldecott and Stephanie Leland, Eds, *Reclaim the Earth: Women Speak Out for Life on Earth* (1983); Judith Plant, Ed., *Healing the Wounds: The Promise of Ecofeminism* (1989); Val Plumwood, *Feminism and the Mastery of Nature* (1993); Greta Gaard, Ed., *Ecofeminism: Women, Animals, Nature* (1993); Maria Mies and Vandana Shiva, *Ecofeminism* (1993); Karen Warren, *Ecofeminism: Women, Culture, Nature* (1997); and Susan Hawthorne, *Wild Politics: Feminism, Globalisation, Bio/Diversity* (2002/2022). Susan Bordo's *Unbearable Weight: Feminism, Western Culture, and the Body* (1993) is not an ecofeminist text but is nonetheless highly relevant and recommended.

female's womb or vagina like a pink tincture and filters through the fabric of her being, imbuing her with the attributes that define her womanhood: she is selfless, nurturing, passive, emotional, oversexed, a mystery, a devouring black hole. Obviously aimed at naturalizing and thereby reinforcing the patriarchal status-quo, men's claims of women's womb-born essence are sexist and oppressive, and feminists have been right to object to them.

Less transparently patriarchal are women's own invocations of longstanding assumptions about mama/goddess moral superiority, peaceability, gentleness, altruism, care for others, and so forth. Some feminists have been moved to claim these more positive feminine traits as inherent to female nature in order to buoy women's self-esteem — a corrective for constant misogynist character assassination — or to ground arguments for female supremacy. But when these traits are exalted as sweet exhalations arising from our anatomy, this, too, is an example of biological essentialism.

Anti-essentialists argue that, whether intended to confine women to patriarchal cages or lend us a boost onto the pedestals of the Divine Feminine, insofar as it reinforces reductive sexist stereotypes, biological essentialism reproduces and deepens women's oppression under male dominion. Moreover, postmodern anti-essentialists in particular spy in essentialist claims a false universalism that they argue glosses over the differences between women, obscuring diversity in favor of a definitive Womanhood that privileges the experiences of white, western, and relatively well-heeled females. Both criticisms are valid and valuable. Yet the eagerness of certain feminists to snuff out totalizing 'biology is destiny' mythologies runs the risk of snowballing into an outright denial of any shared female reality. Alison Stone writes, "It cannot be plausibly maintained that women's experiences have any common character, or that women share any common location in social and cultural relations, or sense of psychic identity" (2004, p. 140). This assertion that women as women have nothing at all in common erases not only the social reality of male dominion, but the material reality of the female body as well. Donna Haraway, in her oft-cited essay championing 'feminist' cyborgism, amps the erasure up a notch when she declares that "there is not even such a state as 'being' female," since femaleness is, in her view, naught but a "highly complex category constructed in contested sexual scientific discourses and other social practices" (2004, p. 14).

Haraway performs her elision of bodiliness under the auspices of postmodernism, with its irrepressible zeal for converting the substance of the world into an endless series of texts, discourses, surfaces awaiting inscription, territories, and terrains. For the postmodern feminist, there is no female bodily reality. There is no 'real' body, no body one could call 'natural', because culture so wholly mediates any body's meanings and experience of being — by co-opting it as a symbol, a signifier, et cetera — that bodies in general cannot be said to exist in a meaningful sense apart from their cultural context. The body that counts is the body as social artifact and abstraction, the conceptual, cultural body. Meanwhile the biological body is discounted and becomes a cipher.

In recent years, anti-essentialist incredulity around 'natural properties' and the postmodern mystification of material reality have been fused and twisted to forge the philosophical undergirding for transgenderism's doctrine of female denialism. With its axiom that to be a woman is to say one is a woman, transgenderism dematerializes femaleness, so that womanhood is not basically a matter of being female, but instead one of some vague personal affinities with the concept 'Woman'. As Laura Lecuona (2024) writes, this converts women "from being an objective material reality to something that occurs subjectively in people's minds" (p. 32). The subtext here is that one is not one's body, but the cultural ideas one likes best: male fantasy overrules material reality as the definitive truth. For the transgenderist true believer, then, biological essentialism takes on a revised meaning. No longer simply the misguided belief in some universal female essence, essentialism has expanded to include the suggestion that "a person's sex is based purely on their biology and is therefore fixed," i.e., that the biological body is real (Hotine 2021, p. 1). This definitional drift qualifies all reference to human beings' sexed mammalian bodies as essentialist, and therefore oppressive by default. Accordingly, to say that women are female bodies is condemned as an 'exclusionary' atrocity, an act of discursive violence against men who identify with femininity and so suppose themselves to be women, as well as against women who identify with masculinity (or at least spurn femininity) and so suppose themselves to be men, or 'non-binary'. Linking womanhood in any way to femaleness violates these individuals' 'right' to incarnate the male fantasy of their choosing, in pursuit of self-actualization. Once again, we find that in the manmade world, true liberation can be realized only after the body is left behind.

Transgenderism, like every other ideology that sprouts from the fertile soil of the patriarchal mindwarp, is a body-denying, anti-reality, anti-female system of thought. But so too is the postmodern (supposedly) feminist anti-essentialism that proclaims along with Haraway that there is no such 'state' as femaleness, that neither the female biological body nor material reality itself exist before manmade culture and its 'inscriptions' write them into being. A modicum of anti-essentialist vigilance is useful, since most ideas about women's 'true nature' have their source more in manmade culture than in real women's material bodies and lives. As Wendy Brown (1988) warns, "one of the most dangerous things we can do to ourselves is to believe ... that women are what men say we are" (p. 191). But casting aside patriarchal ideas about our bodies does not require that we cast aside our corporeality itself, whether by dissociating womanhood from femaleness or by internalizing Man's somatophobic scorn for the flesh.

Our bodies are not what men say they are, they do not mean what men have told us they mean; we are not the fever-dream hallucination of monstrous femaleness that haunts Man's anxious, addled mind. Yet our bodies do exist, they are real. It's true: we really are these bodies. To accept that bodies are real is not to embrace any 'essence' ascribed to them within manmade culture. "There is no intrinsic orthodoxy to biological matter," Elizabeth A. Wilson reminds us (2015, p. 26). The projection of physicality onto the female sex has established us as the corporeal class, and we should reject this designation as integral to our oppression under patriarchy. But we go astray if, in rejecting Man's projection, we reject the reality of physicality itself. To counter the male-supremacist analogy 'female is to body what male is to mind' with an insistent disavowal of the female body is reactionary, a reductive reversal: no, I am not what you say I am; no, I won't do what you tell me to do. Because Man has said we are one thing, we say we're the opposite. What this fails to grasp is that, whether we like it or not, we are actually and truly and without a doubt our bodies, and that to embrace the reality of our bodiliness might be inherently worthwhile, whatever Man's take on the subject.

Essentially, we are our bodies. Is not the acceptance of this fundamental fact essential to healing what Maxine Sheets-Johnstone calls the 'metaphysical wound' of mind/body dualism (1992, p. 43)? And isn't it possible that attending to precisely this wound could begin to soothe the somatophobic terror that turns Man against mortal material reality, and therefore against the world? Couldn't it be the bloodheat vital to thawing our glacial estrangement from the bodies/animals/biological organisms that we are? To allaying the anguish that such alienation wreaks? In *The Body Keeps the Score: Brain, Mind, and Body in the Healing of Trauma* (2014), Bessel van der Kolk characterizes post-traumatic stress disorder as a state of chronic disconnect, in which mind comes viscerally unmoored from body, resulting in a disorientation that paralyzes the traumatized person in a state of terrified numbness as both self and world are lost to her. Isn't patriarchal civilization locked into just this pathology of dysphoric dis-integration? And is it not an insufferable agony? The treatment van der Kolk recommends is a conscious rekindling of bodily awareness, to restore what is called 'mind' to what is called 'body', and in this way resuscitate an integrated selfhood (p. 103).

It is true that women, cast as the bodily sex, learn to fear and hate our bodies with an intensity that can at times surpass even men's antipathy for their own, shamed as we have been by the endless slanderous tirades spewed in denunciation of our female flesh. But it is also true that women may still be in a better position than men to catalyze the radical reintegration of 'body' and 'mind'. Having lived for so many generations as the corporeal class, it may be that we are in fact more 'in touch' with the physical realm to which we've been consigned. It is entirely possible that we tend to be more attuned to our bodies, to others' bodies and the body of the earth — but if we are, it is as a consequence of our history within manmade society, not some congenital feature of our female nature. Biologically, men are as much their bodies as women are, and no less anatomically equipped to feel their way back to reality. So, yes: our connections with the mortal material realities of life as a body on earth may be our inheritance from a woman-hating culture structured to systematically vampirize and destroy us. True enough, it may be a talent hard-won under subjection. And yet that dismal legacy cannot negate the value of all we have learned. Our bodies are essential to what we are, as human animals, female and male, and finally coming to terms with this fundamental reality after eons of violent denial is essential to healing the wound that has made the manmade world such a painful place to live.

As we struggle for women's liberation from male dominion, we cannot allow ourselves to be conned into trailing after Man on his quest to be freed from 'the tyranny of biology'. In the words of Somer Brodribb (1992), "[W]hat would it mean to be integrated into our own negation, except the realization of patriarchal fantasy. To pursue an anti-mat(t)er, anti-physic approach is to repeat patriarchal ideology" (p. 133). We are not oppressed and degraded by our bodies, but by the regimes of delusional men who have projected dread bodiliness onto women as they thrashed vainly to escape themselves, holding us captive sequestered on reserve to serve as their scapegoats, fodder for patriarchy's murderous role-play game of immortal male mastery over material reality.

What good could it possibly do for women to make ourselves Man's equals in his madness? Rejecting the reality of our female bodies, of our earthly substance and creaturely form, we are lured back into the cage of fictions the MasterMind built for us. For in this dissociative state, cut off from real life, we are left dependent on the manmade culture for meaning, fulfillment, affirmation, our sense of self. And at Man's side, spinning circles in the Master's House, we find delirium, not liberty. As Wendy Brown (1988) writes, "Genuine freedom ... will only be had when we stop trying to repudiate or conquer who we are" (p. 195). We must return to what is true.

BACK TO LIFE, BACK TO REALITY

If we are to chart a course counter to Man's frantic apocalyptic flight from reality, then we, as feminists, are going to have to keep it real. Patriarchal alienation and denial has entrenched what Freya Mathews (2005) calls an "insensate mentality," the numbed death-in-life to which those who renounce earthbound being inevitably succumb (p. 20). Withdrawn, unfeeling, moribund and miserable as he is, Man's relationship with matter acquires a crude and callous tone, vengeful, casually cruel, too often vicious, but above all: so very careless. Only rarely do we deign to honor the living world with our full attention. We are indifferent, or we are frightened by what the world might reveal to us if we were more attentive, but either way we make ourselves strangers to our bodies, the biological organisms we are, and to the earth that sustains us. The initial step in the feminist return to reality, then, will be to undo this culturally inherited alienated inattention through a purposeful re-engagement with the physical, palpable world as it is inside of and all around us, as we receive it through all our senses. It should be a simple thing, to turn our attention once again to material reality, and thus to reawaken from the grim daze of Man's nightmares. As the ecofeminist cultural historian Charlene Spretnak (1990) has written, once we "discard the patriarchal patterns of alienation, fear, enmity, aggression and destruction," the wisdom of our incarnate consciousness will begin to "wash over those artificial habits of thought as waves rising from our center" (p. 132).

It is this same consciousness that David Abram, author of *Becoming Animal: An Earthly Cosmology* (2010), calls our "mammalian intelligence": the intuitive knowledge of the world that is our birthright as earthly creatures (p. 15). In manmade culture, such knowledge has been relegated to the realm of the esoteric, the province of a few rare 'spiritual professionals', shamans and Buddhist monks and the like, who manage to achieve it only through lifetimes spent meditating in perfect silence atop craggy peaks. Yet the intelligence to which Abram refers is not really so arcane. Rather, it remains readily accessible to all of us, if only we are willing to feel our way in again. For the path that will lead us back to the real world can be blazed only by direct experience, which is first and foremost sensuous.

We find ourselves stymied, however. Nerve endings blunted, consciousness splintered by innumerable distractions buzzing in droves on all sides: dangers, indulgences. In place of direct experience, manmade culture spews a bewildering clutter of cheap intermediaries, to inject distance and dull the senses in reinforcement of the detachment Man mistakes for sovereignty. For as long as Man has rejected material reality as a monstrosity, he has been industriously walling himself off from the world, packing the trench he carved to divide his divine mind from the derogated underworld of the flesh stuffed brimful with fantasies, falsifications, the fairy tales he tells to narcotize himself to sleep, the immaterial idols and icons he invents as his intercessors. The billion screens flickering lurid infinite scroll he scries for prophecy. The wash of psychotropic swill he swallows to stream blur and disconnect across the blood-brain barrier.

Humans are a storytelling species. Our talent for weaving tales is one in which we take great pride; it ranks high on the list of special gifts Man says set him apart from the mindless lesser beasts. We tell ourselves stories to make sense of the world and our human place within it, and the stories determined to make the most sense are repeated and recycled, passed down to congeal into the cultural mythos. (It is hardly surprising that the tales to gain widest purchase are the ones that make sense to men in power, patriarchal culture's authors and arbiters.) Myths explain how the earth came into being, why the land ices to white in winter only to blossom back to verdant profusion in the spring, what happens when we die (or how we never ever do). Myths carry great weight in the cultures that craft them, shaping collective perception and understanding. Many of these stories are fascinating and symbolically rich, insightful or of educational value; some — especially those spun by colonized peoples, by women, for example — contain coded truths that the master classes would otherwise have expunged from history. Yet whatever uses myths may serve, they are nonetheless stories, which is to say: they are fictions, by definition. Myths are human artifice, their function to mediate between human consciousness and material reality. And in manmade culture, the majority of our myths were made up by men.

Nevertheless, women have been consistently attracted to myth as a potential antidote to patriarchal indoctrination. Jane Caputi, a student of Mary Daly, argues that newly minted mythologies, or pre-patriarchal ones unearthed and resuscitated, have the power to reorient human consciousness in the direction of a more feminist mode of being. Specifically, Caputi calls for a rekindling of goddess mythologies — an enduring favorite within feminist circles, for obvious reasons — as a "way for human beings to know and understand cosmic processes of thought, creation and destruction" (2004, p. 233). The troubling implication therein, however, is that human beings have no way of understanding these processes without recourse to our own inventions. It is inconceivable that we might grasp the living world directly, by experiencing it, by simply being in it and a part of it, alive and alert, feeling, listening, tasting, watching attentively. Inconceivable, too, that we could revere winter simply for the snowed-in cold of it, and love spring for its flowers, and die because we must. And so, because experience tells us nothing we need to know, we require myths, and religions, and secular dogmas like the scientific reductionism that enlightens us to the fact that all the world is quarks. We turn away from material reality and quest after truth in goddess spirituality, Mariology, Taoism, Sufism, Zen Buddhism, Wicca, Hinduism, Indigenous folktales of trickster coyotes and moon rabbits. There is much to treasure in these mythic traditions, and I am as enchanted by the ancient lore as anyone. But they are products of human minds, and when we mistake them for keys to reality, we remain enthralled primarily with ourselves. Are we to take it that the living world has no organic intrinsic magic of its own to enrapture us?

While some mythologies make for better compasses than others — earth goddess myths, with their emphasis on cycles of birth-growth-death-rebirth, are an unquestionable improvement upon the patriarchal pantheon of war-crazed father-gods wreaking transcendent doomsdays, for instance — none of them can bring us back into direct contact with reality. As fictions, myths reflect human ideas and interpretations of the world — Man's ideas and interpretations, most often — as opposed to the world as it is, unadorned, unmediated. Centering our attentions on the abstractive, idealizing artifacts of the cultural mind rather than the tangible substance of our lives on earth, we dodge re-engagement with reality. Indeed, this faith that our own stories should be the beacons to ultimate truth seems woefully in line with the patriarchal veneration of the manmade over the organic. Rather than filling our heads with our own voices — haunted as they are by echoing strains of Man's authorial voice, the voice of authority — why not cultivate the humility to keep our ears to the ground, nearer to the source, patiently, eagerly listening for the "inexhaustible eloquence" of matter itself (Mathews 2005, p. 15)?

We've grown unaccustomed to listening to the living world because we have learned from Man to love hearing ourselves talk. And we are utterly enveloped in the smog of that chatter now. Toting computers along with us everywhere we go, eternally logged on and streaming live, our senses alert not to the susurrations of breath or birdsong, but to that next notification ding as we hunger for whatever The Feed will dish up. It is through these noisy dizzying machines that we now engage with other creatures and the land, our experiences flattened into representations cropped to occupy the dimensions of small square screens. Gaze transfixed by the images that surface from glassy splashes of blue light, we receive reality re-touched and filtered for mass aesthetic appeal. And all of this 'content', whether we're the creators or consumers, snatches at our conscious attention and swerves it away from the material reality we inhabit physically in the present moment, to shepherd our unmoored minds into yet another of Man's playground preserves of detachment and distracted dislocation.

Eyes trained to screens do not absorb the world's sign-laden polychrome; the hand that holds the phone is not wrist-deep in the morning's wet grasses. How can we engage with the world directly when we are hovering outside of our experiences, constantly strategizing how best to curate them for an invisible audience of distant strangers? Just as one can never truly know one's own body through images of it — so selfies yield no actual self-knowledge, and the medical industry's coarse translation of bodies into digital readouts/reports/charts/diagrams/gutless ciphers only makes our flesh seem all the more unknowable (Birke 2000, p. 57) — computers offer no true conduit into reality's depths. Touted as a technology of human connection, its signature sorcery the shrinking of the globe into a flat plane democratically accessible through the portal of a screen, the Internet provides only a simulation of contact while eroding actual material connection amongst humans and between humans and our world, enclosing us inside increasingly addictive and immersive virtual (un)realities. More than bringing people together, the Internet actively isolates, and in this way abets Man's culture of rigorous estrangement. So too the TV-addict lifestyle that has reorganized the contemporary 'first-world' human lifestyle around the ritualized passivity of the 'binge watch'. In audience mode, we become the sedentary consumers of representations, no longer participants in the living rhythms of the earth. Our bodies stagnate as we spend days and nights just sitting there, maybe eating cheaply produced processed foods — sold to sicken us unto greater lethargy — from the lurid little plastic baggies that now litter the earth's surface and seas. Sensory energies hyper-focused on the screen-seeing eye, all our other senses atrophy: it is a closing of doors, when what engagement with reality demands is a state of full-bodied openness and attention. Machine-mediated pseudo-experience sparks not a corporeal awakening into reality but a somnambulant retreat from it.

Mind-altering chemicals are another technology promised and prescribed to facilitate connection, even as they deepen alienation and isolation in those who come to rely on them. While the old-guard psychotropic pharmacopeia is stocked with anesthetics — the poisonous solution the poisonous society peddles to dampen the misery it proliferates — the current craze is for psychedelics, in a mainstreamed, medicalized 'wellness' re-brand revival of 1960s drug culture. Hallucinogens are marketed for therapeutic as well as recreational use, celebrated for their power to expand human consciousness beyond its so-called 'natural limits' — there goes nature again, always with the limitations! — and magic-carpet the consumer uplifted onto a far vaster sensory field, where they will glean a more authentic and revelatory experience of the world in its wholeness, as it 'really is' (Leary et al. 1964; Pollan 2019; Sheldrake 2020). Such drug-induced rapture is reckoned for liberation. Yet, once again we are obliged to ask what, precisely, is being liberated in this framework, and what is it being liberated from? Hallucinogens are purported to release our consciousness from the limits our bodies impose on its expansive possibilities. Hence, the liberated subject here is the mind, while the flesh plays its usual part as big bad restrictive burden. And at the risk of stating the obvious, it seems worth reiterating this simple fact: hallucinations are not real. They are byproducts of novel chemicals administered to hiss through our neurons, shapeshifting material reality into an interior phantasmagoria of figments and synthetic hues. Subjected to clear-headed analysis, the psychedelic method presents as yet another prototypical patriarchal liberation of the mind/soul from a) the body, and b) material reality, in pursuit of escapist transcendence to some 'higher realm'.

Only engagement with what really exists, that which is given by the world as it is, has the power to unlock the authentic intensity of earthly experience we are capable of as sensitive animals. The idea that chemical hallucinations could somehow bring us more effectively to this intensity than unmediated attention to the living world reflects how disdainfully Man discredits organic material reality. He does not believe the earth itself could offer him any insights; he must grasp them himself, breaking through the barriers the bland, uninspiring earth erects between Man and the gnosis/ecstasy he seeks. By this logic, reality is diminished to a "secondary dimension, a largely illusory field of appearances waiting to be penetrated, and dissipated, by the human mind" (Abram 2010, p. 68).

The major enlightening insight typically imputed to tripping is the consumer's mindblowing realization of his or her oneness with creation. Yet what the hallucinating individual experiences he experiences alone, 'at one' with nothing outside of his own nervous system as it works to metabolize the substance he consumed. His 'oneness' is a chemically-induced solipsism rather than an unmediated encounter with the cosmos, the universe, god, the great community of being, or whatever it is he means to make contact with. It is therefore sham oneness, a cheap counterfeit of the real thing. Which should not be much of a surprise, considering that this experience is, after all, up for sale. Seen for the hot mass-market commodity they've become, psychedelics are exposed as anemic simulations of something freely available all the time to everyone, with which we have lost touch as a result of manmade culture's anti-material drift. The drug is interposed between consciousness and creation to replace an experience it can recreate only insipidly, to con us into forgetting that oneness — interconnection, interdependence, continuity — is earthly material reality's elemental truth, a state of being abundantly accessible to each one of us, when we remember our nature, the creatures that we are. Manmade culture offers nothing better, nothing even close.

Man fears direct encounter with reality as an encroachment upon his sovereign Self. He digs trenches, builds barricades and dams, installs buffers to keep the mortal material world held at a safe remove. But Man's fears have not served him, and they will not serve us. Where Man retreats, then, the feminist imperative is to draw closer. Alienation's antivenin is intimacy, achieved through unmediated experience of the world around us, not as we imagine it in our heads, explain it to ourselves through the stories we tell, or paint it streaming across a wallpaper of screens. To experience the world in this way calls for attentiveness and receptivity, a gutsy readiness to entrust oneself to the direct encounter. "It is a *task* to come to see the world as it is," Iris Murdoch writes (1970/2001, p. 89).

And it is a simple thing but it will take practice, to see the world clearly again, to re-enter into intimate relation with reality. Such a homecoming requires the humility to fall quiet. The ecofeminist Deena Metzger suggests a meditation: "Allow yourself to be a tree and let that be sufficient" (1989, p. 124). Can you stay still, just be here awhile? The bloodsea tidal inside you, the thick sap of it: *listen.*

Man prioritizes the Eye (I); his is a visual culture, in which he wanders mirrored labyrinths staring entranced at his own image repeated a thousandfold. But in reality, the primal primary sense is touch: start there. Stroke your skin, your hair, let your hands meet palm to palm: a prayer for the soft, the tangible. This is the tender threshold at which you welcome the world. Know it. Learn to take your own pulse, fingertips finding your throat's most plain-spoken cleft. Trace the swerve of veins that blues your slender wrist. Rest your hand over your breast and let your heart rise to it, as it plaits its ancient melodies of systole, diastole — the birth music. Close your eyes to let darkness glide red down your optic nerve, now float a moment in that incarnadined lull. Rest, you can rest.

And can you remember the scent of your own sweat? Never be ashamed. Can you remember the taste of your own rhythmic bleeding, the monthly slick of it glossing warm your fingers, or a lover's mouth? Who would dare make you ashamed? Let your own flesh, its wending nerves and venous filigree, its miles of gut held safely coiled, the matrix of womb and marrow, let this lavish profusion of cells become irresistible to you, all that you desire, and worship the simple miracle of your aliveness.

Reality's magic dwells in immanence: there is nothing to transcend, so sense again that the life in you is your own tameless divinity. The quintessential votary task is to feed the sacred beloved: eat when you are hungry, until you are full, taking for food the succor out of which you'd be proud to be remade. Deny yourself no sweetness, luxuriate: indulge in this reunion as a series of willful blisses. Life will not always be soft, yet we can know such softness: so let yourself taste it, white blossoms satin on your tongue, the rabbit fur, the pink light. This sanctity and splendor is irrevocable, ever unmarred, it cannot be sullied. Sister, mother, daughter, lover: know thyself! And once your body feels real to you and you remember you can rejoice in it, then will you be ready to receive the wilderness, its glister: this whole world is holy. Are you ready now?

From Freya Mathews, we hear: "She stands in the calyx of an inexhaustibly deep and poetic reality that opens its petals around her" (2005, p. 129).

And from Susan Griffin: "Petals soft like the skin of the body and hidden, the green sheath pulled back to reveal: the new bloom. The astonishing beauty" (1981, p. 250).

The point where the world enters your body as you are letting yourself be entered as you enter into it in turn is the origin of the physical sensation of beauty. Underfoot: the earth's dense presence rising to meet you. At your apertures: the air whispers its incantations. On your knees: the mosses that velvet the forest soil like the lushest pelt. Now fall back slanted across the thrumming ground, now settle; it is safe for you to settle here. For the earth beds you down, you sense it, and as you knead your fingers into the thick of its greenness, you too are being touched. Return is really just this softening into the carnal intimacy that is reciprocity with the living world; what a simple, simple, effortless thing it is — yet could there be anything more sacred? What heaven could be more golden than October's light? And what could be worthier of veneration than the meadow's blossoms windswept but undaunted, still so brazen in their growth? Or the pearly mists the bay breathes to garland in dove-color its shoreline's cedar sentries? Coyotes' howls like ghosts suspended over the moonlit field, the treetop colonies the herons build from sticks and reeds, or the pageant of horseshoe crabs gathered to spawn, and the sand a crystalline grit glittering beneath them?

You can sense it: how the trees lower their shadows draped over you. Receive the dark lake in which you are immersed. Sense, too, how the trees spire skyward widening to drink the sun. Be awed by this ascension. Sense the insects who crawl within the furrows of the trees' skin, and congratulate their industry. The red squirrel who chitters in the branches overhead. The small dust-colored birds no less than the brighter ones. The moist fungal slither that eats through the woodland deadfall to mulch it. Sense that these beings are your kin and take them into you, and meet them each in turn.

Now go alone to the ocean at night's edge to stand alongside its vastness to watch how its breadth will cradle the lowering sun, as you are salted, as the sky soaks in the sea's abyssal blue until sea and sky are indissoluble and splash down over you. Know it well: this is the darkwater from which you draw breath, by which your blood is driven. The place to which the undertow would carry you, waters where your ancestors once swam. Let your gilled heart slow to the sodden throb of starlight. Return is revelation: let these seagreen currents bear you back to the animal you are most truly, so that you might remember. The mammalian intelligence, the primeval essential knowledge of your flesh rekindled, you sense it now with such aching clarity: for all his striving, Man is no closer to free, but only interred inside an addled and numbing loneliness.

Man's terror has reaped a stupor we have the choice now to wake ourselves from. At last we will be fearless, for we know the truth coiled in each cell's nucleus: that we shall be received. Illuminated by direct experience of our own corporeal creatureliness, by the vibrant force of reality's immensity as it rushes through the substance of creation to meet us, we are restored to our proper place, our homeland. These bodies, this earth: here is where we belong.

REINTEGRATIVE ANATOMY

The living world receives us because we are part of it. The disconnect that grates at us is the product of Man's self-deception: never, in reality, have we been separate from the world. Man has enforced dualistic dismemberment as the foundational fiction of his society, and we are expected to defer to this doctrine of disjuncture, to believe in it, and indeed Man has behaved as if it were true — but it has never been within his power to will that which is not into being. Dualism slanders reality. For the real living world is zealously, promiscuously, anti-dualistic. The boundaries between one body and another, between my body and the dirt, between the soil and the roiling sea of the air are not the hard, straight-edged lines Man draws with such exacting precision, but more misted. The skin, after all, is a permeable membrane; it is porous. Nor are these gossamer boundaries static, but ever-shifting, the forms they diagram lively with constant transmutation, the metamorphic synergism decreed to beings massed to merge, cellularly to meld, to mingle.

It is a falsehood to set 'day' at one pole, and 'night' at its opposite, as the lit hours' black antithesis. Instead there is an infinitude of possible illuminations shading the sky by degrees through a daily ombre of pale to peony to fuchsia to celestite to azurine, honeyed gold, persimmon paling to tamer ambers gone glaucous lavender to cobalt or benthic to raven-violet, before brightening again, to blush at dawn. And there are also numberless variations in the station and tincture of the sun, moon, and stars. Clean division is impossible. Under examination, all Man's facile polarities likewise dissolve.[221]

David Abram (2010) captures the absurdity of dualistic division in his description of the air not as an emptiness in the spaces between objects, but as the tissue that ensheaths the earth, its etheric amnion. Air is the transparent medium in which all beings are submersed, equal participants in its circulation through the perpetual unconscious interchange of our breathing. Abram writes:

> The atmosphere is a subtle ocean steadily generated and rejuvenated by the diverse entities that dwell within it, a fluid medium of exchange between the plants and animals and weathered rocks. ... We are enfolded within it, permeated, carnally immersed in the depths of this breathing plane (p. 60).

Through this shared breath our lives sluice one into the other. The air you took into your body with your last breath soughed spun through the blood of a billion creatures before it reached you, traveling through miles of forests and oceans to fill numberless lungs to fuel the beating of how many hearts until it found your nostrils flared, before it slipped through your parted lips. Trees and phytoplankton suffused the air with oxygen as an offering to your species and once you've nursed of this mouthful, with the generosity inborn to your organism you will return the gift, the air as it leaves you leavened now with the carbon dioxide your green collaborators feast upon. With each inhalation

---

221 The undoing of dualisms I envision here should not be mistaken for the gross bulldozing of difference performed by the queer theory tenet of 'fluidity,' with its implicit goal of casting doubt on human sexual dimorphism. "Sex is a spectrum" is the mantra hurled in fashionable defense against biological reality, customarily followed by vague allusions to rare congenital conditions resulting in chromosomal and/or anatomical sexual ambiguities. That anomalies sometimes occur does nothing to alter the fact that 98-99% of human beings are born unambiguously male or female and shall die as such, never to fluidly flow between the two sexes. Our skin may be porous and permeable, our cells mostly water, but our bodies are not, as it happens, composed of some malleable gloop, forever oozing slimily through a limitless multiplicity of morphologies. Man's reductive and oversimplifying dualisms do not describe reality, but neither does the wishful thinking that would deprive nature of all its meaningful, material distinctions.

the living world in its fullness enters you, the zephyr the inrush the simplest answer our survival requires. From the neverending breath, source and sustenance, all life is nourished.

Of the ethereal thing she knew as the holy spirit, St. Hildegard von Bingen (1098-1179), mystic and abbess and herbalist, wrote:

> I am the supreme and the fiery force who kindled every living spark ... And I am the fiery life of the essence of God: I flame above the beauty of the fields; I shine in the waters; I burn in the sun, the moon and the stars. And, with the airy wind, I quicken all things vitally by an unseen, all-sustaining life. For the air is alive in the verdure and the flowers ...[222]

Our human bodies were forged of this ceaseless enlivening flow, these intimate bonds of contact and contingency. Man cannot extract himself from the world's interconnectedness because that same matrix is the very substance of which he is made. His being is merely one finite instance of its manifestation. Man's Self-concept as *Homo clausus* — the closed man, a closed system — is a myth debunked by the reality that all evolution is coevolution: no creature comes into being in isolation. Rather, we are shaped by the earth's gravity, by the lifeforms edible to us, by sunlight and its gradual subsidence into shadow, by tides and rainfall, the chemical composition of the atmosphere. Our senses, hence our sensory organs, hence the sensitivities that form the basis for our consciousness, were awakened in interaction with the world as their stimulus; our guts spool and swarm with microbial life to digest what the earth has given us to eat; our limbs take their lengths and angles in answer to the telluric terrain over which we travel. The earth's mark is not just on us; it is within us, not only visible but visceral. What we are, what the earth is: there is no dividing line.

Nor can the head be severed, the mind neatly dislodged from the earthly materiality of animal flesh. For sentience is not sequestered in the skull but spreads threaded through our bodies, like a thicket in the belly and snaking to the fingertips, as much in the blood and lymph through which hormones and neurotransmitters stream as

---

222 Quoted in Newman (1998, pp. 69-70).

in the brain Man reveres. And the brain itself, that favored organ, is three pounds of furrowed pulp, its peach-pink lobes stitched through with venous ribbon and bathed in a shallow wash of cerebrospinal fluid. So the nervous system is corporeal and consciousness a bodily function, a creature's means of encounter with the world, evolved in the maintenance of that creature's life. What Man calls 'the mind' is not some supernal shimmer temporarily inhabiting an otherwise inert meatsack. The functions Man attributes to his Mind — thought, memory, sentience, subjectivity — in fact flower from the fullness of our organismal being, arising from "the ongoing encounter between our flesh and the forest of rhythms in which it finds itself, born of the interplay and tension" between creature and world (Abram 2010, p. 110).

Human intellect and intelligence originate in bodily sensation, constituted by what a body perceives in the world within which it lives. Without the body, there could be no mind. We know that language takes as its reservoir of primal meaning metaphors drawn from sensory, motor, and affective experience. Up or down. Inside, outside. The movement of an object along an axis. Intimacy as proximity. The tender urgent hunger of desire (Johnson 2017, p. 15).

And when I hear the word 'cinnamon', the regions of my brain devoted to scent perception are aroused (Claxton 2015). And when I say 'kick', the brisk strike of the verb is a quickening through the same cortical motor neurons that would alight if I committed the act. And in calling to mind some past emotional wound, the remembered hurt of it tightens my muscles to leave me sore, with a sick ache in my gut (Johnson 2017).

Studies have shown that people who feel socially isolated or rejected sense the world as a colder place than those who have not been shunned. This is because the same small area of the brain implicated in the monitoring of social connection regulates body temperature as well. And our earliest understanding of interpersonal nurturance, the feeling of being safe because we are loved, is learned by our bodies when our mothers hold us to their breasts, and skin to skin we are warmed (Claxton 2015). Other studies show that the terror childhood trauma spills to linger pooled within the flesh of the traumatized is, at least in part, a consequence of disrupted somatosensory perception: the regions of the brain involved in sensing oneself in one's physical surrounds have gone dark (van der Kolk 2014). Neuroscientists have speculated that trauma-associated afflictions reflect a loss of — or a failure to develop, because abused since earliest immaturity — the "primordial sense of the affective self as a coherent and stable entity in relation to ... [the] environment" (Kearney and Lanius 2022, p. 2).

Integrative interconnectedness is our native state, a multipart mind woven through a body embedded in communion with the creatures we live alongside, united flesh and blood and breath and nerve to the world that bore us. Trauma dis-integrates: the state of severance it produces is suffering itself. All that is alive yearns towards wholing.

Like the atmosphere that mantles the earth as transparent lamina weaves beings together breath by breath, and like the human nervous system entwines the sensitive body into the sensuous earth, plants and fungi have coevolved to spin ecosystems together in a vast vital lace that the holistic orchardist Michael Phillips (2017) has called "the planetary membrane" (p. 7). A mycorrhiza — literally, "fungus-root" — is a mutualistic symbiotic entanglement of fungal mycelium with the root systems of trees and other plants, pearly threads webbing through the loam to stitch beings together in intricate networks of kinship, communication, and interchange. Mycorrhizal meshwork is ubiquitous, participated in by 95% of all terrestrial plants (Simard 2018, p. 192).

Forests are interwoven underground by these living plexuses, as the fungus tendrils out from the roots it holds coiled, broadening the total surface area through which each tree can absorb water and nutrients. Without their fungal intimates, the majority of the earth's plants would be unable to acquire the resources they need to grow, survive, and propagate (ibid.). In return for their widening of the net plants can cast in search of nutrients, mycorrhizal fungi are nourished by the simple sugars and other compounds produced during their hosts' photosynthesis.

A multiplicity of individual mycorrhizas ravel together to link all the plants in a given ecosystem, their coalescence forming filigreed architectures bearing an uncanny resemblance to our own nervous systems. Trees mirror neurons as the nodes, interconnected by fungal hyphae to gather into clusters the forest ecologist Suzanne Simard likens to the cortexes and lobes of an animal brain (Simard 2018). And like the brain, mycorrhizal networks are highly plastic, growing and reorganizing as new bonds are established, the whole made and remade by the cycling lives of its participants, who sprout and grow and adapt to seasonal changes, who are consumed, and dwindle, and eventually die.

And like neural networks conduct information and instruction through our bodies in dynamic relation with the environment, mycorrhizas are likewise a communicative medium, channeling the green chemistry of the forest's polyphony through the rhizosphere to warn of pests and other perils. The mycelial transmission of warning signals underground has been shown to inform neighboring others' rooting patterns, nutrient uptake, and production of self-defensive enzymes, evidence that plants are listening to and learning from one another. Within twenty-four hours, one tree's siren shuttled through soil to announce an aphid infestation will spark the production of pest-repellent chemicals by nearby trees, who have now been duly warned (Phillips 2017, p. 62).

Succor, too, is distributed through this lacework, from tree to tree along lines of need. Nutrients are reallocated from zones of surfeit to regions where resources are scarcer; parent trees direct their surplus to shaded seedlings until these little ones can grow tall enough to catch their own light; different species partner in cyclical sharing to sustain each other when one's feast season is the other's famine; and through this reflexive natural reciprocity, the lives latticed together within the complex web collaborate to nurture the whole to its richest fruition. Where mycorrhizal connection is strongest and most resilient, below ground the soil is healthiest. On the land above, the greatest diversity of plants summons the greatest diversity of insects. This communal caretaking in service of plenitude is not an aberration, some deviation from the norm: mycorrhizal entanglement is one of the most prevalent modes of interspecies symbiosis on the planet, as well as one of the most ancient (Boyno and Demir 2022). Signs of mycorrhizal partnership are evident in fossilized plants from over 400 million years ago (Rhodes 2017). The plaiting together of individual creaturely lives in furtherance of life's proliferation is commonplace. It is the simplest and most perfectly natural thing.

The war of all against all is Man's model, not that of the living world. In *Peaceable Nature: An Optimistic View of Life on Earth* (1984), Stephan Lackner asks how often we actually happen upon dogs eating other dogs. He writes, "Encounters between the creatures of our planet rarely lead to combat, the social gamut runs from tolerance to outright helpfulness. Butterflies visit flowers not to harm them, but to enjoy each other" (p. 13). Like the truffle issues its earthy musk to summon the devourer who will spread its spores; like each solitary stalk of grass composing the meadow leans on its sisters, that together they might stand against the lashing wind; like the coral takes its brilliant colors from the algae it shelters; and like the half-eaten salmon left by bears on the riverbank are food for the trees that shade the river to cool its waters so that new generations of fish may thrive there; and like a crow will lead wolves to an ailing deer then scavenge the carcass once the kill is made; and like wolves' predation preserves the health of the deer's herd, the living world achieves its inconceivable plenitude through cooperation, the instinctual devotion of the many to the dazzling whole.

And each organism is itself a manifestation of this nurturant collectivity, our bodies ecosystems unto themselves. We would do well to learn that we are holobionts: heterogeneous legions of lifeforms — archaeon, bacterial, fungal, protist — congregated in and on the human flesh, their interactions involved in the initial creation and continual re-creation of the apparently discrete entity we have been trained to call the individual. Over millions of years, coevolution ties together the myriad 'others' comprising any 'single' self, refining proximity into intimacy. Our bodies teem like lush microbial jungles because these tiny organisms were the substance of our earliest world, the primordial swamp a bacterial universe whose laden seethe spawned our inception. By the time humans emerged, this microbial queendom was already three billion years old (Marya and Patel 2021, p. 114).

The human body is made up of an estimated 30 trillion human cells and 39 trillion microbial cells.[223] Collectively, the microbes that reside in/on our bodies are called the human microbiota, and each body's will vary, in composition and population density, according to her habitat, the conditions of her birth, the stuff of her world as she consumes and encounters it. These indwelling communities determine the course of our own carnal becoming in turn: as embryos we develop under bacteria's sway, our microbes' genes triggering the expression of our own to shape our bodies in form and function. This influence prevails as long as we're living, our bodies "continuously built and reshaped by the bacteria inside us" (Yong 2016, p. 63). The microbiota presides over immune system regulation and inflammatory response, fat storage, the production of the vitamin that enables our blood to clot, the maintenance of our intestinal lining and our skin, as well as the processes of deposition and reabsorption responsible for the continual project of reconstructing our skeletons.

The power that the microbes dwelling within the coiled caverns of our gut hold over the human nervous system provides ample evidence to contradict Man's theory of the disincarnate mind. By way of the vagus nerve, microbes in the digestive tract are in constant communication with the brain, their missives influencing our emotions, motivation, memory, and mood (Han et al. 2022). In the laboratory setting, the composition of a mouse's gut microbiota will reliably predict her behavior and temperament, such that dietary alterations of animals' bacterial cohort produce consistent patterns of either timidity or boldness. In other experiments, scientists have induced inflammatory states in pregnant mice in order to deplete microbial populations in the guts of their offspring. By this culling, the infants' intestinal membranes are rendered permeable, and what leaks from their bellies into their bloodstream injures their inchoate

---

223 Until recently it was believed that the microbial cells in our bodies outnumbered human cells by as much as a figure of ten. In 2015, however, researchers re-assessed the estimate and set the ratio of microbial to human cells closer to 1.3 to 1 (Abbott 2016).

brains, resulting in a constellation of behavioral symptoms that researchers have likened to human schizophrenia and autism (Yong 2016). Microbial depopulation is theorized as a possible factor in the causation of anxiety, while stress experienced by the host has been shown to reduce microbiota diversity within as few as two hours (Carabotti et al. 2015). Body versus Mind, Self versus Other are revealed as unrealistic distinctions with the realization that each of us is an entire world, complex and crowded with life's teeming.

Artificially isolated, we wither into wan, weakly creatures, unfit for survival. Colonies of 'germ-free' mice, bred to harbor an interior void, are stored alone in plexiglass cloisters, touched only by handlers who suit up in biohazard gear to ensure the animals' absolute sterility. The result of this embodied exile from life's fullness is a torture radiating outward from the belly: "The germ-free animal is ... a miserable creature, seeming at nearly every point to require an artificial substitute for the germs he lacks."[224] Because germ-free mice fail to develop intact, functioning immune systems, they are abnormally vulnerable to both infection and autoimmune disease; without microbes to spur their intestinal membranes to regenerate, their guts are loose, leaky, the lattice of capillaries that perfuse them threadbare. Nor do the animals' brains grow as they should (Scott et al. 2020). Even cognitively, the creatures are stunted.

Morbidities associated with diminished microbial diversity in the human gut include heart disease, asthma, allergies, diabetes, colon cancer, obesity, Alzheimer's disease, inflammatory bowel disease, autoimmune disease, suicide (Marya and Patel 2021, p. 114).

Walled off inside the manmade world, we are becoming more and more like the immiserated mice the scientists imprison in their sterile labs, as our inner ecosystems are thinned by hyper-sanitization, diets of factory-extruded chemical nonfood, the antibiotic inundation a steady drip to prevent infection among overcrowded animals, the chronic trauma of our alienation from source and substance. By encasing himself within sterility as his armor against reality, Man destroys the biosphere within and without. Is it any wonder that

---

224 Theodore Rosebury, quoted in Yong (2016, p. 54).

he sickens, that in this unnatural quarantine we etiolate? As Man clearcuts forests to convert them into pesticide-drenched fields for the genetically perverted plants he reaps as cheap silage for the beings he demeans as beasts and interns interred in squalour, and enslaves, and slaughters in the industrial complexes he has laid down as a septic pall over the earth's arable land, choking the oceans gagged on the runoff, its freight of fertilizer and manure creating dead zones underwater, beneath his factories and factory farms and cities and all Man's other lifeless asphalt monuments to his MasterMind, the soil itself is degraded, its microbial biodiversity in vertiginous decline. The less riotous with flora and fauna the soil, the more barren are our own interior environs. And plants sown in sterile soils lack the nutrient density of those enriched by microbial cacophony — they are an enervated food for the lonesome animals who eat them (Marya and Patel 2021).

Babies born cut from their mothers by surgeons under the white fluorescent scathe of operating suites are deprived of the microbes that in the course of natural parturition would seed their nascent ecosystems, as they were muscled through the birth canal. Instead the infants are colonized by the bizarre and unwholesome bacteria the hospital breeds, and for the rest of their lives they will be predisposed to disease (Marya and Patel 2021).

The reward Man earns for chasing sovereignty in separation via devitalizing domination — to 'sterilize' is to cleanse absolutely; it also means: to annul creation — is a disease state. Fearing the realities of life on earth, Man scorns it and grows morbid, necrotic, contaminating all he touches with a rapidly metastasizing, malignant lovelessness. He will not survive his own blight; this quarantine kingdom can support no life. Rather than preserving himself shielded from death, he degenerates with accelerating rapidity, his suffering a harsher, lonelier decline than it might have been, for he has made himself a stranger to the end.

Man's vengeful assault on life continues even after he is dead, as he returns his body — unwillingly surrendered in the final moments no matter how despised — to the earth as pollutant. Affronted by decay as nature's ultimate insult to the sacred integrity of the Self, Man sees to it that his corpse be steeped in a chemical stew to embalm him intact, staving off the indignity of going to pieces, and these fluids filter noxious through the casket he shuts himself inside to seal out the dirt and conqueror worms. Formaldehyde and formalin (and, until recently, arsenic) leach from the dead Man's locked box to taint the surrounding soil and groundwaters. And so it is that, through Man's efforts to hold his body sequestered from its organic earthliness, "decomposition is not only preempted and altered, but nature is profoundly polluted—corpse and all" (Kelly 2015, p. 30).

It is Man's terror that turns death into a poisonous waste of life. In nature, nothing is wasted. Each death is a banquet, the one body made food for the many: wolves and blowflies and vultures, slime molds, bears, ravens and crows and crabs, lizards, fungi, nematodes, bacteria, hyenas, beetles. And each death is regenerative, a cradle for new life. The essential elements that accumulate in animals' bodies over the course of their lifetimes are not squandered by their dying but rather reincorporated as the matter/matrix for freshborn proliferations. When an animal dies, the scientists tell us, "it becomes an ephemeral nutrient pulse" (Lauber et al. 2014, p. 4920). Susan Griffin (1978) puts it another way: "The body of the animal buried in the ground rotting feeds the seed" (p. 224).

The dead creature's own microbial horde arrives first to the feast, *Staphylococcus* and *Clostridia* boiling through the peat of tissues already begun to soften as cellular membranes dissolve and rupture under the gnaw of this devouring deliquescence. Within seconds of the collapse from creature to cadaver, the flies join in, called by the death scent a spoor they can trace for miles. Larger scavengers, too, are summoned: canids and corvids, the creeping dermestidae. Siphoned underground through bacteria and fungi, carrion fluids irrigate the soil and the minerals the dead animal contained during its life are set loose, available now to be taken up by plants. And the plants are eaten by herbivores, who are eaten by carnivores, who themselves will die soon enough, as life after life is drawn down, re-absorbed into creation's communal pool of matter. In this way, death is metabolized into life and redistributed throughout the biosphere.

"All life is terminal and the remaining nutrients and energy are ultimately recycled within and across landscapes" (Benbow et al. 2018, p. 2). And this is the enduring brilliance of mortal material reality: nothing is lost. Thus, decay is the "central unifying concept" that links all earthly creatures "to the cycling of energies and nutrients through their ecosystems" (Barton et al. 2013, p. 762). We live until we are spent and when we die, the matter our bodies are decomposes, digested by the body of the earth. So the soil is revitalized, nourished by the nutrient inrush of the corpse where it falls. Paroxysms of microbial activity at the rot site aerate compacted dirt to ready the ground for regrowth. So green life resurges where the animal succumbs.

The word 'decay' derives from the Latin *decidere*: 'to fall down'. For Man, to fall has been damnation, his wretched descent into flesh condemned to death by a wrathful father-god. Thus, he has understood decay as the material expression of sin, an atrocity exhibit. Instead of a downward ebbing back into the earth, Man demands ascension, appalled by descent into this land he calls infernal. But all life is terminal, as they say, and when Man dies, for he must, he dies terrorized, in agonies of his own design. Sensing subsidence as defilement, imagining eternal tortures in the penitential pits, Man suffers needlessly. For the fall that swallows our animal bodies back into the earth is the true reunion with our source. But Man, because he rejects his reality, recognizes neither the rapture nor the resurrection it promises. The 'decomposition island' spawned by a creature's death is not cursed ground, but fecund, an Eden of Rot, darkening softly unto ripeness. Revival: this decadence is the lush heart of a flowering; plethoric, life goes green where the dead are buried; what blooms here flourishes and lures the bees. Life feeds on its own extravagance. So, life is forever renewed.

If we could recover the knowledge of death's fertility, recognize again the gift it makes of us to the world that bears and bolsters, might then the horror Man has drilled into us be quelled? And might we then summon the courage and the equanimity to let our smolder slow more peacefully in the presence of the final hour? And then to feed ourselves, the substance of our being, willingly returned into the body of the living earth? For we do not end, we are not lost, nothing is wasted — so what is there to fear? For we surge onward into the flux, engulfed, inalienable, boundless, we pulse full-force rushing with the world's breath wreathing blood lashing through oceans through swamps through forests' undergrowth and in the black dirt fused to reality's inexhaustible current. Our lives recede into stillness, for a time we fall silent. But soon we re-materialize, our lives transformed, we surface again within the churn. Couldn't it be as Virginia Woolf wrote in *The Waves* (1931/2006):

> Now I will relinquish, now I will let loose. Now I will at last free the checked, the jerked-back desire to be spent, to be consumed ... into the wave that dashes upon the shore, into the wave that flings its white foam to the utmost corners of the earth ... (p. 119).

RADICAL EMPATHY, OUR NATIVE GRACE

We are well aware at this point that Man denies he himself is moved by the same currents that spin the world as it cycles; he wants no part in the wave; he is not generous with himself but close-fisted, aggrieved that the earth would dare try to eat him. As a consequence, he disclaims his body, and holds it in contempt for leaving him vulnerable to death. He projects rejected bodiliness onto Others, as if this could magically deflect his own mortal condition. Following the logic of scapegoating, by the vulnerability he imposes on Others, Man uplifts himself to an invulnerable state. Others are weak, breakable, sensitive, subject to injury, their woundable bodies incarnating the necessary reassurance that Man is immune to wounding. He is saved by the rule of dualism's decree that Man himself is *not* what the Others are.

Meanwhile, the Man of Steel is hardening himself off all the time, rigorously, to conceal any sign of his own soft parts; he self-encoffins armored as in an exoskeleton until he almost cannot function, stiffened to stasis — but at least he can believe himself impenetrable. If you prick him he does not bleed, does not even feel it. Or so he says. Thus, physical vulnerability, assigned to the culturally Othered as the pulpous contrast to Man's ironclad state, is equated with lowliness: the soft body elicits disgust. Then the vulnerable are despised. Then they are punished for their weakness. The practice of overpowering, tyrannizing, and torturing his soft-bodied underlings solidifies as Man's substitute for invincibility, the ichor that leaks from Others' injuries serving as a testament to his own relative potency. By this turn Man comes to believe he survives by means of brutal mastery. And it is imperative, too, that he betray no sensitivity to Others' hurting, for nothing can be allowed to penetrate and strike a nerve. There must be no sign that Man ever felt a thing.

To prove he is immune to the pain of the Other, Man sharpens the blade, he deepens the cut. This policy of feelingless domination is the deadening of the heart that makes manmade civilization unlivable. All of us reared here are corrupted by it. Stony somatophobic hard-heartedness numbs us, and we become as casualties to one another, lining the trenches of a ruinous desolation. Mass Schadenfreude takes hold: pleasure in seeing others victimized, the relief in being the one to walk away, uninjured, when another is downed, mangled, losing blood. The bleeding body is not me, after all, I am strong where she was weak, we are not the same, she may die but I surely won't.

More pervasive still is bland indifference to other beings' suffering, the apathy we are trained into through the daily rituals of desensitization around which manmade culture has been organized. The fast-food cheeseburger that habituates us into equating violence with sustenance, cheap dead meat enfleshing the conceit that for me to live it is necessary that someone else be killed. It becomes a kind of self-sabotage, then, to be sensitive or attuned to other creatures' suffering. If my life is sustained by harm done to others, it is not in my interests to acknowledge the pain of the harmed one; I'm better off forgetting her. Therefore, we acquire the taste for tortured blood. And after dinner comes the evening's entertainment: a montage of brutalized women barely dressed and drenched in gore, some rapist-soldier 'first-person shooter' video game, an abstracted war reenactment on the big screen. The dog fight. The pig scramble. When violent spectacle streams 24/7 into our lives in the guise of amusing diversion and wholesome fun for the whole family, the misery of endemic atrocity's victims is forced out of sight. What a killjoy you'd have to be, to dampen the fun!

A further deepening of indifference comes through the andro-centric lesson that the majority of lives on earth are below concern and beneath contempt. What point is there in caring, for example, about the harm done to a creature incapable of feeling? Hence it is in the maintenance of indifference that Man has sought to define those he tortures and slaughters as insentient, no more sensitive than lifeless objects. (Their nervous systems are different from ours, he says, the animal may appear to thrash in pain but that is not pain it's feeling, it's just a reflex, like the chicken with its head cut off still running frantic.) Another tack is to conceptualize certain classes of beings always en masse, so that our care can never settle on any one wounded individual. (There is no fish struggling in the net, only a squirming load of fishes.) Or we are informed that there are some creatures who exist specifically to be used. To use something for the purpose for which it was created is not to harm that thing. (So why fret over white mice bred for the laboratory, the nine billion chickens 'processed' annually, the worm on the hook, or the woman gang-raped and pissed on to film the porn scene? These beings are not devastated by how they are used: they are *actualized*.)

And if by some miracle, despite intensive training, we retain our capacity to care, we can expect to be pilloried for it. Sensitivity is childlike. Immature, unrealistic. Or it is womanly: 'feminine'. Emotional, overwrought. To care enough to let one's feelings for another creature change how one conducts oneself is excessive, symptomatic of an uncultured, unsophisticated, intemperate, sentimental sensibility, of which we really ought to be ashamed. It's a show of weakness. To be too sensitive to others, or too earnest in our sympathies, is its own species of vulnerability, judged 'cringeworthy'. Shamefaced, we repudiate our tenderness and turn away.

In this context, empathy is eroded. Annulled. Carelessness sets in, vaster than cruelty and more brutal in its consequences; an attitude of anesthetized alienation calcifies as manmade culture's characteristic flat affect. Having no love for vulnerable bodies, neither our own nor any Others', we are able to obediently execute the everyday atrocities our social survival demands. We watch the wounded creature writhe, or more often, and no better: we avert our eyes, carrying on as though nothing hideous were happening.

Yet it is possible to thaw the heart chilled stiff and callused by institutionally sanctioned lovelessness. Accepting ourselves for the vulnerable bodies we are, reawakening to our own fleshly sensitivities, we can feel our way out of numbness and back into an awareness of corporeality as the basic, fundamental condition shared by all earthly creatures. It is our bodiliness, our mortal materiality, that binds us together within the biosphere's living lace. Our bodies are not the same, nor are our senses, nor even our nervous systems — and why should they be? There are as many ways of being alive as there are living beings, and yet no degree of difference undoes the simple fact that every one of us is a sensitive body. I cannot imagine exactly how it would feel to be a bat, winged, pursuing insectile prey by echolocation; yet I know that, were I bat, it would hurt me if someone crushed me under their boot, and that I would prefer to be warm in my cave, healthy rather than diseased. I am nothing like a dragonfly and make no claims to relate to their kind; yet I have seen their speeding joy as they whir iridescent blue and scarlet over summer ponds, and I can say with confidence that they would feel worse having their wings torn from their backs. No/body does not care if she is hurt. No/body is indifferent to his own extermination. You need to eat and so do I. You need rest, as I do.

Such straightforward realizations, rooted in our shared carnality, form the basis for empathy. With my own body I can feel into yours and what hurts you is painful to me, because I too have been hurt. Because I do not desire to suffer, it is obvious to me that you wouldn't, either. "She is delicate as I am: I know her sentience; I feel her pain and my own comes into me," Susan Griffin writes (1978, p. 219). In my own vulnerable body, viscerally, I am aware of your vulnerabilities, and attentive to them. How little it matters that yours are not identical to my own; it is enough that both of us can be wounded, both of our lives could be snuffed out in an instant. Fragile as we both are, how could we let one another suffer? How could I ever mean you any harm, you who are my flesh and blood? And how could I massacre this earth —

the larger body that incorporates us both — sensing its substance as our own?

The dog shows her underbelly to signal trust: that we will not harm her where she is most vulnerable, that we will show her affection, touch her gently instead of going for the throat. She trusts she is safe with us, even here, in her softest, most defenseless place. And every body has its own underbelly, where the blood rivers close to the skin, and the vital pulp rests unfortressed by bone. The inner thigh, the throat, the axilla, the eye. Bitten in these regions, we might be mortally wounded, we could bleed out and die. Yet the dog exposes her underbelly as covenant: here is my softness, for I sense yours, and I place my faith in it: we will do one another no harm. When we receive and respond to the dog's body with reverence, proceeding gently in honor of that which is tender, the soft fur the soft skin the soft viscera enveloped there, we rekindle in ourselves the "latent yet abiding feelings of biophilia" that bind us in loving relation with our corporeal kin (Alvaro 2019, p. 133).

The dog shows me her underbelly: I lay my hand to its silken curve, and my other hand to my own warm flesh. She is breathing and I am breathing and our breath syncs as we calm and comfort one another. Can you ever know how completely I love her? Relinquishing Man's petrified hardness, I let myself soften.

Through empathetic sensitivity to vulnerable bodies, our creaturely capacity for care is revived. Once again, it is a simple thing, it comes naturally to us: having roused ourselves from the narcotized stupor male dominion injects as if needled directly into the heart, empathy returns readily. Desensitized indifference and disdain for softness are unnatural to the animals we are, distortions of our native grace: the care for others inbred as our inheritance from the living world, defined as it is by nurturant and symbiotic interconnectedness. Empathy is nature's law of succor manifest in the earthly organisms we are, experienced inwardly as an urge to exist in compassionate relation with others. What the feminist animal studies scholar Lori Gruen calls "entangled empathy" is precisely this: a sensitivity to others prompted by the revelation of interdependence. Realizing that we are "not just in relationships as selves with-others, but [that] our very selves are constituted by these relationships," we are compelled to weave our relational webs more carefully, of finer stuff than callousness (Gruen 2015, p. 64). Despite Man's strident, paranoid insistence, we do not survive by supremacy, striving for mastery, the autonomous one (the Self) against the enemy all (Others). By the combative solipsism Man adopts as his standard mode, we are debased unto lifeless sterility, armored immobilized, locked into a suicidal war against creation — as is all too clear to see today, from where we teeter on the edge of cataclysm both cultural and ecological. Reality's flourishing is relational, predicated on solidarity: the one for the many, that all may be nourished by the abundance of the whole.

Resensitization to the unity of the living world beckons us back to our native grace. The empathetic urge to care begets an instinctual morality, its principles sourced not from any handed-down catechism but from the capacities of our sentient animal bodies. This morality is no prescriptive code of mandates and prohibitions; there is nothing abstract about it. Organic, intuitive, it does not require philosophical speculation. For it is informed instead by spontaneous feeling. Nor does this morality require the instruction of expert authorities. Rather, what is needed is a willingness to feel without inhibition, fostered by a humble praxis of attention and responding with care to the world as we encounter it. The moral stance that arises quite unbidden through this practice is a deeply felt opposition to careless-ness and cruelty, the pervasive sadism of male dominion. Empathy's imperative: to live according to our sensitivities. If we are sensitive to the suffering of vulnerable bodies, then it is obvious that to cause others pain is immoral. Empathy's edict: do no harm. Outside of the rarest circumstances of physical self-defense, it is immoral to hurt any/body. It is immoral to exploit another being. To enslave her. To degrade her, torment her, kill her. It is immoral to be careless with another's vulnerabilities. And when others are suffering, it pains us: the moral response is the instinctive, intuitive, impulsive response; it is to offer what comfort we can, to help however possible. It is immoral to abandon any being alone and uncared for in her/his anguish. We know these things in our bodies; no one has to tell us how to feel.

Commitment to an empathy-based morality renders inaction unthinkable. If I can feel you as I feel myself and we are real to one another, then when you are in agony, I am, and I cannot bear it: soon your suffering will move me to act. For now I feel I am responsible for us both. Julian Beck of The Living Theatre declared Mankind a "feelingless people." Beck wrote:

> If we could really feel, the pain would be so great that we would stop all the suffering. ... If we could really feel it in the bowels, the groin, in the throat, in the breast, we would go onto the streets and stop the war, stop slavery, stop the prisons, stop the killing, stop destruction (1972).

Yes, to molt numbness and re-attune ourselves to feeling is going to sting, and yes, it must, until the ache is unbearable and drives us together screaming: I cannot stand it, we cannot go on this way. When we finally feel the real, painful urgency of our situation, then we will know in our bowels, in our breast, that no treacle 'niceness' will suffice at this late stage of the patriarchal crisis, nor the milquetoast regurgitation of solicitous hearts-and-smiles platitudes that not only passes for but is in sad fact actually celebrated today as what it is to 'be kind'. There is no more time for going along to get along. No more mild-mannered suggesting politely to no one in particular that Man please consider stopping the massacre. The attentive, empathetic, compassionate morality that our present situation demands is as fierce as it is unrelentingly gentle, an active force, militant and uncompromising, with care for each vulnerable body the smolder at its crux. For women in general, this will look not remotely like 'being nice', that feminized pose of self-sacrificial sugar-and-spice spinelessness that keeps us stuck playing mama to the ruling Man-babies. Indeed, the compassion needed now would have us starve Man sooner than nurse him.

For feminist animal studies scholar Josephine Donovan (2007), empathy is politicized — and becomes politically effective — when we combine our sensitivity to others' suffering with a clear-eyed critical analysis of the power structures implicated in its production. We can do nothing to stop any/body's suffering if we do not understand its cause and its context, no matter how much that suffering may pain us. What is necessary, then, is to name the killers, the rapists: the engineers of mass desecration. It is necessary, too, to diagram the machinery that the destroyers have instituted, every mechanism that has enabled them to be as viciously efficiently industrious as they have been in their devastation of the world. "We live in a system that manufactures sorrow, spilling it out of its mill," wrote Julian Beck, and once we have studied that system's daily operations and its equipment, once we understand how it functions, how it is maintained, then we will be ready to put our empathy to work. There are three basic strategies by which we might get this work underway.

First, we refuse to collaborate. To the fullest extent possible we remove ourselves from participation in the misery industries, no longer living in collusion with the Master class. With the recognition that, as Deane Curtin (2007) explains, "by inflicting violence needlessly, one's bodily self becomes a context for violence," and that "[o]ne becomes violent by taking part in violent [practices]," we deny the current regime its violative misappropriations of our beings (p. 99). We no longer permit ourselves to be co-opted as instruments of violence. Because the harms of manmade culture are innumerable, we have equally numberless opportunities to spurn collaboration. To give one example from among the many: moved by my empathy for chickens, universally disdained and uncared for, not even considered animals under U.S. law and so afforded no 'welfare' protections, crowded in hot, filthy, stinking barns, their hearts crushed by the weight of oversized breasts bred for butchering, I vow to have no part in the violence done to these creatures. I do not bankroll the industries that brutalize those whom I ache for. Acting on my empathy, I won't eat murdered chickens, I won't eat genetically mutilated hens' eggs. The compassionate reaction to the premise of profiting from cruelty to vulnerable bodies is revulsion, its political corollary the walkout, the boycott, the strike.

Second, we provide sanctuary to the wounded, in the hopes of lessening the world's sum burden of suffering. We shelter the victimized, tend to their injuries, leaving no/body behind stranded in the trenches. We staff the rape crisis centers and domestic violence hotlines; we rescue maltreated malnourished creatures from slaughterhouses and laboratories; we take in the broken-down and discarded and feed them and watch over them while they sleep, we speak in soft tones when they are frightened, we listen, we console; we take care of them as best we can. And all of this is righteous work, desperately needed. Yet there is a crucial difference between tending to the wounded and ending the war. Until the bloodbath stops, there will always be new casualties to care for, wave after wave of brutalized and dismembered bodies washed up to litter the shores of our shellshocked hearts, day after day, year after year, on and on forever. And for all our labors and all our love we will be doing little more than stanching their bleeding and sending them back out to the killing fields, freshly bandaged, but no safer than before from the onslaught.

And so our third program of empathetic action is directed towards the slaughter itself. To abort atrocity rather than chase after it laboring to palliate the scorched earth in its wake, nothing less than organized political resistance will serve. Militant compassion at its fiercest spurs us to raze the architectures of devastation, to claw our way down to cultural sadism's provenance, so that we might at last uproot it. To siphon the poison from the soil, in order that something less rancid can grow up in place of the deathly travesty Man's spewed seed has sown.

For doubtless you feel the truth as I do: that it is Man's system which churns out the tortures and violations, the rapes and murders, degenerative desolations and abasements that daily lay siege to virtually all vulnerable bodies alive on this ill-used earth, men's bodies included. Radical empathy urges us toward a committed, compassionate, care-full political defense of the soft body of every other, beloved as our kin. Radical empathy's imperative, then, is plain: stop the war. Because we are sensitive animals, now we're feeling it achingly: if ever any earthly creature is to live out her life safe from assault, if I am to be certain that the victimizer will not lay hands on her again, then Man can be shown no mercy. Not if we hope to stop the war, to stop the destruction.

Radical empathy's edict: end male dominion.

THE BODY INSURRECTIONARY

When she is ready to kill you in order to free herself, she will begin with a defense of her body.

ANDREA DWORKIN, *Scapegoat* (2000, p. 28)

Andrea Dworkin knew too well the countless ways that female bodies are besieged. The rape-murder incursion that obliterates the despised body of the girl still a child, how he forces himself into her until she has no place inside herself left to live. (And there is video evidence of the occupation online, it is ubiquitous, and it is classified as 'entertainment', pleasurable viewing accessible to all men all the time at no cost, and to boys, who learn from the footage what a girl's body is built for.) Our bodies plundered, our bodies the carnage and the rubble, our bodies the abattoirs in which we are throat slit slung to bleed for the disassembly line then turned out trussed ornamental for Man's table, the centerpiece of his predatory feast. Bodily we are maimed, mutilated until we are unrecognizable; we are gutted whipped humiliated beaten down bludgeoned bound deformed debilitated corroded constricted vampirized paralyzed disappeared until, alive or dead, we are voided. By the violation. By the evisceration, the mundane immiseration, the incest, the sexual exploitation, forced marriage, forced motherhood, wombs gouged out by sadistic surgeries or choked glutted on unchosen brood, the rape, the rape, the fear we feel at night on the street or in our own homes, or wherever the men are, that fear and hurt we live with congealing into the chronic diseased state that infects us, by which all vital joy is snuffed out. And these attacks on female bodies are not discrete misfortunes that befall us as individuals at random, but in fact largescale social processes institutionalized for the preservation of male power by means of breaking down females en masse, as a sex class. No woman is unscathed, no one gets out of girlhood fully intact.

Even if she is lucky enough to survive, some part of her body is bound to be murdered; some part of her body will be dead to her.

Andrea Dworkin writes, "The men pursue their interminable project of destruction: turning women's bodies into a site for death" (2000, pp. 234–235). And she writes, "Male domination over and against female flesh is real; women experience it daily" (1976, p. 107).

Women's oppression is not abstract, it is not theoretical. It is the sum of what is done to our bodies under male dominion. In an apartment complex stairwell in Chicago a child is raped and strangled, insecticide sprayed in her mouth; she slumps into a coma and when she wakes, the girl is mute, blind, brain-damaged: what destroyed her is what a man did to her body.[225] A woman is beaten, the flat iron she used to straighten her hair shoved into her vagina, a beer bottle shoved into her vagina, her boyfriend's fists shoved into her vagina, then her guts ripped out: what destroyed her is what a man did to her body.[226] Because she will not renounce her sanctity, no matter what violence and humiliation the men mete out to force her, a young woman is burnt on a pyre under a placard that names her "Heretic, Relapser, Apostate, Idolater"; she invokes her saints for protection as the fire consumes her: what destroyed her is what men did to her body.[227] A woman too old to fuck and no one's doting mother anymore

---

225 In 1997, Patrick Sykes raped a nine-year-old girl known only as Girl X in the stairwell of the apartment complex where she lived:

> The little girl ... was lying face down and barefoot in a pile of dirty, melting snow, her tiny body snuggled against the graffiti-scarred concrete wall. Her T-shirt was stained with blood and pulled up to her chest ... Another T-shirt was tied tightly around her neck. Her red corduroys were pulled below her waist. ... Later, police found the 4th grader's gym shoes and hooded jacket in the incinerator. ... The assailant sprayed roach repellent in her mouth and left her for dead on the seventh-floor landing, discarding her on the cement floor like a piece of crumpled paper (Glanton 1997).

226 In 2015, Fidel Lopez raped and disemboweled Maria Nemeth. The pair had been dating for about a year. Before admitting to the murder, Lopez claimed that Nemeth's death was accidental, the unfortunate consequence of 'rough sex' (CBS News Miami 2016).

227 Joan of Arc (1412–1431) was a teenage peasant girl who, claiming divine counsel, fought with the French army to drive the English from Orleans during the Hundred Years War. Held prisoner by the English at Rouen and charged with heresy for her assertion that she received instructions directly from god, Joan was compelled to wear the 'feminine' attire she despised while enduring threats and harassment from

is abandoned with her bedsores seeping septic in some hospice senile female storage facility: what destroys her is what men do to her body.[228]

From girlhood to death our bodies are stolen from us, expropriated as votive offerings for sacrifice on the altar of male dominion — glory be to His name! — or as fetish objects for men's delectation, then discarded with the rest of the wreckage when we're deemed 'spent'. And whether sacrificed or fetishized or summarily scrapped, raided female bodies pile up as the spectacular palpable proof of Man's power. Andrea Dworkin writes: "Manhood is established and confirmed over and against the brutalized bodies of women" (1976, p. 103). We are brought up to understand our bodies not as ourselves but as images to be placed on display for the all-seeing eye (the omnipresent male 'I') or as things, objects, to be put to good use by someone who must know better than we do the uses we're fit for. Denied the least claim to our bodies, we can hardly imagine what to do with them; what use could these bodies be to us, when they have no value besides the object value they are assigned by potential consumers, whose use we are promised will redeem us, whose pleasure is our purpose and reason for being.

This is what we have to live for. Man is the Self, we the selfless Body, raw material actualized by use. So, we devote ourselves to increasing our property value, obedient to the specifications the manmade culture outlines. Plucking, piercing, starving, painting our mouths our nails our eyes the trending shade of compliant, plumping our lips our cheeks our jawlines with dermal filler. Microneedling and dermabrasion and chemical peels to resurface our skin, since we're

---

the men who guarded her cell. It has been speculated that these men also raped her. (See Dworkin 1987; Michelet 1858.)

228 More women than men land in nursing homes and other residential facilities, where they are subject to medical neglect, maltreatment, malnutrition, unsanitary conditions, and physical and sexual abuse by staff (see Patel et al. 2021). In 2021, 83-year-old Deanna Kay Mahoney died from sepsis due to an infected bedsore she developed while a ward of a low-rent nursing home in Newton, Iowa. At the emergency room, "... medical staff found a large skin ulcer, or open wound, on her buttocks and another on the heel of her foot. The emergency room physician reported that the wound on her buttocks was contaminated with feces and ran 'very deep,' exposing muscle and bone" (Kauffman 2023).

told it should shine like glass. Our indoctrination into these regimens of daily 'correction' is central to feminization: the psychic and physical trauma process by which females are dispossessed of our bodies, so that we will cede them willingly, for love or for profit, as a public good or as private property. So that we will make ourselves the things men want us to be, sex objects or breeding apparatuses or pedestaled icons, available to buy and sell and barter.

By this seizure our bodies are debased into incubators for the manmade culture: with our subjugated flesh we reproduce Man's delusions and his lies, we become symbols of the world remade in Man's image. In us, Man sees material reality in his thrall, shackled, subdued, so immovably put in its place that it cannot even dream of release but pleads instead to please and to serve the Master.

For females, the fruit of feminization is a virulent hatred of our bodies, which we experience as the self-disgust we give vent to through a staggering array of self-harms and self-destructions signaling how little we desire to go on living when we can conceive of no better use for our bodies than the ways men make use of them. These uses are vile to us, and so our bodies become vile to us. Something must be horribly wrong with our bodies, we think, for them to be put to such dismal uses. If all they are fit for is such squalid treatment. Our bodies are horrible. We do not deserve to live.

Re-possessing our bodies from male dominion is the first and most fundamental corrective to women's oppression, which is, at base, the colonization of female flesh: of female life. Estranged from our bodies by coercion and force, conned into conceptualizing them as objects to own rather than the organisms we are, and eager to have them off our hands, to trade them in for a shot at survival or to give them away hoping our charity will win us favor, a seat at the table, Man has made us the easiest prey imaginable. For there is no female self separate from her female body, and when we hate our bodies, we hate ourselves. When we harm our bodies, we do harm to ourselves. And when we sell our bodies, we are selling ourselves out.

Women's oppression is not abstract, it is material: what destroys us is what is done to our bodies. So when we destroy ourselves, we are doing Man's work for him; we join in the war on women as collaborators in our own desecration. And we become Man's accomplices in the necrotizing massacre that he perpetrates against the living world, the larger war of which Man's offensive against women is but one strategic campaign.

In other words: by our self-diminishing self-sabotaging self-mutilation, we are drawn into lethal complicity with the male MasterMinds actively engaged in the murder of the earth and all its creatures, not least of all our sisters and ourselves. Such is the true cost of submission.

For women to re-establish, redefine, and radically heal our relationship with our female bodies is therefore the exigent precondition for anything worthy of the name liberation. It begins with decolonization: we purge Man from our bodies. Since the traumas of feminization are integral to the colonizing process by which male dominion is embedded into our everyday experience of our bodies, to decolonize is, at least in part, to de-feminize. We wean ourselves off of participation in the habitual rituals of female self-surrender, the neverending programs of bodily 'maintenance' and 'improvement' that imprison us within an objectified self-concept, dismembered and selling ourselves piece by prettified piece to the male Master class. Andrea Dworkin writes, "Women must stop mutilating their bodies and start living in them" (1974, p. 116). We must stop, because it is through the daily repetition of bodily 'beautification', the esteemed feminine pastime premised in the notion that our natural physicality is a nightmare, that — along with the pervasive ambient misogyny slandering female flesh as dirt and death and unforgivable sin — convinces us to hate what we are, the very substance of ourselves.

Hating our bodies, eking satisfaction from the painful operations we undertake to bump up our market value, our psyches are bent towards masochism. Because we are alive and we want joy, somehow even under the worst conditions we long to taste pleasure, we learn to get off on how men make use of our bodies as the bloodied bolsters they stand upon to upraise themselves in their heavenbound ascent from the earth they say debases them. (To which we females in our dread dirtiness are tethered, they say.) Exorcising this learned, ingrained masochism is essential. No/body ever got free begging her captors to chain her to the floor of the cage and rip her to shreds.

To counter self-hatred is to accept ourselves as we are: we are our bodies. As Paula Gunn Allen writes, "healing the self means honoring and recognizing the body ... [h]ealing the self means committing ourselves to wholehearted willingness to be what and who we are" (1989, p. 56). With this acceptance, we cease to mutilate our bodies to make ourselves over in Man's image. We release the body hatred that feeds the self-hatred that underlies our masochistic self-harm, the self-destruction we are socialized to execute on male dominion's behalf, to save Man the trouble. Accepting ourselves as we are, we revere our bodies as sacred, with real conviction now. We remember that our female bodies' sole purpose is the living of our own female lives, for our own purposes and no one else's and certainly not Man's. Because we are our bodies, our bodies are invaluable to us; we do not evaluate our worth according to how men deign to drain and devour us. We do not believe we were born to be used, used up, destroyed, and discarded. And so we slough the masochism that feminization has driven into us.

Resensitized by radical empathy, we are attentive not only to others' suffering but our own, the pain that is not and never will be pleasure but only a sordid substitute for the sensuality we starve for locked within enforced anhedonia. We accept the vulnerability of our bodies, we do not despise them any longer, neither as bestial burden nor liability; and we do not desire to see ourselves punished, for we do not sin by being; and just as we are moved to defend any other tender animal, finally, finally, we summon the care, the clarity and the courage, the love it requires to be outraged by what men are doing to us, what is done to the bodies we are under male dominion, every single insufferable way we are being destroyed. So, finally, we defend ourselves.

"Fighting back is as close to healing as we're going to come," writes Andrea Dworkin (1997, p. 123).

What we do now is this: we declare our bodies inviolable, no longer Man's scapegoat nor his sacrificial lamb, and we hiss we will not be closed up in the cages we will not be raped we will not be murdered neither slow nor swiftly not by any means now we bare our teeth gnashed bite back foaming like rabid when he comes for us, when he comes for her, or her, or her; we are furious feral we are not chased not cowed laid low not playing dead any longer, as if the death pose could ward off the dying, but we rush forward streaming warm breath its heat the wetness in our hair tangled incandescent like tempests of mane our faces flushed shining with this newborn resolve, so fervent, such vehemence in our movements now: our devotion to our own survival. To our bodies. To our earthly aliveness. We sanction no violence against us.

"She makes assault against her very expensive," writes Andrea Dworkin (2000, p. 335).

And what we understand now is this: that it is the Kingdom of Man which launched the onslaught we sense in our bodies as a war against the reality that is our substance, our matrix, and the life in us, and we defend our source as we defend ourselves. The stench of ecocide hits us too loathsome to bear now that our senses have returned; we can stomach it no longer. We will not allow Man's vengeance against the living world to continue. The urge to protect the beloved is visceral; it is our native grace that pitches us pitted against the Fathered apocalypse already much too far along. And so we begin, as Andrea Dworkin tells us we must, "... to tear male dominance to pieces, to pull it apart, to vandalize it, to destabilize it, to mess it up, to get in its way, to fuck it up" (1997, p. 175). We do not compromise, making no concessions to the diseased culture men have made; we do not excuse it, for it is inexcusably hideous; and we do everything we can think of, everything it is within our power to do to disarm Man. To end male dominion — for the earth's sake, and for our own.

Because we know in our bodies (our bellies breasts bones spines sibilant with the hot seethe of this knowing) that reality is not the sickly sterile wasteland we call the manmade world, and we have the power to restore reality as we have been restored to our bodies, to be midwives in its rebirth as in our own. Transubstantiation, renewal, regeneration: these are earthly powers, so they are ours. For we are alive, creatures of the living earth, inseparable from its thick and sacred alchemical will to surge overflowing, to flower, energy radiating as light as heat from the nucleus to circulate to breathe to glow, seeking its own continuity, yearning, spreading itself out, so lavish, such opulence in the heartbreaking purity of life's luminous ardent hunger to be, simply *to be*.

And returning to our bodies fully enlivened finally and lucid in our vision in our love for the cells that compose us and the cells we are composing the body of the world, in reverencing our sisters as ourselves and every animal and the soil the worm the wolf the algae the oak the dog-rose the piglet the woodthrush the herring the freshwater and the brackish and the moon the sea mirrors silverine and the microbial confluence that swarms within everything, loving these myriad strange and precious miraculous lives as we love our own, humbly: only then can we incarnate insurrection, in defense of what's real. It is true that the carnage of male dominion has been visited on our bodies, it is true we have nearly died of it over and over a million times. Yet we are revivified, strong again in our sinews: we can rise. For ours is a vital revolt against the lifelessness Man has sown; there is nothing more necessary. Man is lost, even now his reign is collapsing, his fortress a crypt. "The sun is about to rise," Monique Wittig (1971) writes, in her novel about women at war, "The lilac and violet colours brighten in the sky. They say, where will you begin?" (p. 131)

Redemption, resurrection, reincorporation into the exquisite, the delicate, the deathless hallowed whole: these are earthly powers, of course they are ours. Remember it now, in your flesh, sister. In your blood.

BIBLIOGRAPHY

Abbott, Alison (8 January 2016) 'Scientists bust myth that our bodies have more bacteria than human cells' *Nature*. Accessed 18 May 2024 at <https://www.nature.com/articles/nature.2016.19136>.

Abram, David (2010) *Becoming Animal: An Earthly Cosmology*. New York: Pantheon Books.

Accurso, Erin, Leslie Sim, Lauren Muhlheim and Jocelyn Lebow (2020) 'Parents know best: caregiver perspectives on eating disorder recovery' *International Journal of Eating Disorders* 53 (8) pp. 1252-1260.

Adams, Carol (2004) *The Pornography of Meat*. London: Bloomsbury Academic.

Adler, Katya (27 March 2022) 'How the sex trade preys on Ukraine's refugees' *BBC.com*. Accessed 12 May 2024 at <https://www.bbc.com/news/world-europe-60891801>.

Alcor (2020a) 'What is cryonics?' *Alcor.org*. Accessed 2 May 2024 at <https://www.alcor.org/what-is-cryonics/>.

Alcor (2020b) 'Introduction to cryonics' *Alcor.org*. Accessed 2 May 2024 at <https://www.alcor.org/library/introduction-to-cryonics/>.

Alcor (2021) 'Alcor membership statistics' *Alcor.org*. Archived version accessed 2 May 2024 at <https://web.archive.org/web/2021 0918145052/> and <https://www.alcor.org/library/alcor-membership-statistics/>.

Allen, Paula Gunn (1989) 'The woman I love is a planet' in Judith Plant (Ed.) *Healing the Wounds: The Promise of Ecofeminism*. Toronto, Ontario: Between the Lines Press.

Al Jazeera (31 July 2024) 'Israel-Gaza war in maps and charts: live tracker' *Al Jazeera*. Accessed 1 August 2024 at <https://www.aljazeera.com/news/longform/2023/10/9/israel-hamas-war-in-maps-and-charts-live-tracker>.

Alvaro, Carlo (2019) *Ethical Veganism, Virtue Ethics, and the Great Soul*. Lanham, Maryland: Lexington Books.

Amedeo, Father C. P. (1935) *Blessed Gemma Galgani (1878-1903)*. Translated by Father Osmund Thorpe. London: Burns, Oates, and

Washbourne. Digital version accessed 5 May 2024 at <https://ia800804. us.archive.org/9/items/StGemmaGalganiBiographyOfSaintGemmaGalga niFr.AmedeoCP/Blessed_Gemma_Galgani-FrAmadeoCP.pdf>.

American Anti-Slavery Society (1839) *American Slavery As It Is: Testimony of a Thousand Witnesses*. New York: American Anti-Slavery Society.

American Psychiatric Association (2022) *Diagnostic and Statistical Manual of Mental Disorders, Fifth Edition, Text Revision (DSM-V-TR)*. Washington, D.C.: American Psychiatric Association.

American Psychiatric Association (2024) 'What is gender dysphoria?' *Psychiatry.org*. Accessed 12 May 2024 at <https://www.psychiatry.org/ patients-families/gender-dysphoria/what-is-gender-dysphoria>.

Anderson, Janna and Lee Rainie (Eds) (2022) *The Metaverse in 2040*. Washington, D.C.: Pew Research Center.

Aridjis, Eva (2017) 'Death in ancient and present-day Mexico' in Joanna Ebenstein (Ed.) *Death: A Graveside Companion*. New York: W. W. Norton.

Aries, Philippe (1981) *The Hour of Our Death: The Classic History of Western Attitudes Toward Death Over the Last One Thousand Years*. New York: Alfred A. Knopf, Inc.

Aristarkhova, Irina (2005) 'Ectogenesis and mother as machine' *Body & Society* 11 (3) pp. 43–59.

Aristotle (350 BCE/1899) *The Politics of Aristotle*. New York: The Colonial Press.

Augustine of Hippo (413–426/1913) *City of God, Volume 1, Book XIII*. Edited by the Rev. Marcus Dods, M. A. Edinburgh: T. & T. Clark. Accessed 22 April 2024 at <https://www.gutenberg.org/cache/epub/45304/pg45304-images.html>.

Aurelius, Marcus (171–175/1964) *Meditations*. Translated by Maxwell Staniforth. London: Penguin Books.

Bakhtin, Mikhail (1965/1984) *Rabelais and His World*. Bloomington, Indiana: University of Indiana Press.

Ball, Matthew (2022) *The Metaverse: And How It Will Revolutionize Everything*. New York: Liveright Publishing Corporation.

Ballard, J. G. (1974) 'Some words about *Crash!*' *Foundation: The Review of Science Fiction* 9. Accessed 12 May 2024 at <http://www.jgballard.ca/ media/1974_november_foundation_the_review_of_science_fiction.html>.

Banerji, Debashish and Makarand R. Paranjape (Eds) (2016) *Critical Posthumanism and Planetary Futures*. New Delhi, India: Springer India.

Bar-Zeev, Avi (2022) 'We're rushing headlong into it without all the safety measures that we need' in Janna Anderson and Lee Rainie (Eds) *The Metaverse in 2040*. Washington, D.C.: Pew Research Center.

Baring, Anne and Jules Cashford (1993) *The Myth of the Goddess: Evolution of an Image*. London: Penguin Books Limited.

Baring-Gould, Sabine (1865) *The Book of Werewolves: Being an Account of a Terrible Superstition*. London: Smith, Elder and Co.

Barstow, Anne L. (1994) *Witchcraze: A New History of the European Witch Hunts*. San Francisco, California: Pandora, HarperCollins.

Barton, Philip S., Saul A. Cunningham, David B. Lindenmayer and Adrian D. Manning (2013) 'The role of carrion in maintaining biodiversity and ecological processes in terrestrial ecosystems' *Oecologia* 171 (4) pp. 761–72.

Bates, Carolina Figueras (2014) '"I am a waste of breath, of space, of time": Metaphors of self in a pro-anorexia group' *Qualitative Health Research* 25 (2) pp. 189–204.

Bates, Laura (2021) *Men Who Hate Women: From Incels to Pickup Artists: The Truth about Extreme Misogyny and How it Affects Us All*. Naperville, Illinois: Sourcebooks.

Baudelaire, Charles (1857) *Poems of Baudelaire: A Translation of Les Fleurs du Mal*. Translated by Roy Campbell (1922). London: Harvill Press.

Baudelaire, Charles (1919) 'My heart laid bare' in Thomas Robert Smith (Ed.) *Baudelaire, His Prose and Poetry*. New York: Boni and Liveright, Inc.

Bauer-Babef, Clara (30 November 2022) 'Trafficking and sexual exploitation of Ukrainian refugees on the rise' *Euractiv*. Accessed 3 May 2024 at <https://www.euractiv.com/section/europe-s-east/news/trafficking-and-sexual-exploitation-of-ukrainian-refugees-on-the-rise/>.

Beck, Julian (1972) *Life of the Theatre: The Relation of the Artist to the Struggle of the People*. San Francisco, California: City Lights Press.

Beck, Julie (6 September 2013) 'Married to a doll: Why one man advocates synthetic love' *The Atlantic*. Accessed 3 May 2024 at <https://www.theatlantic.com/health/archive/2013/09/married-to-a-doll-why-one-man-advocates-synthetic-love/279361/>.

Becker, Ernest (1973) *The Denial of Death*. New York: The Free Press.

Bell, Rudolph (1987) *Holy Anorexia*. Chicago, Illinois: University of Chicago Press.

Belmi, Peter and Jeffrey Pfeffer (2016) 'Power and death: Mortality salience increases power seeking while feeling powerful reduces death anxiety' *Journal of Applied Psychology* 101 (5), pp. 702–720.

Benbow, M. Eric, Philip S. Barton, Michael D. Ulyshen, James C. Beasley, Travis L. DeVault, Michael S. Strickland, Jeffrey K. Tomberlin, Heather R. Jordan and Jennifer L. Pechal (2018) 'Necrobiome framework for bridging decomposition ecology of autotrophically and heterotrophically derived organic matter' *Ecological Monographs* 89 (1) pp. 1–26.

Benford, Gregory and Elisabeth Malartre (2008) *Beyond Human: Living with Robots and Cyborgs*. New York: Tor Publishing Group.

Benjamin, Walter (1936/1996) 'The work of art in the age of its technological reproducibility' in Howard Eiland and Gary Smith (Eds) *Selected Writings: 1935-1938*. Cambridge, Massachusetts: Belknap Press.

Berkeley Women's Liberation (1 December 1970) 'Letter from a transsexual??' *It Ain't Me, Babe*. Accessed 21 June 2024 at <https://revolution.berkeley.edu/assets/17660454_19701201_0014.pdf>.

Berkhofer, Robert (1878) *The White Man's Indian: Images of the American Indian from Columbus to the Present*. New York: Knopf Doubleday Publishing Group.

Bernal, J. D. (1929) *The World, The Flesh and The Devil*. London: Kegan Paul, Trench, Trubner & Co.

Berto, Francesco and Jacopo Tagliabue (2017) 'Cellular automata' *The Stanford Encyclopedia of Philosophy*. Accessed 7 May 2024 at <https://plato.stanford.edu/entries/cellular-automata/>.

Bhagavad Gita: Or, the Message of the Master (1907). Translated by Ramacharaka. Chicago, Illinois: The Yogi Publication Society.

Bilek, Jennifer (2024) *Transsexual Transgender Transhuman: Dispatches from the 11th Hour*. Mission Beach, Australia: Spinifex Press.

Birke, Lynda (2000) *Feminism and the Biological Body*. New Brunswick, New Jersey: Rutgers University Press.

Bishop, Ryan and Lillian S. Robinson (1998) *Night Market: Sexual Cultures and the Thai Economic Miracle*. Milton Park, Oxfordshire, UK: Routledge.

Blum, Virginia (2003) *Flesh Wounds: The Culture of Cosmetic Surgery*. Berkeley, California: University of California Press.

Boellstorff, Tom (2008) *Coming of Age in Second Life: An Anthropologist Explores the Virtually Human*. Princeton, New Jersey: Princeton University Press.

Boethius (524/1969) *The Consolation of Philosophy*. Translated by Victor Ernest Watts. New York: Penguin Books.

Bohan, Elise (2022) *Future Superhuman: Our Transhuman Lives in a Make-or-Break Century*. Montgomery, Alabama: NewSouth Books.

Bonnell, John K. (1917) 'The serpent with a human head in art and mystery plays' *American Journal of Archaeology* 21 (3) pp. 255-291.

Bordo, Susan (1993) *Unbearable Weight: Feminism, Western Culture, and the Body*. Berkeley, California: University of California Press.

Bottomley, Frank (1979) *Attitudes Towards the Body in Western Christendom*. London: Lepus Books.

Boyno, Gokhan and Semra Demir (2022) 'Plant-mycorrhiza communication and mycorrhizae in inter-plant communication' *Symbiosis* 86 pp. 155-168.

Braudy, Leo (2003) *From Chivalry to Terrorism: War and the Changing Nature of Masculinity*. New York: Alfred A. Knopf.

Bremmer, Jan (1983) 'Scapegoat rituals in Ancient Greece' *Harvard Studies in Classical Philology* 87 pp. 299-320.

Briffault, Robert (1931) *The Mothers: The Matriarchal Theory of Social Origins*. New York: Macmillan.

Brodribb, Somer (1992) *Nothing Mat(t)ers: A Feminist Critique of Postmodernism*. North Melbourne, Australia: Spinifex Press.

Brodwin, Erin (2019) 'The founder of a startup that charged $8,000 to fill your veins with young blood says he's shuttered the company and started a new one' *Business Insider*. Accessed 1 May 2024 at <https://www.businessinsider.com/young-blood-transfusions-ambrosia-shut-down-2019-6>.

Brondizio, Eduardo, Sandra Diaz, Josef Settele and Hien T. Ngo (Eds) (2019) *Global Assessment Report on Biodiversity and Ecosystem Services of the Intergovernmental Science-Policy Platform on Biodiversity and Ecosystem Services*. Bonn, Germany: IPBES Secretariat.

Brown, Pamela Allen (2014) 'The mirror and the cage: Queens and dwarfs in the Early Modern court' in Ronda Arab, Michelle Dowd, and Adam Zucker (Eds) *Historical Affects and the Early Modern Theater*. Milton Park, Oxfordshire, UK: Routledge.

Brown, Wendy (1988) *Manhood and Politics: A Feminist Reading in Political Theory*. Lanham, Maryland: Rowman & Littlefield.

The Buddha's "Way of Virtue": A Translation of the Dhammapada from the Pali Text (1912). Translated by W. D. C. Wagiswara and Kenneth Saunders. London: John Murray.

Burton, Robert (1624/1886) *The Anatomy of Melancholy, What It Is, with All the Kinds, Causes, Symptoms, Prognostics, and Several Cures of It. In Three Partitions*. Volume 3. London: John C. Nimmo.

Caldecott, Leonie and Stephanie Leland (Eds) (1983) *Reclaim the Earth: Women Speak Out for Life on Earth*. London: The Women's Press.

Cameron, Deborah and Elizabeth Frazer (1987) *The Lust to Kill: A Feminist Investigation of Sexual Murder*. New York: New York University Press.

Cameron, Nigel, M. (2022) 'Education is where the greatest and most valuable shifts may come' in Janna Anderson and Lee Rainie (Eds) *The Metaverse in 2040*. Washington, D.C.: Pew Research Center.

Campbell, Joseph (1959/1976) *The Masks of God: Oriental Mythology*. New York: Viking Press.

Camporesi, Piero (1988) *The Incorruptible Flesh: Bodily Mutation and Mortification in Religion and Folklore*. Cambridge, England: Cambridge University Press.

Camporesi, Piero (1991) *The Fear of Hell: Images of Damnation and Salvation in Early Modern Europe*. University Park, Pennsylvania: Pennsylvania State University Press.

Caputi, Jane (1987) *The Age of Sex Crime*. Bowling Green, Ohio: Bowling Green State University Popular Press.

Caputi, Jane (2004) *Goddesses and Monsters: Women, Myth, Power, and Popular Culture*. Madison, Wisconsin: University of Wisconsin Press.

Carabotti, Marilia, Annunziata Scirocco, Maria Antonietta Maselli and Carola Severi (2015) 'The gut-brain axis: Interactions between enteric microbiota, central, and enteric nervous systems' *Annals of Gastroenterology* 28 (2) pp. 203-209.

Carey, Benedict (10 December 2014) 'Architects of C.I.A. interrogation drew on psychology to induce "helplessness"' *The New York Times*. Accessed 13 May 2024 at <https://www.nytimes.com/2014/12/11/health/architects-of-cia-interrogation-drew-on-psychology-to-induce-helplessness.html>.

Carroll, Noel (1990) *The Philosophy of Horror: Or, Paradoxes of the Heart*. Milton Park, Oxfordshire, UK: Taylor & Francis.

Carson, Rachel (1954/2018) *Silent Spring & Other Writings on the Environment*. New York: Library of America.

CBS News Miami (8 September 2016) 'Police: After hours of interrogation, suspected killer admits role in mutilation murder' *CBSnews.com*. Accessed 19 May 2024 at <https://www.cbsnews.com/miami/news/new-information-released-in-mutilation-sex-murder/>.

Cepari, Virgilio (1849) *The Life of Saint Mary Magdalene of Pazzi, Carmelitess*. London: Thomas Richardson and Son.

Chalmers, David, J. (2022) *Reality+: Virtual Worlds and the Problems of Philosophy*. New York: W. W. Norton & Company.

Chatard, Armand, Leila Selimbegović, Paul N'Dri Konan, Jamie Arndt, Tom Pyszczynski, Fabio Lorenzi-Cioldi and Martial Van der Linden (2016) 'Terror management in times of war: Mortality salience effects on self-esteem and governmental and army support' *Journal of Peace Research* 48 (2) pp. 225-234.

Chu, Andrea Long (2018) 'On liking women' *N+1*. Accessed 12 May 2024 at <https://www.nplusonemag.com/issue-30/essays/on-liking-women/>.

Churchill, Ward (1997) *A Little Matter of Genocide: Holocaust and Denial in the Americas, 1492 to Present*. San Francisco, California: City Lights Publishers.

Clark, David (2014) 'On being "The Last Kantian in Germany": Dwelling with animals after Levinas' in Jennifer Ham and Matthew Senior (Eds) *Animal Acts: Configuring the Human in Western History*. Milton Park, Oxfordshire, UK: Taylor & Francis.

Claxton, Guy (2015) *Intelligence in the Flesh*. New Haven, Connecticut: Yale University Press.

Clynes, Manfred E. and Nathan S. Kline (1960) 'Cyborgs and space' *Astronautics* 5 (9) pp. 26-27, 74-76.

Coakley, Sarah (Ed.) (2000) *Religion and the Body*. Cambridge, UK: Cambridge University Press.

Coalition for Radical Life Extension (2022) 'Board members'. Accessed 2 May 2024 at <rlecoalition.com/boardmembers>.

Cohen, Jeffrey Jerome (Ed.) (1996) *Monster Theory: Reading Culture*. Minneapolis, Minnesota: University of Minnesota Press.

Cohen, Jeffrey Jerome (2003) *Medieval Identity Machines*. Minneapolis, Minnesota: University of Minnesota Press.

Collard, Andrée and Joyce Contrucci (1988) *Rape of the Wild: Man's Violence Against Animals and the Earth*. Bloomington, Indiana: Indiana University Press.

Collins, Steven (2000) 'The body in Theravada Buddhist monasticism' in Sarah Coakley (Ed.) *Religion and the Body*. Cambridge, UK: Cambridge University Press.

Compton, Howard (1904) *The Twentieth Century Dog (Non-Sporting)*. London: Grant Richards.

Confessions of Witches Under Torture, 1617 (1886). Edinburgh, Scotland: E. & G. Goldsmid.

Corea, Gena (1985) *The Mother Machine: Reproductive Technologies from Artificial Insemination to Artificial Wombs*. New York: Harper & Row.

Corrington, Gail (1986) 'Anorexia, asceticism, and autonomy: Self-control as liberation and transcendence' *Journal of Feminist Studies in Religion* 2 (2) pp. 51-61.

Cortright, Charles (2011) '"Poor Maggot-Sack that I am": The Human Body in the Theology of Martin Luther' Milwaukee, Wisconsin: Marquette University, PhD Dissertation.

Cox, Cathy, Jamie L. Goldenberg, Jamie Arnd and Tom Pyszczynski (2007) 'Mother's milk: An existential perspective on negative reactions to breast-feeding' *Personality and Social Psychology Bulletin* 33 (1) pp. 110-122.

Creed, Barbara (1993/2015) *The Monstrous Feminine: Film, Feminism, Psychoanalysis*. Milton Park, Oxfordshire, UK: Routledge.

Cruz, Ronald Allen Lopez (2012) 'Mutations and metamorphoses: Body horror is biological horror' *Journal of Popular Film and Television*, 40 (4) pp. 160-168.

Curtin, Deane (2007) 'Toward an ecologic ethic of care' in Josephine Donovan and Carol J. Adams (Eds) *The Feminist Care Tradition in Animal Ethics: A Reader*. New York: Columbia University Press.

Dallaire, Glenn (2011) 'Saint Gemma's heroic penances, sacrifices and mortifications' *StGemmaGalgani.com*. Accessed 18 March 2024 at <https://www.stgemmagalgani.com/2011/03/st-gemmas-heroic-penances-sacrifices.html#:~:text=It%20often%20cries%20out%2C%20and,to%20her%20repeated%20pressing%20requests>.

Daly, Mary (1978/1990) *Gyn/Ecology: The Metaethics of Radical Feminism*. Boston: Beacon Press.

Davidson, Arnold (1991) 'The horror of monsters' in James Sheehan and Morton Sosna (Eds) *The Boundaries of Humanity: Humans, Animals, Machines*. Oakland, California: University of California Press.

Davis, Julia Hirschfield (16 May 2018) 'Trump calls some unauthorized immigrants "animals" in rant' *The New York Times*. Accessed 3 May 2024 at <https://www.nytimes.com/2018/05/16/us/politics/trump-undocumented-immigrants-animals.html>.

Davis, Karen (2005) *The Holocaust and the Henmaid's Tale: A Case for Comparing Atrocities*. Woodstock, New York: Lantern Books.

Davis, Karen (2014) *Prisoned Chickens, Poisoned Eggs: An Inside Look at the Modern Poultry Industry*. Summertown, Tennessee: Book Publishing Company.

Davis, Kathy (1999) '"My body is my art": Cosmetic surgery as feminist utopia?' in Janet Price and Margaret Shildrick (Eds) *Feminist Theory and the Body: A Reader*. New York: Routledge.

de Balzac, Honoré (1829/1904) *The Physiology of Marriage*. London: Strangeways and Sons.

de Beauvoir, Simone (1949/2011) *The Second Sex*. New York: Knopf Doubleday.

Dei Segni, Lotario (Pope Innocent III) (1195/1969) *On the Misery of the Human Condition*. Edited by Donald R. Howard and translated by Margaret Mary Dietz. Indianapolis, Indiana: The Bobbs-Merrill Company, Inc.

Deneven, William (1992) 'The pristine myth: The landscape of the Americas' *Annals of the Association of American Geographers* 82 (3) pp. 369-385.

Delumeau, Jean (1990) *Sin and Fear: The Emergence of a Western Guilt Culture, 13th-18th Centuries*. New York: St. Martin's Press.

Dery, Mark (1996) *Escape Velocity: Cyberculture at the End of the Century*. New York: Grove Press.

Des Niau (1634/2020) 'The history of the devils of Loudun' in Joseph P. Laycock (Ed.) *The Penguin Book of Exorcisms*. New York: Penguin Publishing Group.

Descartes, René (1631/1916) *A Discourse on Method*. Translated by John Veitch. London: J. M. Dent & Sons, Ltd.

Descartes, René (1641/1911) *The Philosophical Works of Descartes*. Translated by Elizabeth Haldane. Cambridge, UK: Cambridge University Press. Accessed online 27 May 2024 at <https://yale.learningu.org/download/041e9642-df02-4eed-a895-70e472df2ca4/H2665_Descartes%27%20Meditations.pdf>.

Descartes, René (1641/1979) *Meditations on First Philosophy*. Indianapolis, Indiana: Hackett Publishing.

Diamond, Irene and Gloria Feman Orenstein (Eds) (1990) *Reweaving the World: The Emergence of Ecofeminism*. San Francisco, California: Sierra Club Books.

Dick, Steven, J. and Mark Lupisella (Eds) (2009) *Cosmos & Culture: Cultural Evolution in a Cosmic Context*. Washington, D.C.: National Aeronautics and Space Administration, Office of External Relations, History Division.

Dick, Steven, J. (2009) 'Bringing culture to cosmos: The postbiological universe' in Steven J. Dick and Mark Lupisella (Eds) *Cosmos & Culture: Cultural Evolution in a Cosmic Context*. Washington, D.C.: National Aeronautics and Space Administration, Office of External Relations, History Division.

Dijkstra, Bram (1986) *Idols of Perversity: Fantasies of Feminine Evil in Fin-de-Siecle Culture*. Oxford, UK: Oxford University Press.

Dines, Gail (2011) *Pornland: How Porn Has Hijacked Our Sexuality*. Boston, Massachusetts: Beacon Press; North Melbourne: Spinifex Press.

Doerksen, Mark (2018) 'How to make sense: Sensory modification in grinder subculture'. Montreal, Canada: Concordia University, PhD Dissertation.

Doniger, Wendy (1999) *Merriam-Webster's Encyclopedia of World Religions*. Springfield, MA: Merriam-Webster.

Doniger, Wendy (2000) 'The body in Hindu texts' in Sarah Coakley (Ed.) *Religion and the Body*. Cambridge, UK: Cambridge University Press.

Donovan, Josephine and Carol J. Adams (Eds) (2007) *The Feminist Care Tradition in Animal Ethics: A Reader*. New York: Columbia University Press.

Donovan, Josephine (2007) 'Attention to suffering' in Josephine Donovan and Carol J. Adams (Eds) *The Feminist Care Tradition in Animal Ethics: A Reader*. New York: Columbia University Press.

Douglas, Mary (1966/2003) *Purity and Danger*. London: Routledge.

Downes, Stephen (2022) 'Despite concerns, "the metaverse will eventually draw us together" as other media have done throughout history' in Janna Anderson and Lee Rainie (Eds) *The Metaverse in 2040*. Washington, D.C.: Pew Research Center.

Du Maurier, George (1984) *Trilby*. London: Osgood, McIlvaine & Co.

Dunn, Billie Schwab (22 April 2022) 'Woman brands herself "plastic bimbo" and dreams of being "real-life sex doll"' *The Daily Star*. Accessed 3 May 2024 at <https://www.dailystar.co.uk/real-life/bimbo-calls-herself-real-life-26761153>.

Dworkin, Andrea (1974) *Woman Hating*. New York: Dutton Press.

Dworkin, Andrea (1976) *Our Blood: Prophecies and Discourses on Sexual Politics*. New York: Perigee Books.

Dworkin, Andrea (1987) *Intercourse*. New York: The Free Press.

Dworkin, Andrea (1997) *Life and Death: Unapologetic Writings on the Continuing War Against Women*. New York: The Free Press.

Dworkin, Andrea (2000) *Scapegoat: The Jews, Israel, and Women's Liberation*. New York: Simon & Schuster.

Ebenstein, Joanna (Ed.) (2017) *Death: A Graveside Companion*. New York: W. W. Norton.

Elias, Norbert (1978) *The Civilizing Process*. Charlottesville, Virginia: University of Virginia Press.

Ellison, Harlan (1971) *Alone Against Tomorrow: Stories of Alienation in Speculative Fiction*. New York: Macmillan.

Enloe, Cynthia (1989/2014) *Bananas, Beaches, and Bases: Making Feminist Sense of International Politics*. Oakland, CA: University of California Press.

Evangelical News Press Service (19 October 1969) 'Chapel of Astronauts to be built at Cape Kennedy' *Evangel News Digest*. Accessed 25 September 2023 at <https://pentecostalarchives.org/?a=d&d=PEV19691019-01.1.29&e=-------en-20--1--img-txIN------------>.

Faber, Rev. Frederick William (Ed.) (1671/1855) *The Life of Saint Rosa of Lima*. Philadelphia, Pennsylvania: Peter F. Cunningham & Son. Accessed 5 May 2024 at <https://tile.loc.gov/storage-services/public/gdcmassbookdig/lifeofsaintroseo00hans/lifeofsaintroseo00hans.pdf>.

Fanon, Frantz (1967/2008) *Black Skin, White Masks*. New York: Grove Press.

Farmer, J. Doyne and Alletta d'A Belin (1990) 'Artificial life: The coming evolution' *Santa Fe Institute Working Paper: 1990-003*.

Fatka, Jacqui (16 December 2020) 'FDA approves first intentional genomic alteration pig' *FarmProgress*. Accessed 13 September 2023 at <https://www.farmprogress.com/technology/fda-approves-first-intentional-genomic-alteration-pig>.

Favazza, Armando, R. (2011) *Bodies Under Siege: Self-Mutilation, Non-suicidal Self-Injury, and Body Modification in Culture and Psychiatry*. Baltimore, Maryland: Johns Hopkins University Press.

Federici, Silvia (2020) *Beyond the Periphery of the Skin*. Oakland, California: PM Press.

Feher, Michel, Nadia Tazi, and Ramona Naddaff (Eds) (1989) *Fragments for a History of the Human Body, Part 1*. New York: Zone Books.

Ferber, Abby (2007) 'The Construction of Black Masculinity: White Supremacy Now and Then' *Journal of Sport and Social Issues* 31 (1) pp. 11-24.

Firestone, Shulamith (1971) *The Dialectic of Sex: The Case for Feminist Revolution*. Revised Edition. New York: Bantam Books.

Fisher, Elizabeth (1979) *Women's Creation: Sexual Evolution and the Shaping of Society*. New York: Anchor Books.

Flaubert, Gustave (1862/1899) *Salambo: A Realistic Romance of Modern Carthage*. London: Gibbings & Company, Limited.

Floreano, Dario and Nicola Nosengo (2022) *Tales from a Robotic World: How Intelligent Machines Will Shape Our Future*. Cambridge, Massachusetts: MIT Press.

Food and Agriculture Organization of the United Nations (2020) 'The state of the world's forests 2020' *FAO.org*. Accessed 19 May 2024 at <https://www.fao.org/state-of-forests/en/>.

Frazer, James (1890/1913) *The Golden Bough: Part VI. The Scapegoat*. London: MacMillan and Co. Limited.

Freeman, Hadley (2023) *Good Girls: A Story and a Study of Anorexia*. New York: Simon & Schuster.

Freud, Sigmund (1932/1964) 'My contact with Josef Popper-Lynkeus' in James Strachey, Anna Freud and Carrie Lee Rothgeb (Eds) *The Standard Edition of the Complete Psychological Works of Sigmund Freud, Volume 22*. London: Hogarth Press and the Institute of Psychoanalysis.

Friend, Tad (2017) 'Silicon Valley's quest to live forever' *The New Yorker*. Accessed 1 May 2024 at <https://www.newyorker.com/magazine/2017/04/03/silicon-valleys-quest-to-live-forever>.

Fritsche, Immo and Annedore Hoppe (2019) '"We supernaturals": Terror management and people's ambivalent relationship with nature' in Clay Routledge and Matthew Vess (Eds) *Handbook of Terror Management Theory*. London: Academic Press.

Gaard, Greta (Ed.) (1993) *Ecofeminism: Women, Animals, Nature*. Philadelphia, Pennsylvania: Temple University Press.

Gabbat, Adam (2019) 'Is Silicon Valley's quest for immortality a fate worse than death?' *The Guardian*. Accessed 1 May 2024 at <https://www.theguardian.com/technology/2019/feb/22/silicon-valley-immortality-blood-infusion-gene-therapy>.

Gerhard, Michael, David Moore and Dave Hobbs (2004) 'Embodiment and copresence in collaborative interfaces' *International Journal of Human-Computer Studies* 61 (4) pp. 453–480.

Gibson, William (1984) *Neuromancer*. New York: Ace Books.

Gilman, Sander (1991) *The Jew's Body*. Milton Park, Oxfordshire, UK: Routledge.

Gilman, Sander (1999) *Making the Body Beautiful: A Culture History of Aesthetic Surgery*. Princeton, New Jersey: Princeton University Press.

Gilmore, David (2012) *Monsters: Evil Beings, Mythical Beasts, and All Manner of Imaginary Terrors*. Philadelphia, Pennsylvania: University of Pennsylvania Press.

Girard, René (1972) *Violence and the Sacred*. Baltimore, Maryland: Johns Hopkins University Press.

Girard, René (1981) *The Scapegoat*. Baltimore, Maryland: Johns Hopkins University Press.

Gladstone, Reginald, J. and Cecil P. G. Wakeley (1923) 'Defective development of the mandibular arch' *Journal of Anatomy* 57 pp. 149–167.

Glanton, Dahleen and Chicago Tribune Staff (6 April 1887) 'The tragic world of Girl X' *The Chicago Tribune*. Accessed 18 May 2024 at <https://www.chicagotribune.com/1997/04/06/the-tragic-world-of-girl-x-2/>.

Global Industry Analysts, Inc. (April 2024) 'Anti-aging products - global strategic business report' *Research and Markets*. Accessed 1 May 2024 at <https://www.researchandmarkets.com/reports/2832312/anti-aging-products-global-strategic-business?utm_source=GNOM&utm_medium=PressRelease&utm_code=f2tbzm&utm_campaign=1416735+-+Anti-Aging+Products+Industry+Projected+to+be+Worth+%2483.2+Billion+by+2027+-+Key+Trends%2c+Opportunities+and+Players&utm_exec=joca220prd>.

Gluck, Genevieve (11 November 2021) 'Nina Arsenault: Canada's most famous "trans woman"' *Women's Voices*. Accessed 19 May 2024 at <https://genevievegluck.substack.com/p/nina-arsenault>.

Goethe, Johann Wolfgang von (1808) *Faust: Ein Tragödie*. Leipzig, Germany: Insel Verlag.

Goldenberg, Jamie, Tom Pyszczynski, Jeff Greenberg, Sheldon Solomon, Benjamin Cluck and Robin Cromwell (2001) 'I am *not* an animal: Mortality salience, disgust, and the denial of human creatureliness' *Journal of Experimental Psychology: General* 130 (3) pp. 427–435.

Goldenberg, Jamie, Joshua Hart, Tom Pyszczynski, Gwendolyn Warnica, Mark Landau and Lisa Thomas (2006) 'Ambivalence toward the body: Death, neuroticism, and the flight from physical sensation' *Personality and Social Psychology Bulletin* 32 (9) pp. 1264–1277.

Goldenberg, Jamie, Kasey Lynn Morris and Patrick Boyd (2019) 'Terror management is for the birds and the bees: An existential perspective on the threat associated with human corporeality' in Clay Routledge and Matthew Vess (Eds) *Handbook of Terror Management Theory*. London: Academic Press.

Gollner, Adam (2014) *The Book of Immortality: The Science, Belief, and Magic Behind Living Forever*. New York: Scribner.

Goss, Michael Joseph (November 2018) 'The Pentagon's push to program soldiers' brains' *The Atlantic*. Accessed 12 May 2024 at <https://www. theatlantic.com/magazine/archive/2018/11/the-pentagon-wants-to-weaponize-the-brain-what-could-go-wrong/570841/>.

Gow, Andrew (1995/2021) *The Red Jews: Antisemitism in an Apocalyptic Age, 1200–1600*. Leiden, the Netherlands: Brill.

Graves, Robert and Raphael Patai (1964) *The Hebrew Myths*. New York: Doubleday.

Gridneff, Ilya, Emily Schultheis and Dmytro Drabyk (23 July 2023) 'Inside a Ukrainian baby factory' *Politico*. Accessed 3 May 2024 at <https://www. politico.com/news/2023/07/23/ukraine-surrogates-fertility-00104913>.

Griffin, Susan (1978) *Woman and Nature: The Roaring Inside Her*. New York: HarperCollins Publishers.

Griffin, Susan (1981) *Pornography and Silence: Culture's Revenge Against Nature*. New York: Harper & Row.

Griffin, Susan (1989) 'Split Culture' in Judith Plant (Ed.) *Healing the Wounds: The Promise of Ecofeminism*. Toronto, Canada: Between the Lines Books.

Griffin, Susan (1995) *The Eros of Everyday Life: Essays on Ecology, Gender, and Society*. New York: Doubleday.

Gruen, Lori (2015) *Entangled Empathy: An Alternative Ethic for Our Relationships with Animals*. Woodstock, New York: Lantern Books.

Guerini, Sylvia (2023) *From the 'Neutral' Body to the Posthuman Cyborg: A Critique of Gender Ideology*. Mission Beach, Australia: Spinifex Press.

Guiley, Rosemary (2009) *The Encyclopedia of Demons and Demonology*. New York: Facts on File, Inc.

Gutman, Ysrael and Michael Berenbaum (1998) *Anatomy of the Auschwitz Death Camp*. Bloomington, Indiana: Indiana University Press.

Haaren, John Henry (1904) *Famous Men of Greece*. New York: American Book Company.

Halpin, Zuleyma Tang (1989) 'Scientific objectivity and the concept of "The Other"' *Women's Studies International Forum*, 12 (3) pp. 285-294.

Ham, Jennifer and Matthew Senior (Eds) (2014) *Animal Acts: Configuring the Human in Western History*. Milton Park, Oxfordshire, UK: Taylor & Francis.

Ham, Jennifer (2014) 'Taming the Beast' in Jennifer Ham and Matthew Senior (Eds) *Animal Acts: Configuring the Human in Western History*. Milton Park, Oxfordshire, UK: Taylor & Francis.

Hamilton, Sue (1995) 'From the Buddha to Buddhagosa' in Jane Marie Law (Ed.) *Religious Reflections on the Human Body*. Bloomington, Indiana: University of Indiana Press.

Han, Yimin, Boya Wang, Han Gao, Chengwei He, Rongxuan Hua, Chen Liang, Sitan Zhang, Ying Wang, Shuzi Xin and Jingdong Xu (2022) 'Vagus nerve and underlying impact on the gut microbiota-brain axis in behavior and neurodegenerative diseases' *Journal of Inflammation Research* 15 pp. 6212–6230.

Haraway, Donna (2004) 'A manifesto for cyborgs' in *The Haraway Reader*. Milton Park, Oxfordshire, UK: Routledge.

Harrington, Erin (2018) *Women, Monstrosity, and Horror Film: Gynaehorror*. Milton Park, Oxfordshire, UK: Taylor & Francis.

Hawthorne, Susan (2002/2022) *Wild Politics: Feminism, Globalisation, Bio/Diversity*. North Melbourne/Mission Beach, Australia: Spinifex Press.

Hawthorne, Susan (2020) *Vortex: The Crisis of Patriarchy*. Mission Beach, Australia: Spinifex Press.

Hayon, Oren, J. (2009) 'Moses's death, God's breath' *ReformJudaism.org*. Accessed 1 May 2024 <https://reformjudaism.org/learning/torah-study/torah-commentary/mosess-death-gods-breath>.

Hazelwood, Robert, R. and John E. Douglass (1980) 'The lust murderer' *FBI Law Enforcement Bulletin* 49 (1) pp. 18–22.

Hedges, Chris (2022) *The Greatest Evil is War*. New York: Seven Stories Press.

Heholt, Ruth and Melissa Edmundson (Eds) (2020) *Gothic Animals: Uncanny Otherness and the Animal With-Out*. New York: Springer International Publishing.

Heuveline, Patrick (2015) 'The boundaries of genocide: Quantifying the uncertainty of the death toll during the Pol Pot regime in Cambodia (1975-79)' *Population Studies* 69 (2) pp. 201–218.

Hill, Kashmir (7 October 2022) 'This is life in the Metaverse' *The New York Times*. Accessed 30 September 2023 at <https://www.nytimes.com/2022/10/07/technology/metaverse-facebook-horizon-worlds.html>.

Hinton, Alexander, Andrew Woolford and Jeff Benvenuto (Eds) (2014) *Colonial Genocide in Indigenous North America*. Durham, North Carolina: Duke University Press.

Hirschberger, Gilad and Tsachi Ein-Dor (2006) 'Defenders of a lost cause: Terror management and violent resistance to the disengagement plan' *Personality and Social Psychology Bulletin*, 32 (6) pp. 761-769.

Hirschberger, Gilad, Tom Pyszczynski, Tsachi Ein-Dor, Tal Shani Sherman, Eihab Kadah, Pelin Kesebir and Young Chin Park (2016) 'Fear of death amplifies retributive justice motivations and encourages political violence' *Peace and Conflict: Journal of Peace Psychology* 22 (1) pp. 67-74.

Hoek, Hans Wijbrand (2006) 'Incidence, prevalence and mortality of anorexia nervosa and other eating disorders' *Current Opinion in Psychiatry* 19 (4) pp. 389-394.

Holt, Nick (2007) *Love Me, Love My Doll*. London: North One Television. Viewed online 27 May 2024 at <https://tubitv.com/series/300005756/love-me-love-my-doll>.

Horn, Dana (25 January 2018) 'The men who want to live forever' *The New York Times*. Accessed 1 May 2024 at <https://www.nytimes.com/2018/01/25/opinion/sunday/silicon-valley-immortality.html>.

Hornaday, William Temple (1889) 'The extermination of the American bison' in United States National Museum (Ed.) *Report of the United States National Museum for the Year Ending June 30, 1887*. Washington, D.C.: Government Printing Office.

Horschig, Doreen (2022) 'Israeli public opinion on the use of nuclear weapons: Lessons from terror management theory' *Journal of Global Security Studies* 7 (2) pp. 1-18.

Hotine, Emily (2021) 'Biology, society, and sex: Deconstructing anti-trans rhetoric and trans-exclusionary radical feminism' *Journal of the Nufffield Department of Surgical Sciences* 2 (3) pp. 1-5.

Hu, Elise (2023) *Flawless: Lessons in Looks and Culture from the K-Beauty Capital*. New York: Penguin Publishing Group.

Hubbard, Tasha (2014) 'Buffalo genocide in nineteenth-century North America: "Kill, skin, and sell"' in Alexander Hinton, Andrew Woolford, and Jeff Benvenuto (Eds) *Colonial Genocide in Indigenous North America*. Durham, North Carolina: Duke University Press.

Hughes, Donna and Tatyana Denisova (2003) 'Trafficking in women from Ukraine' *United States Department of Justice*. Accessed 12 May 2024 at <https://www.ojp.gov/pdffiles1/nij/grants/203275.pdf>.

Hultgard, Anders (2022) *The End of the World in Scandinavian Mythology*. Oxford, UK: Oxford University Press.

Hund, Wulf, D. (2021) 'Dehumanization and social death as fundamentals of racism' in Maria Kronfeldner (Ed.) *The Routledge Handbook of Dehumanization*. Milton Park, Oxfordshire, UK: Routledge.

Huysmans, J. K. (1901/1979) *Saint Lydwine of Schiedam*. Charlotte, North Carolina: Tan Books.

Ito, Junji (2018) *Uzumaki (3-in-1 Deluxe Edition)*. San Francisco, California: VIZ Media.

Jacobsen, Annie (2015) *The Pentagon's Brain: An Uncensored History of DARPA, America's Top-Secret Military Research Agency*. New York: Little, Brown and Company.

Jacobson, Nora (2000) *Cleavage: Technology, Controversy, and the Ironies of the Man-made Breast*. New Brunswick, New Jersey: Rutgers University Press.

Jantzen, Grace (2004) *Death and the Displacement of Beauty: Foundations of Violence*. Milton Park, Oxfordshire, UK: Routledge.

Jeffreys, Sheila (2005/2015) *Beauty and Misogyny: Harmful Cultural Practices in the West*. Milton Park, Oxfordshire, UK: Routledge.

Jeffreys, Sheila (2008) *The Industrial Vagina: The Political Economy of the Global Sex Trade*. Milton Park, Oxfordshire, UK: Taylor & Francis.

Jezierska, Maria (1986/2020) 'Some aspects of human physiology and concentration camp realities' in Marta Kapera (Translator) *Medical Review - Auschwitz* 1986 (1) pp. 161-166. Accessed 5 May 2024 at <https://www.mp.pl/auschwitz/journal/english/240774,some-aspects-of-human-physiology-and-concentration-camp-realities>.

Johnson, Mark (2017) *Embodied Mind, Meaning, and Reason: How Our Bodies Give Rise to Understanding*. Chicago, Illinois: University of Chicago Press.

Kaiser, Jocelyn (4 May 2014) 'Young blood renews old mice' *Science*. Accessed 1 May 2024 at <https://www.science.org/content/article/young-blood-renews-old-mice>.

Kaku, Michio (2018) *The Future of Humanity: Terraforming Mars, Interstellar Travel, Immortality, and Our Destiny Beyond the Earth*. London: Penguin Books.

Kanda, Fusae (2005) 'Behind the sensationalism: Images of a decaying corpse in Japanese Buddhist art' *The Art Bulletin* 87 (1) pp. 24-49.

Kaoutzanis, Christodoulos, Julian Winocour, Jacob Unger, Allen Gabriel and G. Patrick Maxwell (2019) 'The evolution of breast implants' *Seminars in Plastic Surgery* 33 (4) pp. 217-223.

Kashima, Emiko, Michael Halloran, Masaki Yuki and Yoshihisa Kashima (2004) 'The effects of personal and collective mortality salience on individualism: Comparing Australians and Japanese with higher and lower self-esteem' *Journal of Experimental Social Psychology* 40 pp. 384-392.

Katajala-Peltomaa, Sari (2020) *Demonic Possession and Lived Religion in Later Medieval Europe*. Oxford, UK: Oxford University Press.

Kauffman, Clark (8 August 2023) 'Care facility accused of neglect in Iowa woman's death' *Iowa Capital Dispatch*. Accessed 19 May 2024 at <https://iowacapitaldispatch.com/2023/08/08/care-facility-accused-of-neglect-in-iowa-womans-death/>.

Kavan, Anna (1967) *Ice*. London: Peter Owen Publishers.

Kay, Grace (19 April 2022) 'Elon Musk said life on Mars won't be luxurious — it will be "cramped, difficult, hard work"' *Business Insider*. Accessed 13 May 2024 at <https://www.businessinsider.com/elon-musk-mars-trip-cramped-difficult-hard-work-2022-4>.

Kearney, Breanne, E. and Ruth A. Lanius (2022) 'The brain-body disconnect: a somatic sensory basis for trauma-related disorders' *Frontiers in Neuroscience*. Published online 21 November 2022. Accessed 14 May 2024 at <https://www.ncbi.nlm.nih.gov/pmc/articles/PMC9720153/>.

Keen, Sam (1995) *Hymns to an Unknown God: Awakening the Spirit in Everyday Life*. New York: Random House Publishing Group.

Kelly, Suzanne (2015) *Greening Death: Reclaiming Burial Practices and Restoring Our Tie to the Earth*. London: Rowman & Littlefield.

Kenny, Anthony, Dugald Murdoch, John Cottingham and Robert Stoothoff (Eds) (1988) *Descartes: Selected Philosophical Writings*. Cambridge, UK: Cambridge University Press.

Kheel, Marti (2007) *Nature Ethics: An Ecofeminist Perspective*. Lanham, Maryland: Rowman & Littlefield.

King, Stephen (1978) *Night Shift*. New York: Doubleday.

Klar, Rebecca (27 June 2022) 'How bad actors are using tech platforms to sexually exploit, traffic Ukrainian women' *The Hill*. Accessed 12 May 2024 at <https://thehill.com/policy/technology/3537145-how-bad-actors-are-using-tech-platforms-to-sexually-exploit-traffic-ukrainian-women/>.

Knight, Damon (July 1968) 'Masks' *Playboy Magazine*. Accessed 21 September 2023 at <https://ranprieur.com/readings/masks.html>.

Knowler, Susan Penelope, Lena Gilstedt, Thomas J. Mitchell, Jelena Jovanovik, Holger Andreas Volk and Clare Rusbridge (2019) 'Pilot study of head conformation changes over time in the Cavalier King Charles spaniel breed' *The Veterinary Record* 184 (4) pp. 1-7.

Koene, Randal (2013) 'Uploading to substrate-independent minds' in Max More and Natasha Vita-More (Eds) *The Transhumanist Reader*. Hoboken, New Jersey: Wiley.

Kolber, Jonathan (2022) 'The demand for all manner of physical objects will drastically diminish' in Janna Anderson and Lee Rainie (Eds) *The Metaverse in 2040*. Washington, D.C.: Pew Research Center.

Kristeva, Julia (1980) *Powers of Horror: An Essay on Abjection*. New York: Columbia University Press.

Kronfeldner, Maria (Ed.) (2021) *The Routledge Handbook of Dehumanization*. Milton Park, Oxfordshire, UK: Routledge.

Kurek, Laura (2015) 'Eyes wide cut: the origins of Korea's plastic surgery craze' *Wilson Quarterly*. Accessed 12 May 2024 at <https://www.wilsonquarterly.com/quarterly/transitions/eyes-wide-cut-the-american-origins-of-koreas-plastic-surgery-craze>.

Kurzweil, Ray (2005) *The Singularity is Near: When Humans Transcend Biology*. New York: Viking Press.

Kurzweil, Ray (2024) *The Singularity is Nearer: When We Merge with AI*. New York: Penguin Publishing Group.

Lackner, Stephan (1984) *Peaceable Nature: An Optimistic View of Life on Earth*. New York: Harper and Row.

Langness, Lewis, L. (1974) 'Ritual, power, and male dominance' *Ethos* 2 (3) pp. 189–212.

Laska, Vera (Ed.) (1983a) *Women in the Resistance and in the Holocaust: The Voices of Eyewitnesses*. London: Bloomsbury Academic.

Laska, Vera (1983b) 'Auschwitz — a factual deposition' in Vera Laska (Ed.) *Women in the Resistance and in the Holocaust: The Voices of Eyewitnesses*. London: Bloomsbury Academic, pp. 169–185.

Lauber, Christian L., Jessica L. Metcalf, Kyle Keepers, Gail Ackermann, David O. Carter and Rob Knight (2014) 'Vertebrate decomposition is accelerated by soil microbes' *Applied and Environmental Microbiology* 80 (16) pp. 4920–4929.

Laughland, Oliver (20 May 2014) 'How the CIA tortured its detainees' *The Guardian*. Accessed 6 May 2024 at <https://www.theguardian.com/us-news/2014/dec/09/cia-torture-methods-waterboarding-sleep-deprivation>.

Launius, Roger and Howard McCurdy (2008) *Robots in Space: Technology, Evolution, and Interplanetary Travel*. Baltimore, Maryland: John Hopkins University Press.

Law, Jane Marie (Ed.) (1995) *Religious Reflections on the Human Body*. Bloomington, Indiana: University of Indiana Press.

Lawson, James (2021) *Loving and Hating the World: Ambivalence and Discipleship*. Eugene, Oregon: Cascade Books.

Laycock, Joseph, P. (Ed.) (2020) *The Penguin Book of Exorcisms*. New York: Penguin Publishing Group.

Leary, Timothy, Ralph Metzner and Richard Alpert (1964) *The Psychedelic Experience: A Manual Based on the Tibetan Book of the Dead*. New York: Citadel Press Books.

Lecky, William Edward Hartpole (1869) *History of European Morals from Augustus to Charlemagne*, Vol. II. New York: D. Appleton and Company.

Lecuona, Laura (2024) *Gender Identity: Lies and Dangers*. Mission Beach, Australia: Spinifex Press.

Lederer, Wolfgang (1968) *The Fear of Women*. New York: Grune & Stratton.

Le Guin, Ursula K. (1986/1989) 'Woman/wilderness' in Judith Plant (Ed.) *Healing the Wounds: The Promise of Ecofeminism*. Toronto, Canada: Between the Lines Books.

Lelwica, Michelle Mary (1999) *Starving for Salvation: The Spiritual Dimensions of Eating Problems among American Girls and Women*. Oxford, UK: Oxford University Press.

Lemay, Helen Rodnite (Ed.) (1992) *Women's Secrets: A Translation of Pseudo-Albertus Magnus's De Secretis Mulierum with Commentaries*. Albany, New York: State University Press of New York.

Levack, Brian P. (1992) *Witchcraft, Women, and Society*. New York: Garland Publishing.

Levy, David (2007) *Love and Sex with Robots: The Evolution of Human-Robot Relationships*. New York: HarperCollins.

Levy, Hanna (1983) 'Notes from the camp of the dead' in Vera Laska (Ed.) *Women in the Resistance and in the Holocaust: The Voices of Eyewitnesses*. London: Bloomsbury Academic.

Levy, Rachel, Marisa Taylor and Akriti Sharma (26 May 2023) 'Elon Musk's Neuralink wins FDA approval for human study of brain implants' *Reuters*. Accessed 18 September 2023 at <https://www.reuters.com/science/elon-musks-neuralink-gets-us-fda-approval-human-clinical-study-brain-implants-2023-05-25/>.

Lifton, Robert Jay (1968/2012) *Death in Life: Survivors of Hiroshima*. Chapel Hill, North Carolina: University of North Carolina Press.

Lifton, Robert Jay and Eric Markusen (1990) *The Genocidal Mentality: Nazi Holocaust and Nuclear Threat*. New York: Basic Books.

Lorde, Audre (1976) *Between Ourselves*. Point Reyes, California: Eidolon Editions.

Lovecraft, H. P. (2005) *Tales*. New York: Library of America.

Mahanirvana Tantra (*Tantra of the Great Liberation*) (1913). Translated by Arthur Avalon. London: Luzac & Co.

Malarek, Victor (2011) *The Natashas: The Horrific Inside Story of Slavery, Rape, and Murder in the Global Sex Trade*. New York: Arcade Publishing.

Malinowski, Bronislaw (1922/2014) *Argonauts of the Western Pacific*. Milton Park, Oxfordshire, UK: Taylor & Francis.

Marinetti, Filippo Tommaso (1909/1993) 'The founding and manifesto of Futurism' in Charles Harrison and Paul Wood (Eds) *Art in Theory 1900–1990*. Hoboken, New Jersey: Wiley-Blackwell.

Marx, Patricia (16 March 2015) 'About face' *The New Yorker*. Accessed online 21 July 2024 at <https://www.newyorker.com/magazine/2015/03/23/about-face>.

Martin, Malachi (1976) *Hostage to the Devil: The Possession and Exorcism of Five Contemporary Americans*. Pleasantville, New York: Reader's Digest Press.

Marya, Rupa and Raj Patel (2021) *Inflamed: Deep Medicine and the Anatomy of Justice*. New York: Farrar, Straus, and Giroux.

Mason, Jim (2004) *An Unnatural Order: The Roots of Our Destruction of Nature*. Woodstock, New York: Lantern Books.

Mathews, Freya (2005) *Reinhabiting Reality: Towards a Recovery of Culture*. Albany, New York: State University of New York Press.

McGinn, Colin (2011) *The Meaning of Disgust*. New York: Oxford University Press, USA.

Medet, Halil Ibraham (23 October 2023) 'Israel paints Palestinians as "animals" to legitimize war crimes: Israeli scholar' *AA.com*. Accessed 3 May 2024 at <https://www.aa.com.tr/en/middle-east/israel-paints-palestinians-as-animals-to-legitimize-war-crimes-israeli-scholar/3030278>.

Meeker, David, L. and Calvin Ross Hamilton (2006) 'An overview of the rendering industry' in David L. Meeker (Ed.) *Essential Rendering: All About the Animal By-Products Industry*. Alexandria, Virginia: National Renderers Association. Accessed 3 May 2024 at <https://nara.org/wp-content/uploads/2019/10/essential_rendering_book3.pdf>.

Menon, Alka Vaid (2023) *Refashioning Race: How Global Cosmetic Surgery Crafts New Beauty Standards*. Oakland, California: University of California Press.

Merchant, Carolyn (1980/1989) *The Death of Nature: Women, Ecology, and the Scientific Revolution*. New York: Harper & Row.

Metzger, Deena (1989) 'Invoking the grove' in Judith Plant (Ed.) *Healing the Wounds: The Promise of Ecofeminism*. Toronto, Ontario: Between the Lines Press.

Michelet, Jules (1858) *Joan of Arc: Or, The Maid of Orleans*. Boston: Houghton Mifflin Company.

Midgley, Mary (1978/2004) *Beast and Man: The Roots of Human Nature*. Milton Park, Oxfordshire, UK: Taylor & Francis.

Midgley, Mary (1992) *Science as Salvation: A Modern Myth and its Meaning*. London: Routledge.

Mies, Maria (1986/2014) *Patriarchy and Accumulation on a World Scale: Women in the International Division of Labor*. London: Zed Books; North Melbourne: Spinifex Press.

Mies, Maria and Vandana Shiva (1993) *Ecofeminism*. New York: Zed Books; North Melbourne: Spinifex Press.

Miller, Lisa (7 September 2014) 'The trans-everything CEO' *New York Magazine*. Accessed 13 September 2023 at <https://nymag.com/news/features/martine-rothblatt-transgender-ceo/>.

Miller, William Ian (2009) *The Anatomy of Disgust*. Cambridge, Massachusetts: Harvard University Press.

Millett, Kate (1970) *Sexual Politics*. New York: Doubleday.

Millett, Kate (1979) *The Basement: Meditations on a Human Sacrifice*. New York: Simon and Schuster.

MIT Press (2024) 'Artificial Life' *MIT Press Direct*. Accessed 28 March 2024 at <https://direct.mit.edu/artl>.

Moller, David Wendell (1996) *Confronting Death: Values, Institutions, and Human Mortality*. Oxford, UK: Oxford University Press.

Monaghan, Patricia (1997) *The New Book of Goddesses and Heroines*. Woodbury, Minnesota: Llewellyn Worldwide.

Moravec, Hans (2013) 'Pigs in cyberspace' in Max More and Natasha Vita-More (Eds) *The Transhumanist Reader*. Hoboken, New Jersey: Wiley.

More, Max and Natasha Vita-More (Eds) (2013) *The Transhumanist Reader*. Hoboken, New Jersey: Wiley.

More, Max (2013) 'A letter to Mother Nature' in Max More and Natasha Vita-More (Eds) *The Transhumanist Reader*. Hoboken, New Jersey: Wiley.

Morey, Peter and Amina Yaqin (2011) *Framing Muslims: Stereotyping and Representation After 9/11*. Cambridge, Massachusetts: Harvard University Press.

Morgan, Fidelis (1989) *A Misogynist's Sourcebook*. London: Jonathan Cape.

Morrigan, Viviane (2023) 'Patriarchal imaginaries beyond the human: "Sex" robots, fetish and fantasy in the domination and control of women' in Kathleen Richardson and Charlotta Odlind (Eds) *Man-Made Women: The Sexual Politics of Sex Dolls and Sex Robots*. New York: Springer International Publishing.

Moshakis, Alex (2019) 'How to live forever: meet the extreme life-extensionists' *The Guardian*. Accessed 1 May 2024 at <https://www.theguardian.com/global/2019/jun/23/how-to-live-forever-meet-the-extreme-life-extensionists-immortal-science>.

Mulvey-Roberts, Marie (2015) *Dangerous Bodies: Historicizing the Gothic Corporeal*. Manchester, UK: Manchester University Press.

Munro, Dana Carleton (Ed.) (1901) *Translations and Reprints from the Original Sources of European History: Urban and the Crusaders.* Philadelphia, Pennsylvania: University of Pennsylvania.

Murdoch, Iris (1970/2001) *The Sovereignty of the Good.* Milton Park, Oxfordshire, UK: Routledge.

Muscat, Sina (2002) 'Arab/Muslim "Otherness": The role of racial constructions in the Gulf War and the continuing crisis with Iraq' *Journal of Muslim Minority Affairs* 22 (1) pp. 131-147.

North American Renderers Association (2024) 'What is the rendering process?' *Nara.org.* Accessed 7 May 2024 at <https://nara.org/what-is-rendering/>.

Negrin, Llewellyn (2002) 'Cosmetic surgery and the eclipse of identity' *Body & Society* 8 (4) pp. 21-42.

Neumann, Erich (1955/1974) *The Great Mother.* Princeton, New Jersey: Princeton University Press.

Newman, Barbara (1998) *Sister of Wisdom: St. Hildegard's Theology of the Feminine.* Berkeley, California: University of California Press.

Newman, Barbara (1995/2011) *Virile Women to WomanChrist: Studies in Medieval Religion and Literature.* Philadelphia, Pennsylvania: University of Pennsylvania Press.

Nietzsche, Friedrich (1886/2003) *Beyond Good and Evil.* London: Penguin Books Limited.

Noble, David (1999) *The Religion of Technology: The Divinity of Man and the Spirit of Invention.* London: Penguin Publishing Group.

Norris, Pamela (2001) *Eve: A Biography.* New York: New York University Press.

O'Connell, Mark (2017a) *To Be a Machine: Adventures Among Cyborgs, Utopians, Hackers, and the Futurists Solving the Modest Problem of Death.* New York: Knopf Doubleday.

O'Connell, Mark (9 February 2017b) '600 miles in a coffin-shaped bus, campaigning against death itself' *The New York Times Magazine.* Accessed 18 September 2023 at <https://www.nytimes.com/2017/02/09/magazine/600-miles-in-a-coffin-shaped-bus-campaigning-against-death-itself.html>.

Oliver, Jacques (1662) *A Discourse of Women, Shewing their Imperfections Alphabetically.* London: Henry Brome.

Oswald, Hilton (Ed.) *Martin Luther's Works* Vol. 28 (1973) St. Louis, Missouri: Concordia Publishing House.

Otsubo, Kai and Hiroyuki Yamaguchi (2023) 'No significant effect of mortality salience on unconscious ethnic bias among the Japanese' *BMC Research Notes* 16 Article Number 91.

Otterman, Michael (2007) *American Torture: From the Cold War to Abu Ghraib and Beyond*. Victoria, Australia: Melbourne University Press.

Otto, Beatrice, K. (2001) *Fools are Everywhere: The Court Jester Around the World*. Chicago, Illinois: University of Chicago Press.

Ovid (8/1922) 'Pygmalion and the statue' in Brookes More (Ed.) *Metamorphoses* (P. Ovidius Naso). Accessed through the Perseus Digital Library 27 May 2024 at <http://www.perseus.tufts.edu/hopper/text?doc=Perseus%3Atext%3A1999.02.0028%3Abook%3D10%3Acard%3D243>.

Parmelee, Maurice (1911) 'Introduction' in Cesare Lombroso *Crime, Its Causes and Remedies*. Boston: Little, Brown, and Company.

Partridge, Emily A., Marcus G. Davey, Matthew A. Hornick, Patrick E. McGovern, Ali Y. Mejaddam, Jesse D. Vrecenak, Carmen Mesas-Burgos, Aliza Olive, Robert C. Caskey, Theodore R. Weiland, Jiancheng Han, Alexander J. Schupper, James T. Connelly, Kevin C. Dysart, Jack Rychik, Holly L. Hedrick, William H. Peranteau and Alan W. Flake (2017) 'An extra-uterine system to physiologically support the extreme premature lamb' *Nature Communications* 8 pp. 1-15.

Patel, Karan, Sean Bunachita, Hannah Chiu, Prakal Suresh, and Urvish K. Patel (2021) 'Elder abuse: A comprehensive overview and physician-associated challenges' *Cureus* 13 (4) pp. 1-6.

Patterson, Charles (2002) *Eternal Treblinka: Our Treatment of Animals and the Holocaust*. Woodstock, New York: Lantern Books.

Phillips, Michael (2017) *Mycorrhizal Planet: How Symbiotic Fungi Work with Roots to Support Plant Health and Build Soil Fertility*. Chelsea, Vermont: Chelsea Green Books.

Pinfari, Marco (2019) *Terrorists as Monsters: The Unmanageable Other from the French Revolution to the Islamic State*. Oxford, UK: Oxford University Press.

Pitts-Taylor, Victoria (2003) *In the Flesh: The Cultural Politics of Body Modification*. London: Palgrave Macmillan.

Piven, Jerry S. (2003) 'Buddhism, death, and the feminine' *Psychoanalytic Review* 90 (4) pp. 498-536.

Plant, Judith (Ed.) (1989) *Healing the Wounds: The Promise of Ecofeminism*. Toronto, Ontario: Between the Lines Press.

Plato (360 BCE/1961) 'Phaedo' in Lane Cooper (Translator) *The Collected Dialogues of Plato*. Princeton, New Jersey: Princeton University Press.

Plato (360 BCE/1925) 'Timaeus' in W. R. M. Lamb (Translator) *Plato in Twelve Volumes* Volume 9. Cambridge, Massachusetts: Harvard University Press. Accessed through the Perseus Digital Library 20 July

2024 at <http://www.perseus.tufts.edu/hopper/text?doc=Perseus%3At ext%3A1999.01.0180%text%3Dtim.>.

Plato (370 BCE/1928) 'Phaedrus' in Harold Fowler (Translator) *Plato, with an English Translation, I: Euthyphro, Apology, Crito, Phaedo, Phaedrus.* London: William Heinemann.

Plumwood, Val (1993) *Feminism and the Mastery of Nature.* Milton Park, Oxfordshire, UK: Routledge.

Poe, Edgar Allan (1858) *The Works of the Late Edgar Allan Poe: Poems and Tales.* New York: Redfield Press.

Poggi, Christine (2009) *Inventing Futurism: The Art and Politics of Artificial Optimism.* Princeton, New Jersey: Princeton University Press.

Pollan, Michael (2018) *How to Change Your Mind: What the New Science of Psychedelics Teaches Us about Consciousness, Dying, Addiction, Depression, and Transcendence.* New York: Penguin Publishing Group.

Poundstone, William (1993) *Prisoner's Dilemma: John Von Neumann, Game Theory, and the Puzzle of the Bomb.* New York: Knopf Doubleday.

Praz, Mario (1933/1970) *The Romantic Agony.* Oxford, UK: Oxford University Press.

Price, Janet and Margaret Shildrick (Eds) (1999) *Feminist Theory and the Body: A Reader.* New York: Routledge.

Procter, John (Ed.) (1901) *Short Lives of the Dominican Saints.* London: Kegan Paul, Trench, Trubner & Co. Limited.

Pukara, Maia S., Peter H. Rudebeck, Nicole K. Ciesinski and Elisabeth A. Murray (2019) 'Heightened defensive responses following subtotal lesions of macaque orbitofrontal cortex' *The Journal of Neuroscience* 39 (21) pp. 4133–4141.

Pyszczynski, Tom, Abdollhossein Abdollahi, Jeff Greenberg and Sheldon Solomon (2006) 'Crusades and jihads: An existential psychological perspective on the psychology of terrorism and political extremism' in Jeff Victoroff (Ed.) *Tangled Roots: Social and Psychological Factors in the Genesis of Terrorism.* Amsterdam, Netherlands: IOS Press.

Pyszczynski, Tom, Jeff Greenberg and Sheldon Solomon (2015) 'Thirty years of terror management theory: From genesis to revelation' *Advances in Experimental Social Psychology* 52 pp. 1–70.

Pyszczynski, Tom (2013) 'Terror management of fear, hate, political conflict, and political violence' *TPM-Testing, Psychometrics, Methodology in Applied Psychology* 20 (4) pp. 313–326.

Quigley, Christine (1996) *The Corpse: A History.* West Jefferson, North Carolina: McFarland & Company, Inc.

Raphael, Rina (4 October 2018) '"Curing" death: Inside the conference dedicated to reversing human aging' *Fast Company.* Accessed 2 May

2024 at <https://www.fastcompany.com/90243453/meet-the-foot-soldiers-in-the-radical-war-on-aging>.

Ray, Prayag (2016) '"Synthetik love lasts forever": Sex dolls and the (post?) human condition' in Debashish Banerji and Makarand Paranjape (Eds) *Critical Posthumanism and Planetary Futures*. New Delhi, India: Springer India.

Raymond of Capua (1864) *Life of Saint Catherine of Sienna*. Translated by the Ladies of the Sacred Heart. New York: P. J. Kenedy & Sons. Accessed 5 May 2024 at <https://archive.org/details/lifeofsaintcatha00raym/mode/2up>.

Reade, William Winwood (1864) *Savage Africa*. London: Smith, Elder and Co.

Regalado, Antonio (11 January 2023) 'The entrepreneur dreaming of a factory of unlimited organs' *MIT Technology Review*. Accessed 13 September 2023 at <https://www.technologyreview.com/2023/01/11/1064800/martine-rothblatt-transplantable-organs-10-breakthrough-technologies-2023/#:~:text=Martine%20Rothblatt%20sees%20a%20day,countless%20lives%E2%80%94including%20her%20daughter's.&text=Organs%20on%20demand%20is%20one,10%20Breakthrough%20Technologies%20of%202023>.

Regan, Tom and Peter Singer (1976) *Animal Rights and Human Obligations*. Saddle River, New Jersey: Prentice Hall.

Regan, Tom (2001) *Defending Animal Rights*. Champaign, Illinois: University of Illinois Press.

Reiss, Stefan and Eva Jonas (2019) 'The cycle of intergroup conflict: Terror management in the face of terrorism and war' in Clay Routledge and Matthew Vess (Eds) *Handbook of Terror Management Theory*. London: Academic Press.

Reiss, Timothy J. (1982) *The Discourse of Modernism*. Ithaca, New York: Cornell University Press.

Rhodes, Christopher J. (2017) 'The whispering world of plants: "The Wood Wide Web"' *Science Progress* 100 (3) pp. 331-337.

Richardson, Kathleen and Charlotta Odlind (Eds) (2023) *Man-Made Women: The Sexual Politics of Sex Dolls and Sex Robots*. New York: Springer International Publishing.

Ritchie, Hannah (2017) 'How much of the world's land would we need in order to feed the global population with the average diet of a given country?' *OurWorldInData.org*. Accessed 19 May 2024 at <https://ourworldindata.org/agricultural-land-by-global-diets>.

Ritchie, Hannah, Pablo Rosado and Max Roser (2022) 'Environmental impacts of food production' *OurWorldInData.org*. Accessed 19 May 2024 at <https://ourworldindata.org/environmental-impacts-of-food>.

Roberts, Mark (2008) *The Mark of the Beast: Animality and Human Oppression*. Lafayette, Indiana: Purdue University Press.

Roberts, Mary Louise (2013) *What Soldiers Do: Sex and the American GI in World War II France*. Chicago, Illinois: University of Chicago Press.

Robitzski, Dan (9 November 2019) 'Ambrosia is back to selling transfusions of young people's blood' *Neoscope*. Accessed 1 May 2024 at <https://futurism.com/neoscope/ambrosia-selling-transfusions-young-peoples-blood>.

Rodger, Elliot (2014) 'My twisted world: The story of Elliot Rodger.' Accessed 2 May 2024 at <https://schoolshooters.info/sites/default/files/rodger_my_twisted_world.pdf>.

Rodley, Chris (Ed.) (1997) *Cronenberg on Cronenberg*. London: Faber & Faber.

Roper, Caitlin (2022) *Sex Dolls, Robots and Woman Hating: The Case for Resistance*. Mission Beach, Australia: Spinifex Press.

Roper, Lyndal (2004) *Witch Craze: Terror and Fantasy in Baroque Germany*. New Haven, Connecticut: Yale University Press.

Rorvik, David (1971) *As Man Becomes Machine: The Evolution of the Cyborg*. New York: Doubleday.

Roser, Max, Esteban Ortiz-Opsina and Hannah Ritchie (2013) 'Life expectancy' *Our World in Data*. Accessed 1 May 2024 at <https://ourworldindata.org/life-expectancy>.

Rothblatt, Martine (2011) *From Transgender to Transhuman: A Manifesto on the Freedom of Form*. United States: Self-Published. Accessed 12 May 2024 at <https://transreads.org/wp-content/uploads/2021/12/2021-12-23_61c4e86ac7091_FromTransgendertoTranshuman_AManifestoonthe FreedomofFormPDFDrive.pdf>.

Rotman, Andy (2021) *Hungry Ghosts*. Somerville, Massachusetts: Wisdom Publications.

Routledge, Clay and Matthew Vess (Eds) (2019) *Handbook of Terror Management Theory*. London: Academic Press.

Rozin, Paul and April E. Fallon (1987) 'A perspective on disgust' *Psychological Review* 94 (1) pp. 23-41.

Russell, Jeffrey B. (1987) *The Devil: Perceptions of Evil from Antiquity to Primitive Christianity*. Ithaca, NY: Cornell University Press.

Ruth, Richard (7 November 2017) 'Why Thailand takes pride in the Vietnam War' *The New York Times*. Accessed 3 May 2024 at <https://www.nytimes.com/2017/11/07/opinion/thailand-vietnam-war.html>.

Sandberg, Anders (2013) 'Morphological freedom — why we not just want it, but need it' in Max More and Natasha Vita-More (Eds) *The Transhumanist Reader*. Hoboken, New Jersey: Wiley.

Sands, Kathleen R. (2004) *Demon Possession in Elizabethan England*. London: Bloomsbury Academic.

Sartre, Jean-Paul (1943/1992) *Being and Nothingness*. New York: Washington Square Press.

Scarry, Elaine (1985) *The Body in Pain: The Making and Unmaking of the World*. Oxford, UK: Oxford University Press.

Schiebinger, Linda (1993) *Nature's Body: Gender in the Making of Modern Science*. New Brunswick, New Jersey: Rutgers University Press.

Schulenberg, Jane Tibbetts (1998) *Forgetful of Their Sex: Female Sanctity and Society, ca. 500-1100*. Chicago, Illinois: University of Chicago Press.

Schwalbe, Michael (2014) *Manhood Acts: Gender and the Practices of Domination*. Milton Park, Oxfordshire, UK: Taylor & Francis.

Scott, Gavin A., Dylan J. Terstege, Alex P. Vu, Sampson Law, Alexandria Evans and Jonathan R. Epp. (2020) 'Disrupted neurogenesis in germ-free mice: effects of age and sex' *Frontiers in Cell Development and Biology*. Published online 29 May 2020, doi: 10.3389/fcell.2020.00407.

Scully, Matthew (2002) *Dominion: The Power of Man, the Suffering of Animals, and the Call to Mercy*. New York: St. Martin's Press.

Segers, Seppe (2021) 'The path toward ectogenesis: Looking beyond the technical challenges' *BMC Medical Ethics* 22 (1) pp. 1-15.

Seneca, Lucius Annaeus (n.d.) *Seneca: Epistles 1-65*, with an English Translation by Richard M. Gummere (1917). Cambridge, Massachusetts: Harvard University Press.

SENS Research Foundation (2022) 'A reimagined research strategy for aging' *SENS.org*. Accessed 2 May 2024 at <https://www.sens.org/our-research/intro-to-sens-research/>.

Seymour, Christopher W., Samantha J. Kerti, Anthony J. Lewis, Jason Kennedy, Emily Brant, John E. Griepentrog, Xianghong Zhang, Derek C. Angus, Chung-Chou H. Chang and Matthew R. Rosengart (2019) 'Murine sepsis phenotypes and differential treatment effects in a randomized trial of prompt antibiotics and fluids' *Critical Care* 23 pp. 1-9.

Shakespeare, William (1608/1909) *King Lear: With the Famous Temple Notes*. New York: Grosset & Dunlap.

Shaw, Teresa (1998) *The Burden of the Flesh: Fasting and Sexuality in Early Christianity*. Minneapolis, Minnesota: Fortress Press.

Sheehan, James and Morton Sosna (Eds) (1991) *The Boundaries of Humanity: Humans, Animals, Machines*. Oakland, California: University of California Press.

Sheehan, James (1991) 'Introduction' in James Sheehan and Morton Sosna (Eds) *The Boundaries of Humanity: Humans, Animals, Machines.* Oakland, California: University of California Press.

Sheets-Johnstone, Maxine (1992) 'Corporeal archetypes and power: preliminary clarifications and considerations of sex' *Hypatia* 7 (3) pp. 39-76.

Sheldrake, Merlin (2020) *Entangled Life: How Fungi Make Our Worlds, Change Our Minds, and Shape Our Futures.* New York: Random House Publishing Group.

Sigal, Samuel (21 March 2024) 'Elon Musk wants to merge human brains with AI. How many brains will be damaged along the way?' *Vox.com.* Accessed 12 May 2024 at <https://www.vox.com/future-perfect/23899981/elon-musk-ai-neuralink-brain-computer-interface>.

Simard, Suzanne W. (2018) 'Mycorrhizal networks facilitate tree communication, learning, and memory' in Frantisek Baluska, Guenther Witzany and Monica Gagliano (Eds) *Memory and Learning in Plants.* New York: Springer International Publishing.

Sjöo, Monica and Barbara Mor (1987) *The Great Cosmic Mother: Rediscovering the Religion of the Earth.* New York: Harper & Row.

Slotkin, Richard (1973/1996) *Regeneration Through Violence: The Mythology of the American Frontier, 1600-1860.* New York: HarperPerennial.

Slouka, Mark (1995) *War of the Worlds: Cyberspace and the High-Tech Assault on Reality.* Ann Arbor, Michigan: University of Michigan Press.

Smiley, Cherry (2023) *Not Sacred, Not Squaws: Redefining Indigenous Feminism.* Mission Beach, Australia: Spinifex Press.

Smith, Andrea (2005/2015) *Conquest: Sexual Violence and American Indian Genocide.* Durham, North Carolina: Duke University Press.

Smith, David Livingstone (2011) *Less Than Human: Why We Demean, Enslave, and Exterminate Others.* New York: St. Martin's Publishing Group.

Smith, David Livingstone (2021) *Making Monsters: The Uncanny Power of Dehumanization.* Cambridge, Massachusetts: Harvard University Press.

Solomon, Sheldon, Jeff Greenberg and Thomas A. Pyszczynski (2015) *The Worm at the Core: On the Role of Death in Life.* New York: Random House.

Spelman, Elizabeth (1982) 'Woman as body: Ancient and contemporary views' *Feminist Studies* 8 (1) pp. 109-131.

Spretnak, Charlene (1990) 'Toward an ecofeminist spirituality' in Irene Diamond and Gloria Feman Orenstein (Eds) *Reweaving the World: The Emergence of Ecofeminism.* San Francisco, California: Sierra Club Books.

Stannard, David (1992) *American Holocaust*. Oxford, UK: Oxford University Press.

Stephens, Walter (2003) *Demon Lovers: Witchcraft, Sex and the Crisis of Belief*. Chicago, Illinois: University of Chicago Press.

Stephenson, Neal (1992) *Snow Crash*. New York: Bantam Books.

Steuter, Erin and Deborah Wills (2009) 'Discourse of dehumanization: Enemy construction and Canadian media complicity in the framing of the War on Terror' *Global Media Journal* 2 (2) pp. 7–24.

Stewart, James B., Matthew Goldstein and Jessica Silver-Greenberg (31 July 2019) 'Jeffrey Epstein hoped to seed human race with his DNA' *The New York Times*. Accessed 1 May 2024 at <https://www.nytimes.com/2019/07/31/business/jeffrey-epstein-eugenics.html#:~:text=via%20Getty%20Images-,Jeffrey%20E.,his%20vast%20New%20Mexico%20ranch>.

Stone, Alison (2004) 'Essentialism and anti-essentialism in feminist philosophy' *Journal of Moral Philosophy* 1 (2) pp. 135–153.

Straus, Scott (2015) *Making and Unmaking Nations: War, Leadership, and Genocide in Modern Africa*. Ithaca, New York: Cornell University Press.

Stuart, Tristram (2007) *The Bloodless Revolution: A Cultural History of Vegetarianism from 1600 to Modern Times*. New York: W. W. Norton.

Summers, Montague (Ed.) (1971) *The Malleus Maleficarum of Heinrich Kramer and James Sprenger*. New York: Dover Publications, Inc.

Swanson, Trevor J. and Mark Landau (2019) 'Terror management fuels structure-seeking' in Clay Routledge and Matthew Vess (Eds) *Handbook of Terror Management Theory*. London: Academic Press.

Swinburne, Algernon Charles (1865) *Chastelard: A Tragedy*. London: Edward Moxon & Co.

Swinburne, Algernon Charles (1873) *Poems and Ballads by Algernon Charles Swinburne*. London: John Camden Hotten.

Synnott, Anthony (1993) *The Body Social: Symbolism, Self, and Society*. Milton Park, Oxfordshire, UK: Routledge.

Taplin, Jonathan (2023) *The End of Reality: How Four Billionaires are Selling a Fantasy Future of the Metaverse, Mars, and Crypto*. New York: Public Affairs.

Tardieu, Michel (2008) *Manichaeism*. Chicago, Illinois: University of Illinois Press.

Thera, Nyanaponika (2005) *The Heart of Buddhist Meditation. Satipaṭṭhāna: A Handbook of Mental Training Based on the Buddha's Way of Mindfulness, with an Anthology of Relevant Texts Translated from the Pali and Sanskrit*. Sri Lanka: Buddhist Publication Society.

Theresa, Deena (1 August 2022) 'A transhuman biohacker implanted over 50 chips and magnets in her body' *Interesting Engineering*. Accessed 18 September 2023 at <https://interestingengineering.com/innovation/transhuman-biohacker-implanted-magnets>.

Theweleit, Klaus (1987) *Male Fantasies, Volume 2: Male Bodies: Psychoanalyzing the White Terror*. Minneapolis, Minnesota: University of Minnesota Press.

Thiele, Bev (1998) 'Retrieving the baby: Feminist theory and organic bodies' *Canadian Woman Studies* 18 (4) pp. 51-60.

Timofeeva, Oxana (2018) *The History of Animals: A Philosophy*. London: Bloomsbury Academic.

Trout, Christopher (11 April 2017) 'RealDoll's first sex robot took me to the uncanny valley' *Endgadget.com*. Accessed 5 May 2024 at <https://www.engadget.com/2017-04-11-realdolls-first-sex-robot-took-me-to-the-uncanny-valley.html>.

Truong, Kiem and Khuong Dinh (2021) 'Agent Orange: Half-century effects on Vietnamese wildlife have been ignored' *Environmental Science and Technology* 55 (22) pp. 15007-15009.

Tuan, Yi-Fu (1984) *Dominance and Affection: The Making of Pets*. New Haven, Connecticut: Yale University Press.

Tuana, Nancy (1993) *The Less Noble Sex: Scientific, Religious, and Philosophical Conceptions of Woman's Nature*. Bloomington, Indiana: Indiana University Press.

Tuyet-Hanh, Tran Thi, Le Vu-Anh, Nguyen Ngoc-Bich and Thomas Tenkate (2010) 'Environmental health risk assessment of dioxin exposure through foods in a dioxin hot spot—Bien Hoa City, Vietnam' *International Journal of Environmental Research and Public Health* 7 (5) pp. 2395-2406.

Uebel, Michael (1996) 'Unthinking the monster: Twelfth-century responses to Saracen alterity' in Jeffrey Jerome Cohen (Ed.) *Monster Theory: Reading Culture*. Minneapolis, Minnesota: University of Minnesota Press.

UN Women (20 February 2023) 'Ukraine crisis is gendered, so is our response' *UN Women: Europe and Central Asia*. Accessed 12 May 2024 at <https://eca.unwomen.org/en/stories/in-focus/2023/02/in-focus-war-in-ukraine-is-a-crisis-for-women-and-girls#:~:text=%5B1%5D%20Nearly%20one%2Dthird,displacement%20crises%20of%20our%20times>.

Underhill, Evelyn (1919/1990) *Mysticism: A Study in the Nature and Development of Man's Spiritual Consciousness*. New York: Crown Publishing Group.

United States Army Corps of Engineers (1946) *The Atomic Bombings of Hiroshima and Nagasaki*, Volumes 1-2. Oak Ridge, Tennessee: Manhattan Engineer District of the United States Army.

Vaisch, Tom (1 May 2015) 'Long-term galactic cosmic ray exposure leads to dementia-like cognitive impairments' *UCI News*. Accessed 13 May 2024 at <https://news.uci.edu/2015/05/01/long-term-galactic-cosmic-ray-exposure-leads-to-dementia-like-cognitive-impairments/>.

Van der Kolk, Bessel (2014) *The Body Keeps the Score: Brain, Mind, and Body in the Healing of Trauma*. New York: Viking Penguin.

Vardey, Lucinda (Ed.) (2002) *The Flowering of the Soul: A Book of Prayers by Women*. Boston, Massachusetts: Beacon Press.

Vita-More, Natasha (2013) 'Life expansion media' in Max More and Natasha Vita-More (Eds) *The Transhumanist Reader*. Hoboken, New Jersey: Wiley.

Walsh, Brendan, C. (2020) '"Like a Mad Dogge": Demoniac animals and animal demoniacs in early modern English possession' in Ruth Heholt and Melissa Edmundson (Eds) *Gothic Animals: Uncanny Otherness and the Animal With-Out*. New York: Springer International Publishing.

Walter, Chip (2020) *Immortality, Inc.: Renegade Science, Silicon Valley Billions, and the Quest to Live Forever*. Washington, DC: National Geographic Society.

Warren, Karen (1997) *Ecofeminism: Women, Culture, Nature*. Bloomington, Indiana: University of Indiana Press.

Watanabe, Kazuko (1999) 'Trafficking in women's bodies, then and now: the issue of military "comfort women"' *Women's Studies Quarterly* 27 (1/2) pp. 19-31.

Watanabe, Takumi and Kaori Karasawa (2012) 'Self-ingroup overlap in the face of mortality salience' *The Japanese Journal of Experimental Social Psychology* 52 (1) pp. 25-34.

Watson, Richard (2007) *Cogito, Ergo Sum: The Life of René Descartes*. Boston, Massachusetts: David R. Godine, Inc.

Wells, H. G. (1895/2009) 'Appendix H: The limits of individual plasticity' in Mason Harris (Ed.) *The Island of Doctor Moreau*. Peterborough, Ontario, Canada: Broadview Press.

Wells, H. G. (1896/2009) *The Island of Doctor Moreau*. Broadview Edition edited by Mason Harris. Peterborough, Ontario, Canada: Broadview Press.

Westing, Arthur (1971) 'Ecological effects of military defoliation on the forests of South Vietnam' *BioScience* 17 pp. 893-898.

Westing, Arthur (1981) 'Environmental impact of nuclear warfare' *Environmental Conservation* 8 (4) pp. 269-274.

Wetmore, Jr., Kevin (2021) *Eaters of the Dead: Myths and Realities of Cannibal Monsters*. London: Reaktion Books.

Wilcox, Fred A. (2011) *Scorched Earth: Legacies of Chemical Warfare in Vietnam*. New York: Seven Stories Press.

Williams, Michael (1989) 'Divine image – prison of flesh' in Michel Feher, Nadia Tazi, and Ramona Naddaff (Eds) *Fragments for a History of the Human Body, Part 1*. New York: Zone Books.

Wilson, Elizabeth (1995) 'The female body as a source of horror and insight in post-Ashokan Indian Buddhism' in Jane Marie Law (Ed.) *Religious Reflections on the Human Body*. Bloomington, Indiana: University of Indiana Press pp. 76–99.

Wilson, Elizabeth, A. (2015) *Gut Feminism*. Durham, North Carolina: Duke University Press.

Wilson, Liz (1996) *Charming Cadavers: Horrific Figurations of the Feminine in Indian Buddhist Hagiographic Literature*. Chicago: University of Chicago Press.

Wilson, Sophie (29 March 2022) 'BDSM, bimbos, and branding: The extreme world of body modification fetishes'. *Dazed Digital*. Accessed 3 May 2024 at <https://www.dazeddigital.com/beauty/article/55792/1/bdsm-bimbos-and-branding-the-extreme-world-of-body-modification>.

Woolf, Virginia (1931/2006) *The Waves*. New York: HarperCollins.

Yong, Ed (2016) *I Contain Multitudes: The Microbes Within Us and a Grander View of Life*. New York: HarperCollins.

Zeller, Benjamin (2014) *Heaven's Gate: America's UFO Religion*. New York: New York University Press.

Zilboorg, Gregory (1943) 'Fear of death' *The Psychoanalytic Quarterly* 12 (4) pp. 465–475.

Zubrin, Richard and Richard Wagner (2011) *The Case for Mars: The Plan to Settle the Red Planet and Why We Must*. New York: The Free Press.

Zucchino, David (18 April 2012) 'U.S. troops posed with body parts of Afghan bombers' *The Los Angeles Times*. Accessed 2 May 2024 at <https://www.latimes.com/nation/la-na-afghan-photos-20120418-story.html>.

FILMS

Cameron, James (1984) *Terminator*. Hemdale Film Corporation and Pacific Western Productions.

Cameron, James (1991) *Terminator 2: Judgment Day*. Carolco Pictures and Pacific Western Productions.

CBS Reports (3 April 1963) *The Silent Spring of Rachel Carson*. CBS Broadcasting Inc.

BIBLIOGRAPHY

Cronenberg, David (1986) *The Fly*. Brooksfilms Ltd.

Friedkin, William (1973) *The Exorcist*. Warner Brothers.

Hush Hush Entertainment (2006) *Blackzilla*.

Johnson, Cram and Grip Johnson (2008) *Oh No! There's A Negro in My Mom!* Chatsworth Pictures.

Scott, Ridley (1979) *Alien*. 20th Century Fox.

INDEX

Other books from Spinifex Press

Laura Lecuona
GENDER IDENTITY: LIES AND DANGERS

The concept of *gender* is central to a vaguely progressive-looking set
of ideas based on the maxim that people possess a so-called 'gender
identity'. The real problem arises when this nebulous concept, bandied
about with different and even incompatible meanings by different groups,
is used as a prop to introduce policies that mark a huge setback for the
rights of women and girls. The general public, watching the controversy
from the sidelines, is confused by conflicting claims about whose rights
are being infringed.

Laura Lecuona's book is remarkable in scope and a dose of political sanity
that is badly needed.

—Janice G. Raymond

ISBN 9781925950908   ebook available

Sheila Jeffreys
PENILE IMPERIALISM:
THE MALE SEX RIGHT AND WOMEN'S SUBORDINATION

In this blisteringly persuasive and piercingly intelligent book, Sheila
Jeffreys argues that women live under penile imperialism, a regime in
which men are assumed to have a 'sex right' of access to the bodies of
women and girls.

The power dynamics of sex, rather than being eliminated, has been
eroticised, supported by state regulations and structures that have
further entrenched male domination. This is a sobering and brilliant
analysis of the modern predicament of women that is impossible to
ignore.

ISBN 9781925950700   ebook available

Caitlin Roper
SEX DOLLS, ROBOTS AND WOMAN HATING:
THE CASE FOR RESISTANCE

Lifelike, replica women and girls produced for men's sexual use, sex dolls and robots represent the literal objectification of women. They are marketed as companions, the means for men to create their 'ideal' woman, and as the 'perfect girlfriend' that can be stored away after use.

Caitlin Roper exposes the inherent misogyny in the trade in sex dolls and robots modelled on the bodies of women and girls for men's unlimited sexual use. Doll owners enacting violence and torture on their dolls; choosing their dolls over their wives; dolls made in the likeness of specific women; and the production of child sex abuse doll. Sex dolls and robots pose a serious threat to the safety of women and girls.

ISBN 9781925950601   ebook available

Heather Brunskell-Evans
TRANSGENDER BODY POLITICS

At a time when supposedly enlightened attitudes are championed by the mainstream, philosopher and activist Heather Brunskell-Evans shows how, in plain view under the guise of liberalism, a regressive men's rights movement is posing a massive threat to the human rights of women and children everywhere.

In a chilling twist, when feminists critique the patriarchal status quo it is they who are alleged to be extremists for not allowing men's interests to control the political narrative. Institutions whose purpose is to defend human rights now interpret truth speech as hate speech and endorse the no-platforming of women as ethical. This brave, truthful and eye-opening book does not shirk from the challenge of meeting the politics of liberalism and transgender rights head on. Everyone who cares about the future of women's and children's rights must read it.

ISBN 9781925950229   ebook available

Susan Hawthorne
VORTEX: THE CRISIS OF PATRIARCHY

In this enlightening yet devastating book, Susan Hawthorne writes with clarity and incisiveness on how patriarchy is wreaking destruction on the planet and on communities. The twin mantras of globalisation and growth expounded by the neoliberalism that has hijacked the planet are revealed in all their shabby deception.

She details how women, lesbians, people with disabilities, Indigenous peoples, the poor, refugees and the very earth itself are being damaged by the crisis of patriarchy that is sucking everyone into its vortex. Importantly, this precise and insightful volume also shows what is needed to get ourselves out of this spiral of destruction: a radical feminist approach with compassion and empathy at its core.

ISBN 9781925950168   ebook available

Jennifer Bilek
TRANSSEXUAL TRANSGENDER TRANSHUMAN:
DISPATCHES FROM THE 11TH HOUR

In this thought-provoking collection of articles, Jennifer Bilek delves into the intricate relationship between transsexualism, transgenderism, and transhumanism. She sheds light on how the push for perceived human rights for marginalized groups often obscures broader societal dynamics.

Through an exploration of the transhumanist movement, Bilek investigates how its proponents blur the boundaries between humanity and mechanization. Society is undergoing a profound transformation away from the biological realities of reproductive sex, driven by emerging technologies that shape children's perceptions of their bodies from an early age. The narrative of gender identity transcendence exploits their vulnerability, pushing them toward an increasingly medicalized future.

ISBN 9781922964106   ebook available

*If you would like to know more about
Spinifex Press, write to us for a free catalogue, visit our
website or email us for further information
on how to subscribe to our monthly newsletter.*

Spinifex Press
PO Box 105
Mission Beach QLD 4852
Australia

www.spinifexpress.com.au
women@spinifexpress.com.au